TRIBES AND GLOBAL JIHADISM

VIRGINIE COLLOMBIER
OLIVIER ROY
(*Editors*)

Tribes and Global Jihadism

HURST & COMPANY, LONDON

First published in the United Kingdom in 2017 by
C. Hurst & Co. (Publishers) Ltd.,
41 Great Russell Street, London, WC1B 3PL

A Cataloguing-in-Publication data record for this book is available from the British Library.

This book is printed using paper from registered sustainable and managed sources.

ISBN: 9781849048156

www.hurstpublishers.com

Printed in the United Kingdom by Bell & Bain Ltd, Glasgow

The editors and authors of this volume want to express their support to Ismail Alexandrani, who contributed Chapter 4 on Egypt's Sinai. Because of his research, Ismail Alexandrani has been imprisoned in Egypt since December 2015. His contribution to this book, which could not be finalized because of these particular circumstances, is a testimony to his competence and intellectual probity.

CONTENTS

This edited volume is based on contributions by the authors to a seminar on 'Tribes and Jihad' organized at the European University Institute, Florence (Italy) on 8–9 June 2015, with the support of the Norwegian Centre for Conflict Resolution (NOREF). We would like to thank the then-director of NOREF, Mariano Aguirre, for his trust and support.

GLOSSARY

'Aib: Sin, sinful, shameful.

Aila: (pl. ailat) Lineage, extended family.

'Asabiyya: Any group of solidarity bound by personal ties or kinship relations.

Alizai: Major tribe of the Panjpai branch of the Durrani tribal confederation. One of the three biggest tribes in Helmand (see Noorzai and Barakzai for others). Apart from the first Taliban government (1995–2001), they provided Helmand's provincial governors between 1993 and 2005. They live in the north of Helmand, in the ancient district of Zamindawar (modern districts of Baghran, Musa Qala, Kajaki and northern Sangin).

Barakzai: One of the three biggest tribes in Helmand (see Alizai and Noorzai). Mohammadzai branch provided the royal lineage from 1826 to 1973. Concentrated in central Helmand, they control Gereshk. Generally fought under the Hizb franchise during the jihad in central Helmand.

Dawlat-i islami: 'Islamic state'.

Harakat-e Enqelab-e Islami (Harakat): Traditionalist Afghan mujahidin group fighting against Soviet forces. Mohammad Nabi Mohammadi was leader. Operated across southern Afghanistan. Was part of the 'Peshawar Seven' coalition of mujahidin parties. In Helmand, the most important commander was Nasim Akhundzada.

***Hizb-e Islami* (*Hizb*)**: Two factions: Khales and Gulbuddin. Gulbuddin faction prominent in Helmand. Most well-funded mujahidin party, but was dropped by Pakistan upon the rise of the Taliban in 1994. One of the two major mujahidin parties represented in Helmand alongside Harakat. Prominent commanders include Malem Mir Wali, Abdul Rahman Khan and Hafizullah Khan.

Ishaqzai: The most marginalised of the Durrani tribes in Helmand. Important under the Taliban during 1995–2001, they provided senior commanders for the movement. Heavily persecuted by the Alakozai post-2001. Mainly live south of Sangin, Now Zad and Garmsir although there are some in Nad-e Ali, where they moved (illegally) during the jihad.

Jahiliyyah: The time of 'ignorance' that preceded the Revelation of the Prophet Mohammad.

***Jamiat-e Islami* (*Jamiat*)**: Islamic political party in Afghanistan similar to the Muslim Brotherhood of Egypt. Oldest Islamic political party in Afghanistan. Communitarian ideology based on Islamic law but is also considered moderately progressive. From 1968 to 2011 the official leader of Jamiat was Burhanuddin Rabbani. Major commanders include Ahmad Shah Masoud and Ismail Khan. Akhwaendi was the Amir in Helmand.

Jihad: lit. struggle (Arabic). Like the religious terms of any religion this is open to different interpretations. Appears in the Quran as 'striving in the way of God' [as in a mental struggle]; however, can be interpreted to mean physical fighting.

Khalq/Khalqi: More extreme of the two factions of the People's Democratic Party of Afghanistan. Was in power in Kabul in 1978/9; however, the army remained Khalqi-dominated throughout the 1980s. Ideologically defined the militias in Lashkar Gah at the end of the 1980s. Important leaders include Taraki and Amin.

Kharoti: Important Ghilzai tribe. Very prominent in Nad-e Ali, where they compete with the Noorzai for district leadership. Important members include Gulbuddin Hekmatyar (leader of Hizb) and Hafizullah Amin (president in 1979). Closely allied to Taliban narrative in Nad-e Ali.

Mahaz: Mujahidin party led by Pir Gailani. Probably the most poorly funded party because they represented the old moderate (royal) order which the ISI did not wish to re-empower. Many commanders in Helmand allied with Mahaz and then switched when it was unable to provide them with enough weapons and funding.

Mahaz: system cf. nezami system. Channelled, patronage model of Taliban supply and organisation. Very similar to how the jihad was organised with the different parties being analogous to the different mahazes.

Malik: In Afghanistan, traditional clan and village leaders.

Mujahidin: lit. holy warriors. In the context of Afghanistan it means those who fought in the anti-communist resistance, but the fighters currently fighting the government also call themselves mujahidin.

Nezami: system lit. organised or military. cf. mahaz system. A more institutional, centralised form of supply and organisation instituted in 2009 by the Taliban. Not fully implemented in Helmand.

Noorzai: One of the big three Helmandi tribes (see Alizai and Barakzai). Previously, they were marginalised from Helmandi politics due to their location in Now Zad, Washir and Garmsir; however, during the 1990s they occupied abandoned land in Nad-e Ali and Marjeh, as they were in control of the Helmandi police in the post-2001 era. Also significant in Kandahar province.

Parcham / Parchami: Less extreme faction of the People's Democratic Party of Afghanistan (see Khalq). Ruled from 1979 until 1992. Dominated Khad (and its successor organisations) during that time. Important leaders include Karmal and Najibullah.

Pashtunwali: Tribal customs among Pashtuns in Afghanistan.

Qabila: (pl. qaba'il) Tribe, clan.

Qaraba: Kinship.

Qaum: lit. kin group, tribe, race or people. Often used in the sense of a social solidarity group.

Taraki, Noor Mohammad: Afghan president from 1978 to 1979. A member of the more extreme Khalq faction of the People's Democratic

Party of Afghanistan, he was ousted by Amin. Responsible for the reforms (esp. land reforms) that caused so much damage and resentment in Helmandi society. Also a tribe.

Sharia: Islamic religious law.

Sadah: Supposedly descendants of the Prophet; may constitute a local cast of 'holy men'.

Sheikh: (pl. shuyukh) Tribal leader, elder; religious or spiritual leader.

Surge: US counter insurgency directed against the Sunni upheaval in Iraq in 2007.

Takfir: Declaring somebody an 'unbeliever' although they claim to be Muslim and might abide with the main precepts of Islam.

Ummah: The community of Muslims worldwide that are bound together by their religion.

'Urf: Customary law.

Watan: Territory, homeland.

INTRODUCTION

Olivier Roy

When looking at a map of the local Islamic emirates pledging allegiance to either al-Qaeda (AQ) or Islamic State (IS), or to those connected to them like the Taliban in Afghanistan, a strange phenomenon appears: they are all situated in tribal areas, meaning areas where tribal rules and customs are the predominant forms of social and/or political organization. Certainly, tribal areas are often remote and can provide better protection against state or foreign counter-insurgency operations, but this does not suffice to explain the association (Falluja in Iraq and Abyan in Yemen are not remote places). Of course, not all tribal leaders or tribesmen are jihadists (as highlighted by the case of the Egyptian Awlad 'Ali in Chapter 3 by Thomas Hüsken), and not all jihadists come from a tribe; but all 'Islamic emirates' are in tribal lands: Afghanistan, Pakistan, northern Iraq, Yemen, Sinai, Sahel, Somalia and, if we take a more flexible definition of tribes, the area under the influence of Boko Haram.

There is an old tradition of association between tribes and 'fundamentalist' leaders (for instance, the North-West Frontier Province in the British Raj, the Saud in Nejd, without going back to the Almohads and Almoravids). The state/tribe confrontation is not new, and neither is the mobilization of tribes for jihad in the colonial context (the Mahdi in Sudan, the various '*mad mollahs*' in the Pashtun belt, Iraq in the 1920s, for instance, or Libya against the Italians). All used 'jihad' as the justification and tool for their resistance. But the meaning of jihad itself has evolved: the spread in less than thirty years of 'Islamic emirates' in tribal areas, from the Atlantic to the Indus, is very different from the colonial past: the jihadists nowadays do not fight to protect a specific territory; they proclaim a global jihad against a global enemy, and they connect to the global world by pledging allegiance to a global jihadist movement.

A personal encounter

My first encounter with a 'non-state Islamic state' was in August 1985, when I (illegally) crossed the border between Pakistan and Afghanistan somewhere east of Chitral during the mujahidin upheaval against the Soviet invasion. In the early morning, after crossing the Bashgal river, I was stopped at a mujahidin checkpoint and was asked to show my visa for the 'Islamic state' (*dawlat-i islami*), a visa that was supposed to be provided by the Islamic state 'consulate' in Chitral. I did not have one, but was granted a provisional visa to meet the 'amir', Mollah Afzal, trained in the Panjpir madrasa in Pakistan controlled by the Ahl-i Hadith movement (close to the Wahhabis). Because I had known the place for years, it did not take me long to understand that the 'Islamic state' in fact corresponded to the territory of the Kati tribe around Barg-i Matal. The traditional tribal leaders had disappeared, either killed, jailed or exiled, and *sharia* had supposedly replaced the local customs and traditions. There was an interesting consequence: the mollahs were making the men till the land instead of letting their womenfolk do it, in order to allow the women to stay at home and look after the domestic goat breeding, which until then had been men's work. Unfortunately, I was not able to go back later to assess the anthropological consequences of the Salafization of tribal customs. The local Salafis, as all these neo-fundamentalist militants called themselves, were either trained by Wahhabis or in more traditional Pakistani madrasas where the courses became 'Salafized' under Saudi influence, and they rapidly turned anti-Western. The beautifully carved wooden mosques and graves were erased, with the former replaced by ugly cement minarets. The scheme was repeated some years later by the 'amir' Jamil ur-Rahman in the Pashto-speaking area south of Nuristan, which also corresponded to a tribe: the Safi. At the beginning, the only connection to a 'global Islam' was through the Salafi religious networks, which provided money, weapons and grants for study in their own madrasas, either in Pakistan or, increasingly, in the Gulf countries.

A year before, in 1984, I had travelled to the southern part of Afghanistan and discovered a network of madrasas turned into military units (*jabhahs* or 'fronts') stretching from the upper Arghandab valley to Kandahar. They called themselves 'Taliban' and would make the name famous ten years later. The scheme was slightly different: these madrasas were established in the midst of tribal areas, but extended their political control beyond the various tribal and clan boundaries (also because, as Mike Martin describes in Chapter 2, in southern Afghanistan tribes are territorially more intricate). The madrasa cadres came from the different tribes and clans in the area, but usually from clans or sub-tribes with lower status. *Sharia* was supposed to replace '*pashtunwali*', an unwritten tribal ethical code of the Pashtun people (I had no time to check if it worked or not). One last point: Sufi groups, which had been prominent in the area until then, were rapidly disappearing, although lip-service was still paid to some very old '*pir*' (like Pir-i Zakeri around Kandahar). Many Taliban did belong to families with a Naqshbandi tradition (and less often with a Qaderi one), but they gradually turned to Salafism.

In all these areas, the connection to global jihad came progressively and was based on three phenomena: the development of transnational Salafi networks for training and teaching; an expansion of smuggling (from the traditional pressure-cookers to new products like drugs and weapons, and from the strict border areas to Karachi and the Gulf), and last but not least, the rise of AQ, whose strongholds were mainly in Afghan Pashtun tribal areas and never in non-tribal areas. In 1994 the Taliban proclaimed the 'Islamic Emirate of Afghanistan' and provided sanctuary to AQ. In this case it was the global organization (AQ) that pledged allegiance to the local emirate (Taliban) and not the reverse (until some local Taliban groups shifted to ISIS after 2013).

The phenomenon of 'Islamic emirates' spread from Afghanistan to Pakistan, once again exclusively in tribal areas. The same patterns were at work: local mollahs from the tribe took power by bypassing, expelling or killing traditional tribal leaders (*maliks*), whose power was based on their role as intermediaries between the central state and the local tribes. The Islamic Emirate of Waziristan even signed a truce with the central Pakistani government in 2006. Interestingly enough, the rise of these emirates often coincided with endeavours by the Pakistani army to rescind the special legal status of the Federally Administered Tribal Areas (FATA) and impose state federal law instead of the local customary law. The mollahs counter-attacked by stating that they would agree with the cancellation of the special tribal status on one condition: the federal law should be *sharia*. However, because the federal law was not *sharia* and because the 'Taliban' were already implementing it, they argued that they did not need any kind of state supervision, due to the fact that they were ahead of the state in promoting *sharia*. Instead of resisting the state from below, the Salafization of the tribal system allows it to contest the state from above, from the position of a global ideology, and not to maintain local privileges and customs.

In this sense, the Afghanistan–Pakistan (AFPAK) area was the laboratory for the specific connection between tribes and jihad. However, the extension of the phenomenon from the Indus to the Sahel shows that this is not just a local issue.

A comparative approach

This book deals with specific case studies of encounters between tribalism, Salafism and jihadism. Of course, there is no ambition to be exhaustive. The book is just an attempt to make a comparative study of the relationship between tribes and jihad in the context of the extension of Salafism, in order to find some clues. The rooting of jihadism in some tribal areas is taking place in connection with a far larger expansion of Salafism among Middle Eastern tribes in places where the Muslim Brothers and comparable Islamist political movements had usually been unable to attract followers (with the exception of the north of Yemen). The Muslim Brothers were identified with the urban elite (teachers, civil servants, doctors, lawyers) associated with the state apparatuses that were distrusted by the tribes.

Three patterns emerge: 1) the shift towards Salafism and/or jihadism goes along with a contestation of tribal leadership and with a generational and social change within the tribe; 2) this shift is connected with a globalization of tribes, both through an extension of traditional smuggling activities into a more complex supranational market and through the expansion of global networks of Salafi madrasas and jihadist organizations; 3) this globalization of tribes allows them to plug themselves into a regional geostrategic game and to contest the central state from above and not just from below as before.

Do we need to define 'tribe'?

This is not the place for an extensive discussion of the concept of 'tribe' in the Middle East. Such a debate is to be found for instance in Dale F. Eickelman's seminal book.[1] Nevertheless, there is a minimal definition that can apply to most of the field studies that we present in this book: we use the term 'tribe' to indicate a segmented solidarity-based group (even if the solidarity is sometimes more ascribed than real), based on lineage (generally patrilineal and patrilocal), with an internal system of regulation (customary law, mediation to resolve conflicts) which excludes outsiders, an 'ideology' or at least a culture (hospitality, loyalty, honour) and an uneasy connection with state authorities, usually mediated by local notables ('*shuyukh*' or elders).

In this sense, a quasi-ethnic group (first defined by a specific language) can work as a tribe if it is in symmetric opposition to other groups and develops the same kind of solidarity among its members while maintaining ambivalent relations with the state. Loyalty to the group is presupposed and considered a given, which means that even when young members of the group go to town to escape the conservatism of the system, they remain ascribed to their group identity and might use it to find support.

There can of course be differences between different tribal areas, particularly as far as religion is concerned, such as the presence or otherwise of a non-tribal group of religious leaders, like the *sāyyad* in Yemen, or of a tradition of Sufism (a pattern often closely associated with tribes, as in pre-Qaddafi Libya).

We should also be careful not to essentialize tribesmen: they can make individual religious and political choices like everybody else (as

Hüsken shows in Chapter 3). The rooting of a Salafi jihadist movement or the tensions between Salafis and traditional Muslims might happen in the same way as they do in non-tribal areas. Moreover, the self-definition of a tribe might be shaped by an external perception: if the government thinks that tribal solidarity comes first, even if this is not really the case, it may engage in collective reprisals or discrimination against a tribe seen as 'dissident', thus renewing a fading solidarity (for instance, the Kanuri of Cameroon are perceived as supporting Boko Haram, and are therefore discriminated against by the security forces, stirring up some support for the movement).

However, despite the fluidity of identities, both members and non-members of a tribe agree that there are tribes, whatever value judgement they put on the fact and whatever anthropological definition might be given to tribalism. We will not delve further into discussing the scientific terminology of tribalism, but there is definitely a living tribal 'grammar' that underlies local politics.

An apparent contradiction

The connection between tribes and global Salafi–jihadism seems to be a contradiction. Jihadist leaders tend to pit the 'good' global Muslim militants (fighting for the *ummah*) against tribesmen (supposedly attached to narrow solidarities and interests).[2] Tribalism means segmentation, while in their view jihad is a call to unite the *ummah* and bypass segmentation (*'asabiyya*).[3] A tribe is defined by the existence of customary law and lay instances of negotiations, while jihadist organizations and Salafis promote *sharia* and *sharia* courts. Tribal leaders are lay elders, usually from dominant lineages; jihadist leaders are young self-made men who came to prominence either through war or religious preaching, while Salafi religious leaders, whatever their personal familial background, draw their legitimacy from their religious knowledge and their mastery of preaching techniques. Tribes are very often associated with a Sufi order (usually constituting a parallel religious hierarchy distinct from lay tribal notables); Salafism is strongly opposed to Sufism and its practices: Salafis have been destroying mausoleums and graves, and usually contest the two parallel systems of leadership—one 'lay', the other religious. Hence Salafism appears as an onslaught against tribes.

Then why should tribes be attracted by Salafism and jihadism? There are two levels of explanation. Tribes may embrace the jihadist cause for practical and circumstantial reasons, but more importantly their embrace of jihadism might correspond to an internal sociological change and to a repositioning in the regional geostrategic context allowing the tribe to contest the state no longer from below but from above. In this sense, joining Salafi–jihadism is a way to recast tribal structures, not to suppress them.

An empirical and practical alliance

When local tribes are in trouble, they might find in the jihadist movement a useful tool for regaining influence. The fighting capacity of jihadist organizations enhances the status of tribes (Yemen, Taliban on both sides of the borders, Iraqi Sunnis). Tribes gain direct access to resources and the global world by connecting to Salafi and/or jihadist movements. They can maximize their assets in the traditional game of contesting (and instrumentalizing) the central state: they might be recognized as legitimate or at least indispensable actors by the big powers (the West) in order to stabilize a situation or to find a political solution (the 2007 surge in Iraq). This is even more true when these 'central states' have been seriously reduced to fragility by situations of armed conflict. Central states are indeed no longer so centralized or capable when their capacity to impose their rule and authority have been deeply weakened. In short, by translating a local struggle into a regional or even global one, tribes increase their agency. But this 'rational actor' explanation does not explain why tribesmen should stick to a jihadist agenda that might also backfire or attract more repression, not only from the state but also from foreign forces.

Reciprocally, jihadists find in tribal areas a sanctuary: tribes are often (but not always) situated in remote areas; they value hospitality, and any retaliation from the state against tribes may entail greater solidarity with the 'internationalists'; tribesmen are armed and the state apparatus may be absent or weak, reducing its ability to gather intelligence or to launch military operations. Moreover, the central state might even play the role of buffer or mediator between local jihadist tribesmen and foreign military forces (almost always US forces) by convincing the latter that any attack on the tribes will have a destabilizing effect on the central power (a constant game in Afghanistan and Pakistan). Thus, the complex relationship between tribes and jihad is in fact based on a quadrangle: the tribe, jihadist forces, the central state and foreign military actors.

Who manipulates whom? In Yemen and Afghanistan, the tribes seem to have had the final say so far. In Iraq they have been superseded by ISIS. In Pakistan, there is no clear winner and a fragile balance has been established between the state, the tribes and the jihadists.

Joining jihad, for whatever reasons and even when it is just for opportunist motivations, automatically entails a recasting of the power relations within the tribe. It also positions the tribe differently in its traditionally ambivalent relations to the central power. As Mbowou says, 'In this context, the declaration of war constituted a sudden requalification of the local reality.'

Recasting tribalism in a new world order

From smugglers to global jihadists

It is not by chance that most of the tribes we are referring to have a long tradition of smuggling. In most of these cases (Yemen, North Cameroon, along the Durand line, Egypt's Sinai and Libya), the tribe straddles a border, a fact that creates an opportunity to develop an economy based on smuggling. The modern state is both an opportunity (it creates borders) and an obstacle (it fights smuggling). The best economic opportunity for tribes is not to seize the state and erase the borders, but to make the state impotent and transform the border into an economic bonanza.

However, the nature of smuggling has changed: this is no longer just an issue of proximity to the border; smugglers need to extend their networks to more distant places (Karachi and the Gulf for the different Taliban fronts, for instance). This also implies increasing the tribe's military resources. Smuggling has become more 'dangerous' and militarized: in a context of regional wars and with a proliferation of modern weaponry, smugglers must be able to confront the state or regional rivals militarily, instead of the police and gendarmerie. The level of weaponry has increased considerably during the last fifty years: the old

Lee Enfield rifle has been supplanted by the AK 47, rocket launchers and artillery. Warfare has replaced the occasional skirmishes between smugglers and border police. Jihadist military organizations are better adapted to the new situation, recasting the 'benevolent smuggler' narrative into that of jihad. Nowhere is smuggling more 'political' than on the borders between Egypt and Israel, Egypt and Libya, Afghanistan and Pakistan, and Cameroon and Nigeria.

However, in order to extend the space for smuggling operations (which have become global business transactions instead of just illegal border crossings) regional networks are needed, and these networks are often either provided by or based on religious Salafi networks. There is a strong connection between labour migration, business travel and the religious mobility of young men in search of diplomas and status who benefit from grants and scholarships to study in Gulf madrasas. These different kinds of mobility all involve the same people, who can make more money than their fathers (whose potential wealth is based on land and staple products more than on cash). Of course, neither enrolment in foreign madrasas nor the combination of labour and religious migration is specific to tribes. However, in the case of tribes there is an amplifying effect: this kind of business is based on trust and on the need for a stable connection between home and abroad, plus the benefit of armed protection (or of strong enough tribal patronage to deter extortion). The export of 'tribal solidarity' and the capacity of the tribe to re-integrate both estranged and prodigal sons allow it to make the best use of the generational crisis and its members to find or create a new constituency by playing on both the traditional codes and customs and on the need for social change.[4]

There is a strong but indirect link between Salafism and the upgrading of smuggling from a local activity into global business networks. It empowers the youths who are the effective smugglers (Cameroon) or who have had religious education in Salafi madrasas (Pakistan). They master the globalization of both circulation and ideas, and can maximize their newly acquired economic and cultural capital. Tribes that look anthropologically more conservative might in fact be more effective in making room for their returning children than more urbanized societies, because these children keep their 'seat' in the tribal system whatever their personal trajectory, and may turn this seat into a trampoline for acquiring higher status by maximizing their new 'capital' acquired abroad. Their migration is always presented as a success story.

This 'diasporization' of tribes through the displacement of youths may be increased by repression (Cameroon) or invasion (Afghanistan), but in all cases it switches the legitimacy provided by the wealth and/or religious knowledge of traditional elites to new categories of young entrepreneurs, who often belong to less powerful clans because these are the first to leave.[5]

Salafism as a tool for recasting tribal dynamics

We should not equate the process of Salafization with that of jihadism, however: Salafization is a larger phenomenon that does not always lead to jihadism (as for the Awlad 'Ali, studied by Hüsken), but jihadism is always connected with an ongoing Salafization. Both are linked to a mutation of leadership and internal competition within tribes. Radicalization first expresses resentment against traditional leaders, either because they collaborate with the state for their own benefit (Cameroon) or because they are unable to ensure adaptation to change.

In fact, tribes are not egalitarian: polarization between tribal notables and 'commoners' (people of lower lineage and youths) has often increased during recent decades because the economic assets at stake have increased (smuggling, state allowances). Salafism allows new and younger leaders to emerge at the expense of traditional Sufi leaders. Salafism is linked with travel and globalization, because the new religious leaders have been educated elsewhere, and often abroad. Moreover, Salafi leaders can mobilize new sources of revenue (grants to study abroad, funds to build mosques), while the revenues of Sufi orders are mainly local (gifts from believers). The Sufi orders have missed the opportunity to become global in tribal areas (unlike the Sufi orders in western Africa, like the Tijannya, which have become a successful global organization).

Nevertheless, the link between the crisis of tribal structures and the breakthrough of Salafism does not mean that the tribe is disappearing as a tribe. For dominated clans or for would-be leaders it is a good opportunity to contest the power of the traditional elite without antagonizing the tribe as such. They just claim to have greater legitimacy and efficiency (through their belonging to international networks), specifically when the tribe is confronting a foreign assailant (Afghanistan, Iraq). If Salafi leaders are usually not the traditional tribal leaders, they belong to a lineage, which helps (lower lineages versus superior ones). In short, local actors refer to the tribe as a specific entity even if what constitutes this specificity at one time might have changed structurally. In any case, kinship works, at least for the moment.

However, when jihadist movements take over non-jihadist Salafi networks, they may target the very tribal structure by requiring young activists from the tribe to show that their loyalty to the movement is above their loyalty to their parents and lineage, for instance by joining military and security units under the direct command of jihadist leaders (as Boko Haram and ISIS do). This is certainly the point where the interests of the tribe and the interests of the global jihadist organization might diverge.

The generational issue is the key

In a sense, Salafization corresponds to the assertiveness of a new generation of young males who can play the 'holier than thou' game with the older generation. However, it seems that Salafism and jihadism are not just tools with which to challenge traditional tribal leaders. It is not just a matter of competition, as much as of redistribution of traditional roles, including gender roles. Salafism appears as a new way to recast traditional gender and generational patterns for the benefit of young males. It goes along with more exclusion and seclusion for women. Women are first excluded from participation in religious life: religious performances that Sufism and 'popular' Islam used to allow (visits to the saints' graves, rituals concerning fertility etc.) have been forbidden by the Salafists, who have not provided a new position in the public space for women; something the Muslim Brothers did (by setting up the 'association of Muslim women', accepting women into the labour market if they wore the new 'Islamic' garb, establishing separate women's schools, appointing female candidates in elections, etc.). The model that I saw in Nuristan in 1985 spread: women were more and more excluded from farming activities outside the house. The *niqab*, which prevents women from working, is spreading in tribal areas (in

Afghanistan, the *chadri* was mainly a pious urban middle-class attire before it spread to the rural areas). While Islamism recasts the role of urban faithful women, Salafism destroys the niches of female religiosity and social participation in tribal areas.

When the fiercest jihadist groups are in charge, they challenge the traditional patterns of marriage and tend to build an army of 'janissaries', young men living together (as does Boko Haram, and many Salafi madrasas, which are also boarding schools for very young boys who are thus separated from their families for years). A logical consequence might be the kidnapping of would-be brides. An old tribal custom (*ghanima* or booty) is thus sanctified and recast as a religious duty, whether it concerns women or wealth. *Takfir*, or excommunication, of the enemy allows all kinds of plunder and abuse. The consequence is that the recasting of tribal identity into a jihadist one reaches its limits when the jihadist organization goes too far in erasing, instead of manipulating, tribalism.

The debate on tribes between al-Qaeda and ISIS

We have seen that both al-Qaeda and ISIS have found territorial roots among tribes, and only among tribes. Both have global strategies and favour *sharia* replacing local customs. Both acknowledge that 'tribes are tribes', even if they intend that the tribal system will eventually disappear. The big difference is that ISIS considers that the tribal system should be dissolved immediately into the fold of the Islamic state, while bin Laden advocated respecting the tribal system because it exists and is more useful than harmful. The reason for the divergence is obvious: for AQ the priority is global jihad, and not building a local Islamic emirate or state that would become the target of a foreign offensive and would be destroyed sooner or later. For Al-Baghdadi, the priority is to build a territorial Islamic entity that ignores any kind of segmentation or communal identity, whether familial, tribal, ethnic or national. The tribal system is an obstacle to the rise of the Islamic state, even if tribesmen are welcome to join, provided that they reject any kind of tribal loyalty. ISIS means it: it has executed whole tribal clusters which proved to be more loyal to their tribal leaders than to the Caliphate.

Let us compare the two positions. According to William McCants:

> Just as AQAP [al-Qaeda in the Arabian Peninsula] should avoid attacks on the local government, Bin Laden advised them to 'avoid killing anyone from the tribes' (Bin Laden, 'Letter to Nasir al-Wuhayshi', 2). To his mind, the tribes were pivotal to the success of the jihadist state-building enterprise, which would be doomed without their backing. 'We must gain the support of the tribes who enjoy strength and influence before building our Muslim state,' wrote Bin Laden (Bin Laden, 'Draft Letter from Osama bin Laden to Nasir al-Wuhayshi' [English translation]). [6]

Meanwhile, the position of ISIS is more patronizing:

> The Islamic State has an extensive history of building relations with the tribes within its borders in an effort to strengthen the ranks of the Muslims, unite them under one imam, and work together towards the establishment of the prophetic Khilafah [caliphate]. Its practice of attending tribal forums, addressing the concerns of the tribal leaders and accepting their *bay'ah* [allegiance] is regularly met with success. (*Dabiq*, issue 3)

And then in the same journal:

> There the tribe—when intoxicated by *jāhiliyyah* [ignorance]—still acts like a body with some kind of bigoted head or like a gang maddened by the mob mentality of tribal arrogance. They might move like a flock of birds or school of fish, albeit less gracefully due to their extreme ignorance.

In short, the future of a 'good' tribe is to disappear as a tribe and to melt with the Caliphate. But there is a clear 'double-speak' with ISIS: it has established an office to deal with tribes and never hesitates to play the tribal game, by pitching some clans against others.

Needless to say, such a position sooner or later will lead to the moment of truth. Will the jihadist turn be the swansong of the tribe or its Phoenix dance, finding a new life through fire? The coming years will bring an answer. In the meantime, let us assess the present state of the relationship between tribes and global jihadist organizations.

1

IRAQI TRIBES IN THE LAND OF JIHAD

Hosham Dawod[1]

While most Arab Spring uprisings have resulted in civil wars and neo-authoritarian regimes, their most significant outcome remains the dramatic rise of radical jihad in the form of Islamic State (ISIS/*Daesh*). The collapse of state institutions in a number of countries has reduced the amount of leeway that foreign states might have, thus making it inevitable that attempts will be made to connect with local tribes. While we know that tribes usually pledge allegiance to state authorities and even to foreign powers, we are still in the dark about the behaviour of tribes in the land of jihad. This chapter discusses this phenomenon in Iraq, a country struggling with political implosion, an undermined state, a rise of radical jihad, sectarian war and regional and international interference.

A careful study of the Arab–Muslim scene highlights the central role that tribes play in political, military and security issues. It is no secret to anyone that in 2004, a year after its invasion of Iraq, and more specifically from 2006 onwards, the US army started to realize the importance of the tribal issue in Iraq, to the extent that it attempted to copy this model in Afghanistan and other conflict areas reputed for their lack of government authority and the rise of subversive and jihadi movements.

Some twenty years ago, both researchers in the field and political and military figures were compelled to contemplate a concept that grew to become fundamental in the study of the history of societies. This concept presumes that modernization and globalization do not necessarily provoke the disappearance of a battery of socio-historical phenomena (local communities, sub-state entities, tribes), and nor for that matter do they accelerate it. On the contrary, observers have noted serious efforts to re-establish such phenomena in various places, to the extent that the tribal issue is seen to be at the core of conflict resolution. As such, it has become a common practice for the president of the United States to welcome tribal delegations to the White House, whether they be Sunni Iraqi tribes, or belong to a particular ethnic group in Afghanistan or other parts of the world in which the US has intervened. By the same token, it has also become normal for tribal leaders to reach out more to American army generals than to their own national political and military authorities. Thus, we face a somewhat new situation where tribes are motivated not only by their domestic context, but also by their complex and direct contact with the armed forces of the most powerful country in the world.

We must acknowledge, however, that the policy of tribal engagement that the US troops adopted with a significant number of Sunni tribes in its fight against al-Qaeda between 2006 and 2009 did pay off. Until US troops withdrew in December 2011, a majority of these tribes perceived the US military as a shield against the Iranians, or simply against anyone who might attempt to undermine their influence in the region (such as al-Qaeda, in the name of a more radical Islam). Nevertheless, tribal engagement was no easy task to achieve. It followed long years of extremely violent insurgencies and required a drastic change in the strategy of the US troops to be able to establish and maintain contact with this complex section of society. This was made possible through violence, but also through the generosity of the GIs, Marines and Special Operation Forces,[2] financial aid, jobs, integration in the Iraqi army and administration, and some political leverage in various areas. This eventual success was by no means a novelty, as it brings to mind the 'mutually profitable' relationship between Saddam Hussein's regime and most of these tribes.

It is no secret to anyone that Saddam Hussein used to recruit tens of thousands of his loyal forces (Special Republican Guard and Intelligence) among the young men of specific tribes. His rationale proved both simple and effective: in small tribes, the group bond (*'asabiyya*) is powerful, and the degree of kinship and proximity is more significant, which means that when extended to the heart of the state, the phenomenon would ensure that these young recruits displayed an unflinching loyalty to their master. Thus, these recruits not only called Saddam 'president' but also 'uncle' (*'am*); this fictitious kinship between them and him, which dominated their mentality, meant that they were all a family within a greater body (tribe, family or clan) led by Sheikh Saddam. This recruitment model was applied to dozens of small and medium-sized tribes, mainly in the areas of Salahedin, Al-Anbar, Diyala and Nineveh. All these young recruits who found themselves enjoying the easy life of the capital city and the other main cities would gain great power in exchange for total allegiance to their master.

It was with less success that Nouri Al Maliki, the former Iraqi prime minister (2006–14), tried to implement the American model. He would frequently be found meeting tribal leaders, and his office generously distributed money and gave political support to those who proved the most loyal (through what were called 'support committees', *Majalis al-isnad*). In return, Mr Maliki would naturally expect allegiance and loyalty to his persona and his policies.[3] However, even if Maliki represented a high state authority, he was still perceived as the head of the Shiite community in Iraq. This political game of identities, launched from the centre, would undermine the relationship between the capital city and the tribes in the peripheral areas, and pushed a number of Arab tribes in Sunni areas to adopt a wait-and-see policy, while other smaller ones collectively or partially allied themselves with ISIS.

Thus, the folkloric image of the tribe associated with war, raids and unflinching solidarity has in fact vanished. The time has come to address the issue of tribes as a socio-political group, which, while maintaining a predetermined form, will constantly evolve. This chapter aims to analyze the role that the tribe currently plays in Iraq, focusing on the years from the US occupation (2003–11) until today. The concluding part of the chapter will shed light on the relationship between the tribes and ISIS since its occupation of a significant part of Iraq and Syria.

What is the Iraqi tribe?

In the Arab world, two terms are usually used to denote tribe: *'ashira* and *qabila*.[4] In Iraq, the most widely used is *'ashira*. This term refers to a number of individuals and groups of people who speak the same language and sometimes also the same dialect.[5] The tribe is divided into a number of sub-groups known as *fakhdhs* (clans), which in turn are divided into numerous sub-sections of lineage called *hamulas*, comprising a number of houses or *bayts* (extended families). Each *bayt* includes a number of households called *ailas*. In this society, the house (according to Levi-Strauss's expression)[6] is the primary structure for action and political mobilization. For the Iraqis, *bayt* is more important than *aila* in a quantitative and political sense.

The tribe in the Arab Muslim world (with rare exceptions) is also characterized by distant patrilineal ancestry that is not based on actual lines of descent, but on fictive kinship ties.[7] As in other places, it is common for people to manipulate their genealogical ancestry, seeking new

Figure 1.1: An *'ashira* is made of a number of *fakhdhs*, in turn divided into many *hamulas*, comprising a number of *bayts*, then *ailas*.

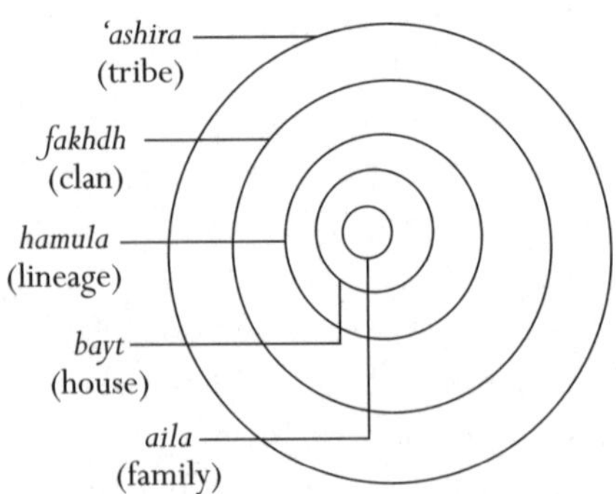

tribal associations. Claiming to descend from a holy line not only earns respect at the social level, but can also lead to the subordination of the whole group. Being the descendant of an ancestral tribal chief (great sheikh) is the necessary requirement to access the status of sheikh.[8]

Another key factor in tribal life is the acquisition of land from another tribe that vows to protect it by force (having inherited it, conquered it, obtained it after using it or having been granted it by the central authority). Today, land that was acquired individually has become the common land of the tribe, even if property transmitted by inheritance in rural areas stays within the same clan and is no longer common property. Nevertheless, people still talk about a property as belonging to a tribe, even if it has become private property and has been divided up. In this way a large portion of the assets of the tribe have been modified and significantly transformed.

Tribes may be of various sizes, but size does not determine their political impact. Saddam Hussein's tribe (Albu Nasser) was one of the smallest and yet it dominated the Iraqi political scene for decades. Some tribes bring together hundreds and even thousands of people around a sheikh and his house. The sheikh claims to control relations among tribe members, and represents the tribal entity and its interests not only to other tribal groups, but also to the central authority or any military, political or even economic foreign or international power (for example, the US army between 2003 and 2011).

Whereas in the past tribes were clearly more compact (living in shared spaces, operating through real interdependencies and led by a powerful and highly respected sheikh), today's tribes continue to look like a group but with a significantly reduced capacity for mobilization and internal and external coercion power. Thus, a member of a tribe enjoys freedom of action and movement. He can even distance himself from his group, a practice that would have been impossible not only after the creation of modern Iraq in 1920, but also during the 1940s and 1950s. Nevertheless, this same individual can still proclaim his tribal belonging in certain contexts in order to benefit from tangible and intangible benefits and protection. In what remains of today's tribal landscape, favouritism is commonly observed. This access to high positions and financial gain explains why in some southern or western provinces of Iraq (for example, in the south-eastern governorate of

Maysan, and in Al-Anbar province in the west of Iraq before the rise of ISIS) the majority of the police force and army is recruited from a limited number of tribes. In these areas of the country, there is a high risk that local conflicts between a police officer and an army soldier could degenerate into tribal conflict, and vice versa.

In the past, most tribes were grouped in big tribal confederations (*'asha'ir*). Each of them was headed by a supreme leader known as *sheikh al-mashayikh* in a kind of leadership model called *za'ama*. In theory, the tribe's sheikh did not possess any hereditary power. He would become sheikh of the tribe by virtue of his fighting skills and his political knowhow in safeguarding the unity of his group. He would play the role of mediator inside or outside the tribe, should he be brought to speak for his tribe. Members of the same tribe would be associated with the sheikh in their control over the tribe's acquired property and resources. The title of sheikh was commonly transmitted from father to son, provided that the new leader was up to the task and knew how to defend himself against potential rivals. Otherwise, a man from the same house (rarely) or from another higher-class house would be entitled to push him aside and take over the title. In this way, since the very earliest times the existence of this title (the power of the sheikh) has promoted the emergence of the house of the sheikh at the expense of other hopefuls. The prevalence of various socio-political ranks inside the tribal structure challenges the segmentarist discourse that emphasizes a hypothetical egalitarianism in Arab tribes.[9]

This factor of differentiation was exacerbated by the socio-political upheavals that Iraq witnessed from the end of the nineteenth century and throughout the twentieth century. The classical model of *'ashira* (Bedouin-type, or operating under the Bedouin model) had already undergone profound changes since the Ottoman reforms in the nineteenth century. The Sublime Porte had made it mandatory to register lands (*tapu*) and distribute them among those who had used them for a period of ten years. These people were entitled to use the land and be exempted from tax by the state, which had the right to claim possession of non-exploited lands. This reform has gradually and irreversibly created a model of private countryside property, and deeply altered social and political interaction both within the tribe and in its relations with the outside world. During British rule, the British authorities amended the Ottoman laws and implemented more drastic measures, especially ones that politically favoured the power of the sheikhs. They were no longer to be 'nominated', but they would impose themselves using their wealth and trans-local political alliances.[10]

Since the establishment of the post-colonial state (1958) and with its later development, tribes have continued to exist through a rather easy integration into the framework of the state, which became multi-ethnic and multi-tribal, mainly by means of violence.

Since then, we have been witnessing societal evolution on three dimensions:

1. A movement that appears at first sight to be contradictory: on the one hand, a real process of modernization initiated by the state and by an authoritarian party, the Baath; and on the other hand, a political structure heading the state and using the resources of tribal logic to consolidate power. In the 1960s and 1970s, Iraqi society witnessed major changes: a total and definitive domination of cities over villages, agricultural reforms, laws limiting the power of tribal sheikhs, generalized access to education, middle-class prosperity, progress in family and marriage models (towards more independence of nuclear families, and monogamous families), a relative emancipation of individuals from their primary groups (tribes and clans), and increased participation of women at the economic, social and even political levels. However, even if this proactive modernization failed to wipe tribes from the social and cultural landscape, it did manage to weaken them and give them a secondary position, thus depriving them of their political role. In fact, the centralized state of Iraq could not tolerate any individual subordination except to its own authority.
2. During the Iraq–Iran War (1980–89), there was a retribalization by the authorities of the social and cultural landscape. Recruitment to some state institutions and army elite units was carried out according to regional and tribal origins, to the extent that some military bodies and police and intelligence services corresponded almost completely with tribal structures. Whereas the period from the 1960s to the 1970s was characterized by a subordination of tribes to the state (a process called 'nationalization of tribes'), the 1980s and 1990s heralded an era of 'retribalization of the state'[11] (in par-

ticular regarding law enforcement). This socio-political tendency was accompanied by a quasi-scientific literature published under Saddam Hussein to praise the role of tribes.

3. It was really after the Kuwait War and the Arab Shiite and Kurd insurgency in 1991 that tribes and their leaders received public recognition of their role.[12] Even though the 1980s witnessed a return of the tribes to the political scene, this was not enough to confirm that the tribal structure dominated the public landscape. It was in the 1990s that this symbolic crossroads occurred, with tribal chiefs pledging allegiance to Saddam and tribalism, mixed with some politicized Islam, Arabism and the glorious Mesopotamian past, becoming the fourth pillar of the Baath regime. With this metamorphosis of the president, Saddam came to consider tribal values (honour, courage, etc.) to be legitimate parts of Iraqi Arab national culture. As a result, prominent state figures regained their tribal names, a practice that had previously been prohibited. This lenience later meant that it turned out that many members of the Special Republican Guard, heads of intelligence, and close bodyguards of the deceased president had actually added 'Al-Nasri' to their names (a derivative of Albu Nasser, the tribe of Saddam Hussein).[13]

Tribes in the early years of the American occupation (2003–4)

The initial political agenda that the Americans had in mind when they invaded Iraq can be summarized in three points: democratization, liberalization and modernization. These three principles are at odds with all the principles that tribes stand for. Nevertheless, following the advice of certain advisers, some voices inside the US civil and military administration emphasized the 'usefulness' of the tribes, which were thought to bring stability on the ground and, more importantly, in issues pertaining to security.[14]

After a few months in defensive mode, in which the US troops refrained from taking into account the tribal variable, tribes reappeared, only this time not as an obvious governance tool but as a socio-political structure that would support the military on the ground. With real challenges arising from November 2003, a document drafted by the US joint staff stationed in Iraq exaggeratedly highlighted the potential that the tribes could have in the reconstruction policy:

> At least three quarters of the population of Iraq belong to one of the one hundred and fifty of the nation's tribes. Many large tribes contain a mix of religions and ethnicities ranging from Sunni to Shia, Kurd to Arab to Persian. Tribal confederacies can date thousands of years, or can be the creation of political expediency in the past decade. If properly engaged by the CPA and CJTF-7, Iraqi tribes can become a key factor in the promotion of a safe and secure environment in Iraq.[15]

Despite the fact that this document overstates the extent to which the Iraqi population belonged to tribes, it clearly proves that the US military had indeed discovered the significant role that tribes can play as political structures: "An individual's stated attachment to a particular genealogical heritage is, at the tribal level, partly a political act (…). In claiming a particular ancestry, people necessarily align themselves with a given political charter and strategy, which cannot be glossed simply as kinship."[16]

From the end of 2003, the American troops undertook a real campaign to exert influence on the tribes. Local Iraqi actors such as Islamic parties (both Sunnis and Shiites) and ethnic groups (Kurds) failed to see the importance of this endeavour (see Appendix I). In the Coalition Provisional Authority, Lieutenant Colonel Alan King, a Lutheran from Arlington Virginia, was in charge of relations with the tribes[17] and communication with the press, and he was appointed director of an office for tribal affairs, officially called the Office of Provincial Outreach. On a tour of duty in Iraq between March 2003 and July 2004, King made every attempt to establish collaboration with the main tribal leaders in the Baghdad area. His work aimed at identifying prominent tribal figures who would be able to assist US troops in their peacekeeping and reconstruction efforts, while still trying to distribute funds on a proportional basis depending on family size (to avoid concentrating power in a few groups that would be harder to control at a later stage).

Along with ethnicity, confession and political party affiliation, the tribe became one of the elements that the coalition relied on to describe Iraq both sociologically and politically.

This reaching-out to tribal authority has been more or less theorized. In a widely-known paper published in many languages at the beginning of 2004, Kenneth Pollack, former CIA official in the Arabian/Persian Gulf and long-time advocate of the Iraq War, suggested drawing support from tribal chiefs to curb the extending insurgency. "The Coalition Provisional Authority (CPA) must reach out to the Sunni tribal community to eliminate their sense of grievance against the United States and so quell their support for the insurgency."[18]

Taking into account their presumed capacity for mobilization or for causing problems on the ground (collusion with jihadi armed groups, non-sabotaging of pipelines against ransom payments), tribal leaders were highly sought after, sometimes even by contradictory parties. They were not only highly solicited by coalition troops (American and British) for security purposes, but also by some Iraqi politicians and political groups to acquire their support on the ground and counterbalance other political opponents, or merely to be used for electoral mobilization.

The Iraqi Sunni tribes between insurgency and General Petraeus' policy

From the end of June 2004 onwards, Iraqis received partial sovereignty and an interim national unity government was formed. In July, a national conference brought together 1,000 people supposedly representing all factions of the Iraqi people, including a limited number of tribal representatives (70 representatives compared to 140 from political parties, and 170 intellectuals). In parallel with this formal political progress, insurgents had already gained control over the majority of the Sunni area and there had been a rise in Shiite activism, mainly by the Sadrist movement.

From the second half of 2004 onwards, and in order to address the expansion of this political and military crisis, the US military made strenuous efforts to engage in successful negotiations with the main tribal groups in the 'Sunni triangle' to regain control over cities to the north and west of Baghdad without having to intervene militarily. The period from April to November 2004 witnessed the peak of the jihadi insurgency in Fallujah.[19]

But then 2005 proved to be a bloody year in Iraq's modern history. For the first time in centuries, a predominantly Shiite regime took power in Baghdad and a constitution taking this situation into account was approved in a referendum. At the same time, still under the shock of 2003, the Sunni population felt alienated and went down the path of sectarian insurgency, offering the jihadi fighters space in which to expand. It is worth noting that the insurgency in western Iraq favoured Sunnis at the expense of other sectarian groups, and this is what characterized the Iraqi jihad from day one: Sunnis against Shiites, Arabs against Kurds, Muslims against an invasion described as a 'crusader war'. Faced with the incapacity of the government armed forces and the stalemate reached within the coalition, the Americans started a massive outreach effort to the main tribal groups in the Sunni triangle in order to gain control of the area.

This phenomenon was emphasized when General David Petraeus took command of the US troops in Iraq in 2006.[20] Influenced by his degree in history from Princeton University, Petraeus surrounded himself with dozens of anthropologists, including former Colonel David Kilcullen[21] of the Australian army and anthropologist Montgomery McFate.[22] For the first time since the Vietnam War, the Pentagon devised a programme to integrate anthropologists on the ground and embed them in combat units, with a budget approaching $40 million per annum (the Human Terrain System).[23]

After numerous failures, the Americans finally came to terms with the fact that granting tribes the role of political actors and negotiators at the domestic level made little sense (given their internal interests and allegiances), except when they were being used for sub-state liaison in territorial and social control: standardization of critical zones, armament of quasi-militias, intelligence-gathering through network infiltration, direct relations with local authorities, etc. In the tribal awakening movement (*sahwa*),[24] the Pentagon used tribes as local power networks in its fight against insurgencies (to provide them with assistance in their strategy to 'win hearts and minds').[25] This tribal policy also involved providing financial resources, support and weapons (tactical airborne support, means of communication).[26] However, the policy led to a certain leniency towards crime (mainly intensive oil smuggling) and to reprehensible practices such as vendettas and a justice system based on codes of honour,[27] thus further destabilizing the already-weakened political regime at a time when the Iraqi security forces were not fully operational, and the rationalization of the judicial system was proving—and still proves—rather difficult to achieve.

At a time when hasty 'experts' wanted to promote the so-called 'stabilization' role that tribes could play,[28] actors on the ground found themselves confronted with the limits and contradictions of the strategy of handing over local power to tribes. Acting pragmatically, these tribes were focused on their political and economic interests and they were even accused of playing a 'double game' in that sense. Some members of tribes would, for instance, sabotage infrastructure and sites that were previously under their control, under the pretext that these sites had been taken away from them. Other tribe members were also involved in the insurgency, joining the ranks of militias and taking part in terrorist activities. In a bid to thwart such practices, the US army multiplied its lobbying efforts with a number of people, while simultaneously pursuing other 'engagement' initiatives with prominent social figures such as businessmen, retired officers, clerics, neighbourhood and village chiefs (*mukhtars*), elected representatives, etc.

In time, it emerged that fostering relations with tribal leaders was not as efficient a way of restoring peace on the ground as relations with mosque *imams* and *mukhtars*.[29] Therefore, the outcome of the tribal awakening at a non-security level (i.e. at the social and reconstruction levels) is questionable. In Al-Anbar province, it was the local population's rejection of al-Qaeda, together with the negative impact the insurgency had on trade (both legal and illegal), that laid the foundations for the alliance between the tribes and the US army. General Petraeus noted that the Al-Anbar tribes 'all have a truck company, they all have a construction company and they all have an import–export business'. And the conclusion was that 'Al-Qaeda was bad for business'.[30] In other words, despite being necessary, alliance with the tribes was not the sole decisive factor in curbing violence and ensuring the security of the country's administrative, military and economic sites. As a result, engagement with tribes at the security level was, in general, limited.

The limits of the tribal *sahwa* were reached with the support given by the US strategy to civilian militias, known by the US troops as 'Concerned Local Citizens' (CLC). These included a number of former insurgents, unemployed youths, soldiers from the disbanded army and even former convicts, reaching a total of nearly 103,000 people (until January 2009, the US military paid them directly the sum of US$10 per day). Geographically concentrated in a zone surrounding Baghdad and in Al-Anbar province, the *sahwa* councils and the CLC gathered the vast majority of the Sunnis (80 per cent). These Sunni Arabs had been secluded in closed communities that the coalition had created using gates, surrounding walls (sandbags and cement walls) and a biometric census. This solution, which consisted in surrounding cities and neighbourhoods with walls, was supposed to bring about calm, but it was a long way from reconciliation. On the contrary, it played a major role in fostering turmoil in the land by creating barriers in the minds of the Iraqis: the Sunnis feared becoming the victims of violence and economic containment once the US troops withdrew, and in turn the Shiites feared that Sunni neighbourhoods and cities would become havens for Salafi terrorist groups. Nevertheless, the US military portrayed tribal councils and the CLC as real tools for preserving local security, protecting critical infrastructure and creating a system for contact and intelligence-gathering in the local community. However, after the US troops withdrew, this achievement proved hard to maintain for various reasons: the tendency of Nouri Al Maliki's regime to favour centralization and to refuse to delegate any power at the regional level or any power-sharing in running the state; the absence of a real national dialogue; and finally the confessional turn that conflicts took not only in Iraq but also throughout the region (especially following the outbreak of the Syrian rebellion in March 2011). Among other issues, these factors were reason enough to hamper the very existence of these organizations.[31]

Sunni tribes: from al-Qaeda to ISIS *(Daesh)*

In Iraq, as elsewhere in the world where the tribal phenomenon prevails, no government or global power is able to rally all tribes around its cause. This remained true even at the peak of the rise of ISIS (*Daesh*) in Al-Anbar and Nineveh in 2014–15. There are always divergent political alignments that result from history, local conflicts, inter-tribal feuds and mostly from political legacy, as is the case in Iraq with the Saddam regime, which was ill-managed by the Iraqi powers after 2003. The split represented by the invasion of Iraq, in addition to the controversial decisions taken by Paul Bremer, the Administrator of the Coalition Provisional Authority of Iraq, exacerbated by successive governments dominated by Shiite religious parties, led to the ousting of old-time military men of tribal origins recruited under Saddam. These were then referred to as enemies and they were stripped of their status, salary and social rank. Some tribal factions that allied themselves with ISIS (*Daesh*) were among them. They include the tribes of Albu Ajeel and Albu Nasser (Saddam's tribe) and some clans of the significant Jubour tribal confederation of the Saladin governorate. Other tribal factions became close to ISIS between 2012 and 2015. These include Al-Luhaib, Al-Hamdon, Al-Juhaysh, Tay, Al-Nuaim, Albu Hamdan, Al-Akeedat, Bani Rabia, Al-Khafaja, Al-Jawalla, most of Albu Mutaywit and a few clans of Al-Obaid tribe in the province of Nineveh. In Al-Anbar province, these groups include part of the Jumeylat tribe, the Al-Meshahdeh tribe (in Fallujah and west of Baghdad), the Halabsa and Albu Issa tribes, Al-Janabat (Al-Anbar), etc. Thus, the tribes that have partially allied with ISIS were mainly the ones that had never really acknowledged the authority of Baghdad after 2003 (see Appendix I).

As we have seen, both Americans and Iraqis made terrible mistakes, but so did the radical jihadis affiliated to al-Qaeda and other groups between 2004 and 2010, when they underestimated and humiliated their tribes and chiefs, particularly in Al-Anbar region (see Appendix II). At that time, al-Qaeda in Iraq was mainly led by foreign jihadi fighters who undertook the fight against what they perceived as American crusades. They would consider any local who proclaimed neutrality or collaborated with the local authorities an enemy. Very quickly, the two doctrines of a globally imported jihad and of the persistent tribal culture found themselves at odds. It is this mismatch that General David Petraeus took advantage of between 2006 and 2008. The fact that members of tribes were not as rigorously religious as those indoctrinated by extreme jihad led to an improvement in the status of normal clerics at the expense of local tribal sheikhs. As a result, tribal sheikhs believed that the time had come to collaborate with the weakened state and particularly with the US army.

After 2010, relations between jihadi fighters and tribes went through many transformations. After the death of the Jordanian Abu

Musab al-Zarqawi (2006) and a joint leadership that lasted four years (the Egyptian Abu Ayub Al-Muhajir and the Iraqi Abu Omar al-Baghdadi, both killed in 2010), al-Qaeda in Iraq was mainly led by Iraqis who were mostly former military men or intelligence agents from the Saddam days. In other words, these were men belonging to former Baath-loyalist groups. This is not to suggest yet another conspiracy theory according to which the Baathists would attempt to use al-Qaeda, then ISIS, from within to come back to power. In reality, these insurgents were profoundly transformed as they stopped being Baathists in the secular sense (before and under Saddam) and instead identified with radical Arab Sunni jihad, eager to seek revenge on Baghdad's Shiite regime and on the Americans, who were perceived as protectors of this regime. Under Abu Omar al-Baghdadi (2006–10) and more particularly under Abu Bakr al-Baghdadi after 2010, al-Qaeda turned into an organization in search of territorial roots in order to be able to lead the local population. The Syrian uprising and then chaos, along with the Sunni insurgency in Iraq, paved the way for what was, a few months later, to become ISIS (*Daesh*). The relations between the organization and some tribes changed. ISIS no longer sought to subordinate the tribes by humiliation, but aimed either to win their support or neutralize them by fighting them, should need be. Both in Syria[32] and Iraq, some tribes aligned themselves with ISIS, whereas others stayed loyal to Baghdad and the international coalition. These two groups have had bloody confrontations in the past and continue to do so today.

How has ISIS invested and worked with some Sunni tribes? First, it allowed them to use their human resources in their areas of influence; it did not force them to join its fighters, but offered security and assured the tribes that they were free to handle their economic affairs. This enabled ISIS to intimidate some tribal leaders through their associates in charge of Sunni provinces, who also represented the tribes in economic and security matters. ISIS gained many benefits from associating with tribes in this way.

Oil business

Since ISIS got its hands on oil wells in north-west Iraq (2014–16), it has been active in the oil trade dominated by tribes who lived near these wells. This opened up a new area of profit for them, and created an opportunity for tribes like some clans of Al-Jubour, Albu Mutaywit and Albu Hamdan. This trade remained a substantial source of income for ISIS, while the tribes were extracting, smuggling and selling the product, which they felt gave them economic freedom.

Transportation business

Tribes in Al-Anbar and Nineveh have always run trucking businesses, which have suffered from difficulties amid economic problems in recent years. But when ISIS took over in a Sunni area, the Syrian border, these trucks no longer faced difficulties moving between the countries and so hundreds of trucks were able to transport goods to and from Syria and Turkey, in addition to oil tankers.[33]

Currency business

Recent surveys show that ISIS has developed the way it deals with the dollar. These reports confirm that ISIS makes between US$20 million and $25 million a month through dollar auctions at the Central Bank of Iraq.[34] These transactions give freedom to banking systems in the ISIS zone, allowing business to grow and bankers to work. These bankers guarantee that millions of dollars every day flow to and from ISIS, which is able to evade international attempts to isolate them from the banking system. In spite of the organization's Sunni fundamentalism, ISIS shows pragmatism when it comes to finances.[35] The movement of money is linked to the funds available from oil and transport businesses, which are run by many tribes. Even those who are against ISIS are part of this economy, willingly or not, because it is based on mutual interest.[36]

I have highlighted the fact that the tribal transformations that occurred a few decades ago deepened the rift between the clans of big houses and sometimes also among notables. This meant that proximity to ISIS did not necessarily include the whole tribe, but just some of its members. In some villages and small cities in western Iraq, the bitterness of the violence is explained not only by the radical character of ISIS, but also sometimes by disputes among factions of the same tribe, or between two groups disputing the same land. Some individuals, and even houses or clans, might have joined the ranks of the jihadis because of internal disputes, local pressure, fear or even financial benefits.

At the sociological level, a new key factor has emerged: the youth of some tribes preferred ISIS over their tribal hierarchy. The elements leading to this factor range from a conflict of generations, to a thirst for vengeance against the regime dominated by Shiite political parties and their regional allies, to an increasing level of individual autonomy, which allows for a total emancipation from the tribe.

The big predominantly Sunni tribal confederations such as Shammar, Obaid, Jubour, Zubaid, Albu Fahd, Albu Nimr, Albu Farraj, Albu Alwan, etc. neither helped ISIS nor pledged allegiance to the organization. They sought to protect their relations with the state, even if it was weakened, and most importantly with representatives of other countries in the region such as Jordan, Saudi Arabia, Turkey, and great powers such as the US.

Conclusion

Many lessons can be drawn from the tribal phenomenon in Iraq and this part of the world. Tribes remain useful actors or, on the contrary, a destabilizing factor in the local order. To confirm their role as main actors, today's tribes need support from the state, when it has both presence and supremacy, and otherwise from other regional powers, and even directly from Western countries such as the US.

Even if at the logistical level tribes need assistance from foreign powers, their own power is reproduced according to local norms and codes. This is exactly the point that jihadi organizations such as al-Qaeda missed between 2004 and 2010. Once again, it is worth noting the example of Al-Anbar province, where the strategy of US Generals David Petraeus and John Allen in 2006–9 was relatively successful. They understood that a jihadi emir would always try to impose himself in the name of an abstract, global and radical Islam. In fact, a major conflict of interests and legitimacy proved inevitable between the Sunni tribes of western Iraq and radical Islamists such as al-Qaeda.[37]

ISIS has tried to avoid the fatal mistake that al-Qaeda made with tribes, and even to alleviate its effects; but there will always be a contradiction between an organization that gets its inspiration from general principles and relies on transversal networks and local groups such as tribes. Unlike al-Qaeda, however, ISIS has a structure that benefits from international jihad while maintaining a territorial freedom that leaves part of the leadership on the ground to be assumed by local militants and jihadis. This pushes ISIS—more than al-Qaeda—to nurture good relations with tribes, and especially those opposing the government.

In this race to win the tribes both the state and the international coalition, however weakened they have become, are the most favoured because of their means, their capacity to spread financial gain and their willingness to delegate part of the local management.

2

KTO KOVO? TRIBES AND JIHAD IN PUSHTUN LANDS

Mike Martin[1]

Introduction

Jihadism and tribalism are similar forces. Both espouse unity; but both tend towards factionalism. Both coexist and interact extensively in the region covered by this book, and have seen a resurgence in recent years. Using data from Helmand province in southern Afghanistan, I will argue that this relationship is best explained when interpreted using insights from scholarship on civil wars.

I will argue that jihadists have only been able to impose their will—that is, the unity amongst the *ummah* that they espouse—when they understand tribal factionalism and use it to achieve their aims. In other words, they must play the tribal game to beat the tribal game. Jihadi ideology, and the legitimacy that it confers, is important for cultivating unity, but it is not sufficient. I will argue that there is also an additional requirement for local political intelligence on tribal factions. That is, who is fighting whom?

This requirement becomes very difficult (if not impossible) to meet in the presence of conflict, because of other ideological, or legitimacy-giving, powers that are competing for the allegiance of the same tribal factions. This will become clearer as we go forward, but there are almost always several outside powers competing for tribal allegiance. This creates a natural advantage for tribal factions on the ground, as they are the source of the political intelligence that outside powers need to enact their ideological programme.

I will illustrate these ideas using the example of Helmand province in southern Afghanistan over the last forty years. I demonstrate that the Taliban administration (1994–2001) was the most successful in terms of both espousing and implementing its ideological programme in Helmand, and of conferring unity on previously disparate tribal factions (this period will be contrasted with the periods before and since). I argue that this was a result of its fine-grained political understanding of the area.[2] I conclude that outsiders seeking to combat jihadism *in situ* could learn from the jihadi movements themselves. In order to defeat jihadi groups, they should focus less on the jihadi ideology and more on the tribal factionalism that it interacts with.

Concepts

A tribe is 'a social division in a traditional society consisting of families or communities linked by social, economic, religious, or blood ties, with a common culture and dialect, typically having a recogniszed leader'.[3] Tribalism, therefore, is simply the 'behaviour and attitudes that stem from strong loyalty to one's own tribe'.[4] Post-colonial scholarship often interprets these concepts as derogatory, implying a form of primitiveness which explains underdevelopment.[5] I do no such thing and use the term neutrally.

People in Helmand habitually define themselves as belonging to a particular social group[6] (they use the word *qaum*, which denotes 'a kin group, tribe, race or people'[7] or *pshe*, meaning 'leg'—English speakers would say 'branch'—of a tribe). Most often, this means that they have a common ancestor, although people do very occasionally change tribes for political reasons (usually to gain protection).[8] In reality, Helmandi tribes continually compete with each other for resources of all types (including access to government positions).[9] Finally, when we discuss 'tribe' in a segmentary patriarchal tribal system like the Afghan Pashtun, it should be considered a shorthand for family, extended family, sub-clan or clan, etc. All are in potential competition with each other. Indeed, 'tribalism' should be considered simply as inter-lineage competition for resources and power—this is the factionalism outlined in the introduction.[10]

In Arabic, the word *jihad* is a noun meaning 'to strive, to apply oneself, to struggle, to persevere'.[11] The term is controversial, however, and can be interpreted as both an inner spiritual struggle and as a physical (violent or non-violent) struggle against the enemies of Islam.[12] Whilst accepting both interpretations, in line with common usage,[13] I use the term *jihad* to mean violent struggle against the enemies of Islam. In this context, jihadism is the behaviour that stems from an acceptance that violent struggle is appropriate against the enemies of Islam.

The concepts of *jihad* and *ummah* ('the community of Muslims bound together by religion')[14] are intimately linked.[15] Jihad is carried out against the enemies of Islam, who are by definition outside the community. For example, the original jihad in the Mohammedan era, and Islam itself, grew out of the tribal society of the Arabian peninsula. This jihad was directed at societies that refused to convert and were considered a threat. Within a century, jihad had spread the message of Islam from the Atlantic Ocean to China.[16]

The original jihadists managed to overcome the factionalism inherent in tribal Arabian society. However, on the Prophet Mohammed's death, this tribal factionalism resurfaced with many Arabian tribal chiefs rebelling and claiming that they owed their allegiance to Mohammed himself as part of a political deal negotiated at Medina, the early Muslim capital. The new caliph, Abu Bakr, disagreed. From his point of view, factionalism, represented by tribalism, threatened the *ummah*, and he crushed the revolt.[17] Today, modern-day jihadists—from al-Qaeda[18] to Hamas[19]—still agree that Muslim unity is a vital goal for the practice and concept of jihad.[20]

Jihadism and tribalism both thrive in areas that are stricken by civil wars—from northern Nigeria, Mali and Libya[21] to the Sinai[22] and Yemen,[23] and from Somalia[24] to Syria[25] and Iraq.[26] This is also the case for the subject of this chapter, Afghanistan and Pakistan. That is not to say that there are not areas of the world where jihadism is practised in the absence of tribalism (for example, western Europe) and where tribalism is practised in the absence of jihadism (for example, the Amazon region of Brazil). Nor is it to say that the two cannot coexist in the absence of conflict, for example in the northern part of the Arabian peninsula (although this region is often identified as a funding source for jihadi groups elsewhere).[27] However, I argue that the linkages between the two phenomena go beyond the casual, and that jihadi groups and tribalism interact in predictable ways in areas of conflict. The question that this chapter sets out to explore is how the two phenomena interact in Helmand, Afghanistan.

Both jihadism and tribalism have seen a re-emergence over the last thirty years. Both revolve around non-state actors, and their re-emergence can be interpreted as a result of the decline of the relative power of the nation state in the region covered by this book.[28] The reasons for this are various, but include the failure of Arab nationalism and the autocracies associated with it,[29] the further integration of the global trade and financial systems coupled with improvements in communications technology—which has exposed poorly-run states to global forces,[30] and the end of the Cold War—which had tended to 'congeal the political terrain of nation-states' worldwide.[31]

In many countries in the region, there has been a direct link between the decline of the state and the rise of tribal and jihadi power, as the leaders of these countries have sought to solidify their power by co-opting non-state actors into fulfilling functions of the state. Examples include Iraq's Saddam Hussein reaching out to tribes in the 1990s,[32] Syria's Bashar Al-Assad supporting jihadi groups in the 2010s[33] and Afghanistan's Najibullah working with both tribes and jihadi groups in the 1980s.[34]

Civil war theory

First among the explanations for civil wars is that they are driven by primordial desires; that is, groups of humans are linked psychologically to certain features of their environment, particularly territory.[35] Later, with the rise of the concepts of ethnicities and cultures, scholars spoke of ancient hatreds of other groups of humans, guided by perceived histories.[36] Both espouse something understood by all: we are 'us' and they are 'them'.[37] The intuitive nature of these explanations is what makes them popular, particularly in the West, where narratives about more primitive, less civilized (other) people are still prevalent.[38] These psychological, sociological and anthropological analyses have been challenged by a substantial body of economic analysis.

Of these, the most influential were a controversial series of papers written by two economists, Paul Collier and Anke Hoeffler, who attempted to create a quantitative model of the causes of civil war.[39] They argued that a 'useful conceptual distinction in understanding the motivations for civil war is that between greed and grievance'.[40] Greed, in their original analysis, referred to economic factors driving conflict, such as control of natural resources and the opportunity to loot. Grievance represented those factors developed from the ancient hatreds explanation, such as ethnic or religious divisions in society and political repression or inequality. Their findings were clear: greed statistically outperformed grievance as a cause of civil war.[41] Collier and Hoeffler's work sparked a vast debate in the literature, which eventually led to scholars advocating arguments based on either 'rationality' or 'identity' when talking about the causes of civil conflict.

Rationality-based theorists of war argue that even extreme events such as genocide can be explained rationally. Their arguments are developed from economic rational choice theory, where individual actors are all free to make rational choices based on the evidence presented to them.[42] Groups (and leaders) are usually seeking either to gain resources or to ameliorate a security dilemma with a neighbouring group.

The identity-driven approach to civil war finds its roots in the ancient hatreds argument. That is, groups go to war because of their identity, often defined in terms of relationships with, and fear of, other groups. Stuart Kaufman, for example, identifies the foundational factors underlying civil war as the presence of myths justifying hostility, fear of group extermination and the opportunity to mobilize.[43] However, all the explanations of civil war discussed here operate at a macro or political ideological level.

Looking at the micro level brings further insight. The seminal example of this approach is Stathis Kalyvas' treatise, *The Logic of Violence in*

Civil War.[44] Kalyvas' theory of selective violence argues that identifying clear political groups and their legitimacy-giving ideologies (i.e. amongst jihadi groups and their ideologies) 'fails to match the vast complexity, fluidity and ambiguity that one encounters on the ground' (i.e. amongst tribal groups).[45] He further argues that there is a subversion of the grand ideological politics of a conflict by local actors, through manipulation of (often opposed) ideological groups. These dynamics are driven by local alliances and cleavages that outsiders simply do not understand. He states that by studying the conflict dynamics themselves, we are best placed to analyze the interaction between ideological (strategic/public) and local (micro/private) levels of civil war, in this case the interaction between jihadism and tribalism. The fusion of the two levels dictates the relationship.[46]

Taking the idea further, it can be shown that there are four commodities that are being traded across this interaction. Ideological outsiders, that is jihadi groups, trade ideology/legitimacy and resources, be they money or armaments. The local actors, that is tribal or lineage groups, provide intelligence (local political information) and manpower. The fusion of these four commodities creates political and conflict dynamics. But where does the locus of agency lie? Or, as Kalyvas quotes Lenin, '*Kto Kovo?*' (Who [is using] whom?).[47] To answer this, we must recognize that the four commodities have different values as they are traded between jihadi and tribal groups.

Thus, tribal leaders need funding and weapons (resources) for the fight, particularly in a zero-sum security environment where if an actor

Figure 2.1: Violence in Internal Conflicts

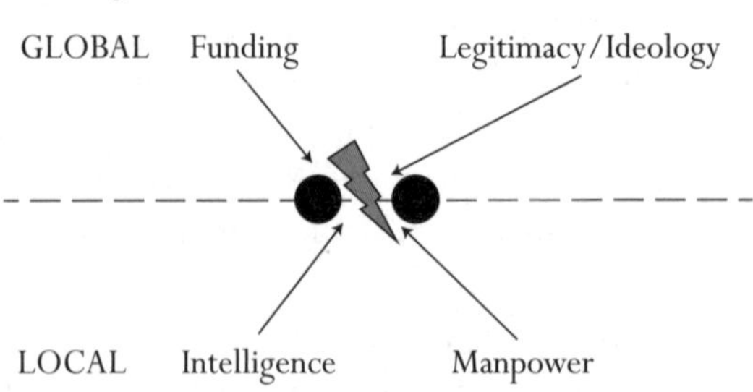

After Kalyvas (2000) *The Logic of Violence in Civil War*

does not secure the support of an external patron, a lineage competitor may well do so instead. Reciprocally, jihadi players need manpower for fighting. These two commodities often get traded equally. For example, the jihadi actor pays for the tribal actor to provide manpower. What is more, because they are both tangible assets, it is easier to ensure that a fair deal is being made.

However, the two other commodities—legitimacy-giving ideology and intelligence—do not share such a straightforward reciprocal relationship. Outside jihadi actors need political intelligence in order to confer their resources and legitimacy/ideology efficaciously. But one of the few sources of this type of political intelligence is the tribal factions themselves. This creates an inbuilt advantage for tribal actors, and one which massively increases with the presence of conflict. This is because of the presence of another outside player who is also seeking to co-opt the tribal factions. Furthermore, due to the intangible nature of the commodities, the jihadi actors have no way of verifying conclusively that the information they are receiving is 100 per cent accurate in the way that they can pay salaries to local men who are fighting for them (although they can, of course, use corroboration from different sources to reduce the risk).

Therefore, local tribal actors have an inherent advantage over external jihadi players in the relationship. And this advantage increases as the scale and intensity of the conflict increases. This is because local dynamics move at a faster pace, become more opaque to outsiders and more open to external competition. Conflicts and violence 'on the ground' end up being more related to local issues than grand ideological splits, even though local splits and issues are often presented within the framework of the ideological cleavage.[48]

The war in Afghanistan has been characterized by many in the West (and seemingly their Afghan clients) through a prism of rival ideologies: Westernized 'modern' values versus Islamist jihadi values.[49] The recent 'rise' of a new jihadi group, Islamic State (IS), in Afghanistan underlines this point.[50] By using detailed oral data from Helmand, this chapter will explore the relationship between the numerous tribal and jihadi groups that have either lived or operated in Helmand over the last forty years.

Tribalism and jihadism in Helmand

The area bounded by the current Afghan province of Helmand has been settled by six (previously nomadic) tribes since at least 1737. In that year, a Pushtun king called Nadir Shah granted these tribes, all members of the Pushtun Durrani tribal confederation, the lands that they largely still occupy in south-western Afghanistan.[51] Thus, the Alizai occupy the north-east (current districts of Musa Qala, Kajaki and Baghran); the Noorzai, the west and the south (Nowzad, Washir, Nad-e Ali and Garmsir); the Barakzai, central Helmand (Nahr-e Saraj, Lashkar Gah and Nawa-e Barakzai—the last of which they share with the Popalzai); the Alakozai, the east (Sangin); and finally the Ishaqzai are somewhat scattered because they suffered the ignominy of having been exiled from the area by King Abdur Rahman, only to be allowed to return some years later to the less productive lands in the province.[52] There are also various Baluch tribes in the far south.

During the 1900s, other tribal groups and ethnicities were encouraged to settle in Helmand. This was achieved with the construction of extensive dams and canals, beginning in the 1910s and ending in the 1970s. This is particularly noticeable in Nad-e Ali and Marjah—two areas that were completely reclaimed from the desert through an extensive canal-building project—where families were encouraged to settle on small packets of land, and often in tribally and ethnically mixed groups. In addition, families and groups were settled within the lands of the six 'traditional' tribes as well. These processes have massively increased the heterogeneity of the province—Nad-e Ali alone boasts thirty-seven different tribes and ethnicities—and make it a particularly good case through which to study tribalism.[53]

This tribal milieu has continued to become more and more complex since 1978, the year of the Afghan communist revolution and the start of the current conflict. This is because the conflict itself and the resulting changes of government and governance over the period have resulted in population movements around, and changes of land ownership in, the province. These movements then often sow the seeds of further conflict.

Helmand has also been a base for several jihadi groups over the period since the mid-1970s, when the jihadi organizations that fought the USSR-backed communist government first began to preach their ideology in Helmand's schools. These organizations were collectively known as the 'mujahidin' (those who do jihad) and were mainly backed by Pakistan, the United States and Saudi Arabia. They were organized into seven parties with differing ideologies. Four of these are particularly important in the context of Helmand: Jamiat-e Islami ('Jamiat'), Hizb-e Islami ('Hizb'), Harakat-e Enqelab-e Islami ('Harakat') and Mahaz-e Milli ('Mahaz').

Although Hizb and Jamiat members disagree as to which came first, the two parties are the closest in terms of their ideology, which is Islamist in outlook and similar to that of the Muslim Brotherhood (Rabbani, Jamiat's leader, was the first to translate Sayed Qutb's work into Dari). They sought to establish a modern state without a monarchy based on Islamic principles.[54] Harakat and Mahaz were the so-called traditionalist parties. Harakat wanted a return to Islamic law—*sharia*—yet did not see any incompatibility between the monarchy and Islam. They were mainly composed of clerics. Mahaz was known as the royalist party. It sought a return to the monarchy and was mainly composed of people connected to the pre-revolutionary order.[55]

In 1994, the mujahidin parties were supplanted by the Taliban, who grew to prominence in Kandahar in the second part of the year and shortly afterwards took control of Helmand. The founding narratives and ideology surrounding the movement emphasize the state of lawlessness in Afghanistan: the Taliban aimed to impose religious law—*sharia*—to return Afghanistan to a state of peace and unity.[56] They would end the civil war between the different mujahidin groups and the terrible depredations that it was inflicting on the population. Removed from power in 2001 by the United States-led coalition, the Taliban movement then re-emerged in Helmand in 2004–5 as an insurgency. Once again, the narratives surrounding the Taliban focused on protecting the population from the predatory Helmandi government, who in reality were the same warlords that the Taliban had chased out of Helmand in 1994–5. Additionally, it harnessed the population's feelings of resistance against the (mostly Western) US-led outside powers who were occupying the country.[57]

In 2014, the US-led coalition left the country, save for a small contingent. Concurrently, in Syria and Iraq a jihadi group called Islamic

State (IS) had risen to prominence. IS ideology is considered ultra-extreme, to the extent that they do not consider Shia Muslims to be Muslims. Towards the end of 2014 and at the beginning of 2015 there were reports of IS groups operating in Helmand and clashing with Taliban groups, whom IS said were not extreme enough.[58] Later on, in 2015, the Taliban overran several district centres in the north of Helmand and even threatened the capital, Lashkar Gah.[59]

This brief synopsis of the jihadi groups that have operated in Helmand over the last forty years demonstrates significant factionalism. In this chapter, for simplicity, the various governments will be treated as single entities, but in reality they have been, and remain, just as factionalized as the jihadi opposition. I will demonstrate that the factionalism within the jihadi ranks has more often than not mirrored tribal factionalism, and that jihadi dynamics have often been led by tribal dynamics, especially in times of conflict. Finally, it is worth emphasizing that none of the jihadi groups (except for IS) espouses fighting other jihadi groups (whatever the practice); instead, they direct their rhetoric and violence towards the various governments and their foreign backers.[60]

The Helmandi conflict, 1975–2015

In the late 1960s and 1970s, two rival ideologies clashed in educational institutions in Afghanistan: communism and Islamism. The leader of Hizb in Helmand, Hafizullah Khan, recounts the tale of Ghulam Mahmad Niazee, a leader of the country's nascent Islamic movement, coming to speak at the high school in Lashkar Gah. As he recalls, the communist students tried to stop him speaking and this resulted in fighting between the two groups, although he was eventually allowed to speak. Malem Mir Wali, the other major Hizb commander in central Helmand, concurs and remembers frequent clashes between the two groups in Helmandi schools.[61] Although these interviewees are self-reporting their motives for their later mobilization against the government, it does appear that the pre-1978 era represents one where ideology was shared across different tribal groups. Indeed, pre-1978 the government was considered powerful. This meant that communism and Islamism—both of which were preoccupations of the university-educated cosmopolitan intelligentsia—were fringe movements: neither had huge resonance in the countryside.

The communist revolution of April 1978 marked a profound change. Extreme left-wing government policies that targeted landowners, tribal leaders and clerics meant that the government in Helmand began to face resistance from the population. Initially, this was in the north and the far south of the province as local groups coalesced around the leaders that the government was targeting. Once the USSR invaded in late 1979, central Helmand followed suit, even though the Canal Zone settlers had previously been supportive of communist ideology.[62]

Thus, the initial response to the government was one of local resistance.[63] Originally, resistance groups rose up without the help of the mujahidin parties along community or tribal lines.[64] The mechanism was that an individual actor—a 'military entrepreneur'[65]—would leverage the perception of a power vacuum created by weakened or non-existent government in a district to improve his own position. For this he needed two things: men to fight and weapons/supplies to equip them with. With the later rise of the mujahidin parties, the leader would come to personify the interaction between local factors and external ones. This was because supplies were more likely to be given out to successful commanders with many men, and men would be more likely to follow a commander who was well-stocked with munitions. This interaction fused the local elements of men and on-the-ground information on the one hand, with the external elements of funding and legitimacy bestowed by an organization—a mujahidin party—on the other. However, at first it was a local spontaneous usurpation of government power.

At that time, most of the northern districts were falling from government control and the mujahidin parties in Peshawar were still forming and reforming, fighting for influence and trying to attract funding (from their own outside backers: the US, Pakistan and Saudi Arabia).[66] Local commanders used different communication networks in order to reach out to Peshawar for membership, recognition and funding. For example, Hizb was a party well-known for recruiting among teachers and the educated youth.[67] Its members often sought links through school or university colleagues to Gulbuddin Hekmatyar, the leader of Hizb, and thus to the supplies coming from Peshawar. Harakat was almost exclusively a clerical party,[68] with those that reached out to it often doing so through religious teachers. Mahaz, led by Pir Gailani and seen as the royalist party, organized itself along connections either generated around the royal government or through teacher–pupil relationships in Gailani's Sufi order.[69]

The conflict in Helmand entered a new phase in mid-1980, when the Soviets deployed troops to Lashkar Gah to protect it from mujahidin encroachment. Locally, this increased the level of fighting as many locals sought to attack the outsiders. Nationally, the Soviet intervention had massively increased the amount of funding that mujahidin parties received from the US: before the intervention they had been 'more or less dormant' due to a lack of funding.[70] The groups of resistance fighters solidified their interactions with the mujahidin parties and ostensibly began to adopt their ideas. As a result, the population became able to indicate which party a commander was affiliated with,[71] even though most commanders 'wouldn't have been able to say who Hekmatyar (the leader of Hizb), Zahir Shah (the previous king) or the Muslim Brotherhood were or what they stood for'.[72]

However, this worked both ways: 'the [parties] who gave [them] weapons had no idea how they were being used'.[73] This is a clear example of local actors exploiting the mujahidin parties for instrumental purposes, something they were able to do due to the latter's ignorance of the complexity of local politics. Which particular ideology was espoused by which mujahidin party was of secondary importance; membership of any mujahidin party bestowed the outside legitimacy that was needed by the local tribal groups.

As the conflict intensified, it became more and more difficult for the parties located in Peshawar to understand the local dynamics in Helmand. This was especially the case in northern Helmand, where there was no government presence—the conflict in northern Helmand was largely a conflict between two Alizai families, those of Rais Baghrani (previously mentioned) and Nasim Akhundzada, both of whom had evicted the government from their respective districts, Baghran and Musa Qala. Although the two were from different clans of the Alizai, they originally allied themselves with the Harakat party (a clerical party). Soon they fell out and Baghrani joined Hizb (which espoused a Muslim Brotherhood-type ideology), Harakat's main competitors in the province. Thereafter, Baghrani joined Jamiat, another

Muslim Brotherhood-style party, because it made him a better offer regarding supplies.[74]

The conflict between Harakat and Hizb dominated the province, and in northern Helmand it accounted for much more fighting than that between the government and the mujahidin. However, at its base it was a conflict between several families which changed mujahidin group affiliation to suit their ambitions in their local political contexts. The contest between the outside ideological players meant that more power was given to the local tribal actors who controlled the required political intelligence. None of the outside players fully knew what was going on.[75] This allowed Nasim to accept money from the government as well as, the Harakat mujahidin party, and to tax the opium crop in his area of control. He used the money to attack his tribal enemies. Nasim was eventually murdered by an old tribal foe from another Alizai clan, although it was depicted in the media as a Hizb killing. His brother Rasoul, however, was able to build on his gains and eventually installed himself as provincial governor in 1993.[76]

Central Helmand exhibited a different dynamic. The canal settlements had created a unique social mix, with different tribal and ethnic groups populating different villages, while some villages were completely socially mixed. Different villages tended to be aligned with different jihadi groups as well, and all of the parties were represented. However, Nad-e Ali did not suffer from the major infighting that was present elsewhere. There were several reasons for this. First, the presence of the government meant that the different groups had a clear target for their activities, and most of the different groups in Nad-e Ali shared a common cause due to the fact that they had arrived at the same time. Second, in Nad-e Ali there were a number of councils that kept together all of the fighting groups in a tribe, regardless of the jihadi party they were from. The refore 'Hizb'–'Harakat' fighting was not to reach Nad-e Ali until the end of the 1980s.[77]

For example, the Kharoti were the largest tribal community in Nad-e Ali at the time of the Soviet intervention.[78] Like many communities and lineages, they used a strategy of bridging ideological divides by deliberately placing people in influential positions on both sides.[79] In their thinking, the unit of currency that had to survive was the community group (tribe). During the conflict, the outside players were unable to determine what was occurring. Thus, the Kharoti leader, Wakil Safar, was appointed senator by Karmal. However, the village that he came from, Shin Kalay, and another closely-related Kharoti village, Naqilabad, were utterly dominated by 'Hizb' groupings (Hekmatyar, the leader of Hizb, was also a Kharoti).[80] Ironically, it was the arrest of the respected Wakil Safar during the Taraki era that had pushed the village to reach out to Hizb for supplies. Shin Kalay provided multiple fighting groups, with each commander leading men from their own lineages.[81]

The third major grouping of Kharoti in Nad-e Ali was made up of those whom Noor Mohammad Khan (also a parliamentarian in the 1980s)[82] had settled around Khwashal Kalay and Noor Mohammad Khan Kalay. Previously *kuchis* (nomads), they were slightly looked down upon by the other Kharoti, who had already been landowners before they came to Nad-e Ali.[83] The Kharoti in Shin Kalay and Noor Mohammad Khan Kalay had been feuding at a low level for years. Although Noor Mohammad's son, Haji Jamalzai, originally joined Hizb 'for lack of other parties', the villages soon broke with the rest of the Kharoti and affiliated with Harakat under Mullah Baz Mohammad (Taraki) from Marjeh.[84] The switch in mujahidin party affiliation was driven by the low-level feud with Shin Kalay. This dispute was to prove surprisingly stable during the jihad, however, with only minor skirmishing between the groups, usually over who could get supplies from different sections of the population.[85]

This stability was largely due to the presence in the aforementioned Kharoti council of Hizb and Harakat commanders, and to members of the tribe being in the government. In other words, Kharoti tribal interests were allied across the memberships of several opposed ideological organizations. Disputes between different Kharoti mujahidin groupings would quickly be resolved before they escalated, and the tribe was able to maintain a foot in all camps while sharing information amongst itself, thus allowing it to avoid involvement in the government–mujahidin fighting.[86] As far as the jihadi parties based in Peshawar knew, all the groups were fighting the government.

Eventually, the Soviets decided to leave Afghanistan in 1989. There was concern that the Afghan government would not be able to survive the withdrawal, and so it embarked on a massive militia programme, starting in 1987,[87] which both diminished the recruitment pool for the resistance and increased the government forces. The militias were employed to defend major population centres and government sites in Lashkar Gah and Gereshk, which were all that the post-Soviet government could realistically expect to hold. One of the main mechanisms of militia recruitment was to buy mujahidin bands wholesale; another was to use tribal leaders to create militias using their lineages. For the tribal leaders, having their members in different parts of the 'government' and the 'mujahidin' was a perfect way to enhance their position—it allowed them access both to two types of legitimacy and to funding.[88] Neither the mujahidin groups nor the government managed to achieve their aims, and, as a result of the competition between the two, tribal actors were able to take advantage of the largesse of both.

The Soviets continued funding the Afghan government up until 1992. It then rapidly collapsed. The conflict in Helmand had become one between Rasoul, Nasim's brother, and those who opposed him. Commanders and their men continually switched sides, between different mujahidin parties and between the government and the mujahidin. Everyone was acting on micro-security concerns largely predicated on the opium crop, and arranged their alliances and feuds within this context, irrespective of ideology or any remaining legitimacy that it might confer. Neither the government nor the mujahidin parties were able to control the conflict dynamics. Indeed, various mujahidin bands began working with various parts of the government against other mujahidin bands, who were also working with other parts of the government. This caused the government in Helmand to collapse, and at this point the Harakat mujahidin forces allied with the Parcham government faction, and the Hizb forces with the Khalqi faction. This reshuffling of the deck was based on a combination of tribal membership and alliances.[89]

Initially, the Helmandi government was composed of individuals in the Hizb/Khalq alliance—mainly Barakzai and Noorzai. This was completely divorced from the national situation, where a mujahidin government was rapidly becoming dominated by the Jamiat faction, in consort with the Parchamis (who were also ferociously fighting Hizb on the outskirts of Kabul). Jihadi ideology had ceased to have any meaning.[90] Shortly after a period of intense communal fighting, the Rasoul-led Harakat grouping—the majority of whom were Alizai—

managed to seize power in 1993. On a much finer scale, smaller groups opted for or against one of the alliances (and often changed sides) according to their micro-security situation and the alliances of the local groups that were threatening them. Due to an agreement between Russia and the United States,[91] the latter also stopped funding the mujahidin and so the local groups in Helmand largely resourced themselves by controlling the opium crop.

Rasoul's period in power was considered peaceful. Aside from Harakat's ideology, Rasoul was a strict Islamist and focused heavily on law and order, and actions deemed un-Islamic, such as smoking tobacco. However, in order to get into a position where he was able to espouse his ideology openly, he had had to spend his last decade breaking and forming alliances with the communists, other mujahidin groups and different tribal factions. He was successful in attaining his position because he was so good at playing politics to accrue resources and vanquish his foes. The Helmandis call this period of government '*andiwali*', meaning a government of friends, i.e. a power alliance of previously fighting mujahidin. However, Rasoul soon died of cancer and his brother, Ghaffour, took over.[92]

Ghaffour had barely settled into the job when a movement of students called the Taliban arose in neighbouring Kandahar. Its ideology was not much different to Ghaffour's, and in any case its main narrative of bringing peace and unifying mujahidin factions under an Islamic banner did not apply to Helmand, which was relatively unified and at peace. However, it wanted control of Helmand's poppy crop and its members understood well the political and tribal terrain in Helmand.

The Taliban approached Rais Baghrani, the commander in Gereshk, and reached an agreement that he would affiliate himself with them, breaking his deal with Ghaffour (an ex-Harakat commander). The Taliban were aware of the long-running and temporarily suppressed feud between Ghaffour's family and Baghrani's family. Six Talibs then organized an 'official' meeting with other Helmandi government 'officials' and Baghrani. An eyewitness related how they used the Taliban's soon-to-be well-known narratives, imploring them to work with the new movement and be good Muslims, saying, 'We want you to go [forward] under the Qur'an; we want the Qur'an to be raised up high.' Khalifa Shirin Khan was slightly incredulous: 'We have been fighting against the Soviets for fifteen years; we have been doing jihad; we are not *kaffirs*,' he retorted. The meeting broke up—the Taliban's ideology was not enough on its own.[93]

Shortly afterwards, the Taliban and Baghrani's forces began to evict all the other jihadi commanders from Gereshk. Once this was complete, the Taliban approached Ghaffour in Lashkar Gah with a deal: they would remove the other jihadi commanders from Helmand, and he would be left with control of the Alizai territory in the north of the province. In return, he had to give up Lashkar Gah.[94] Ghaffour considered what had happened in Gereshk and realized that he had no choice: with Baghrani on their side, the Taliban would be undefeatable, even though they had not yet sent any serious forces to Helmand.[95] Ghaffour fled to Musa Qala and Taliban forces occupied Lashkar Gah peacefully. The Taliban were clearly an organization with a strong ideology, yet they also had very good knowledge of the local Helmandi context—as evidenced by the secret negotiations with Baghrani and then the approach that they made to Ghaffour—which enabled them to shape events in their favour. Within a couple of months, they controlled the entire province and exiled all other jihadi commanders.[96]

The period of Taliban control ran from 1995 to 2001. The era is characterized by Helmandis as peaceful, and in interviews almost all commented favourably on the law and order that came with Taliban rule, even at the expense of a lack of development and slightly harsh (by Helmandi standards) punishments for transgressions. Helmandis also commented on the strength of Taliban ideology, i.e. Helmandis knew where they stood, and the government was seen as fair. Interestingly, unlike other periods covered in my research, the interviewees described the era in terms of Taliban co-option of the population, rather than population manipulation of the Taliban.[97]

As well as espousing a strong ideology, the Taliban utilized subtle political control. First, for key provincial and district-level positions they brought an entire set of appointees with them, mainly from Uruzgan, but beyond this they treated each area differently, often choosing tribal minorities who would be reliant on their patronage in the exercise of power. They did this even where it meant that they would have to choose a (previously) Hizb-aligned group, despite the fact that the Taliban were ideologically much closer to Harakat's clerical government-based ideology than Hizb's Muslim Brotherhood-based one.[98]

Thus, for example, in Garmsir, Mullah Naim was appointed from the Alizai, a minority community, even though he had fought with Hizb during the jihad (approximately 10 per cent of the district's population were Alizai, and the Alizai were largely excluded from governance in the rest of the province).[99] In Gereshk, the Taliban utilized Harakat networks to govern, thus relying on a minority of Barakzai from the smaller of two Barakzai clan coalitions. Hizb-affiliated commanders (the majority in Gereshk) were excluded, and so Khalifa Shirin Khan, the mujahidin district governor, stayed at home. The approach in Nad-e Ali was similar—working with minorities. Thus, Haji Mullah Paslow, the Popalzai Harakat commander, was an official in the government, while his nephew, Akhtur Mohammad, was a judge.[100]

Now Zad, however, offers a striking example where almost the entire district was supportive of the Taliban administration. Indeed, some of the most powerful commanders involved in fighting for the Taliban nationwide were supplied by this district. The Taliban managed to broker an alliance between the major Noorzai and Ishaqzai communities: the district governor had fought with Harakat and the military commander with Hizb.[101] This was quite an achievement after the amount of infighting between the two during the jihad (the Noorzai had largely aligned with Hizb and the Ishaqzai with Harakat).

Beyond these macro-level decisions, the Taliban also selected individuals from marginalized families and sub-clans. One particular young man, Murtaza, was a Kharoti tribesman from Shin Kalay. Shin Kalay was not well represented in the Taliban administration, mainly because it had been so closely aligned with the communists and Hizb, and it was the largest tribe in Nad-e Ali. Murtaza, however, came from the smallest of six Kharoti clans in Shin Kalay, the Shabakhel. This was either a reflection of the Taliban policy of empowering minorities, or the fact that Murtaza saw it as a way of breaking out of his life as a member of one of the less powerful clans in the village, or both. Before long, Murtaza was in command of a group fighting in the north of the country and was eventually arrested by the US and sent to Guantanamo at the end of 2001.[102]

Towards the end of the 1990s, people were starting to feel less positively about the Taliban government. The war in the north of the country between the Taliban and the Northern Alliance was interminable and was drawing large numbers of Helmandis into conscription. The Taliban then decided to ban opium, the mainstay of the Helmandi economy. Finally, there was a massive drought. Even in the face of these three factors, the Taliban still managed to remain in control of Helmand, an area that traditionally revolts against its leaders. This was quite a testament to the Taliban's social control abilities.[103]

The national Taliban government was removed from power through a combination of US bombing and the Northern Alliance once they had been re-monetized by the US. In Helmand, the Taliban who were from outside the province left, and those who were Helmandis went home. The new Helmandi government was formed of the same mujahidin commanders that the Taliban had chased out of the province in 1994–5. There was little talk of jihadi ideology—everyone was now a 'democrat', in line with the new US-backed Karzai government. Apart from this cosmetic change, for the population the situation remained much the same: the commanders grew opium, terrorized the population and fought proxy wars against each other.[104]

The complete failure to solve the traditional problem in Afghanistan—that of predatory government—meant that once again the population began to seek protection. In Helmand, as during the jihad against the Soviets, this meant reaching out to jihadi elements in Pakistan: the exiled Taliban council in Quetta. The aims of local Helmandi groups—tribes, villages and communities—were aligned with those of extra-territorially-based jihadi groups: the overthrow of the government.[105] Once again, local groups provided manpower and intelligence and the Taliban council provided resources and a clear ideology: a jihad to defeat the Western-backed, *kafir* Karzai government.

This dynamic became a fully-fledged insurgency during the period 2004–6. This occurred for two reasons. First, the (ex-)mujahidin commanders were all removed from government by the US due to their abuses. They all immediately began working with the Taliban to undermine the new Helmandi government whilst insisting publicly that they were still pro-government (and pro-democracy, etc.). Naturally, they were simply protecting their interests in power and the opium trade. Neither the Afghan government nor the US was wise to this for some time afterwards. At the same time, the Taliban also approached communities that had been abused by these same commanders and recruited them to fight against the new government. They thus managed to build a coalition of two previously antagonistic collections of groups through political skill backed up with a jihadi narrative about the non-Islamic nature of the new government.[106] It was a masterstroke.

The second reason was that the British deployed thousands of troops to Helmand in order to contain the nascent insurgency (previously there had been a small contingent of US special forces). This reinforced the Taliban's jihadi narrative and sparked a massive uprising, similar to that which faced the Soviets when they deployed troops to Helmand. In fact, the sequence of events leading to the proliferation of the Taliban insurgency, right down to the order in which the district centres were attacked, was almost exactly analogous to that which had occurred twenty-five years earlier with the rise of the mujahidin rebellion. This is because exactly the same tribal dynamics were at play.

Initially, the Taliban-sponsored groups made great gains and managed to pen the foreign-backed government forces into the district centres. Due to a lack of external competition, the Taliban managed to exert control over much of the province. This amount of control, and the apparent success of the jihadis, immediately attracted foreign—mostly Pakistani, but also some Arab—volunteers to fight in the south of Afghanistan over the summers from 2006 to 2008. Lacking in military training, most were killed or went home complaining that the jihad was not the religious war that they thought it would be, and that it actually revolved around power, land and opium.[107] Their presence often enraged local Helmandis, who did not see any benefit in having one set of foreigners fight another in their villages and fields. From then on, the conflict remained a local one.

The intensity of the fighting steadily increased as the British, and then the US, reinforced the number of troops in Helmand (by 2011 there were 30,000 Western troops in Helmand—ten times the initial number deployed in 2006).[108] They also massively increased the amount of other resources, such as spending on development and the raising of militias. These factors heightened the complexity of the conflict dynamics and provided another competitor to the Taliban, which made it much more difficult for the Taliban council in Quetta to understand the conflict and achieve its own aims. That is, their intelligence, mostly gained from the communities who were fighting for them in Helmand, began to reflect more the communities' aims than the Taliban's. This was evidenced by repetitive switching of local groups between the Taliban and the government, tribal councils that straddled the government–Taliban divide to the benefit of the tribe, and the fact that prominent commanders acted for both sides.[109]

The Taliban made a concerted effort to enforce their ideology and will on 'their' fighters in an attempt to shape the conflict dynamics in 2009–10. Previously, the Taliban in Helmand were organized in a *mahaz* system, a patronage system maintaining figureheads in Quetta to source and distribute military supplies. These *mahaz* commanders would have a number of fighting groups, but they were not always in the same area, and could be spread across the whole of southern Afghanistan.[110] The most important element of the *mahaz* system is personal links to particular commanders and areas. This is comparable to the situation in 1978–9, when commanders would develop and use links with those who were in a position to fund them.

This 'system' created a very confused situation, with several fighting groups operating in the same area but answering to different leaderships and funding. This can be considered analogous to the various jihadi parties operating in a contiguous space during the 1980s. And just like the inter-mujahidin group fighting that occurred in the 1980s, this too occurred with different Taliban commanders belonging to different *mahazes*.[111] This infighting caused the Taliban central leadership to decide to enact a centralized *nezami*—meaning military or organized—system that was to be led by a man called Zakir.[112] The *mahaz* system should be seen as the Helmandis reaching out for patronage in order to help them fight their local enemies. By contrast, the *nezami* system should be seen as outsiders reaching in and trying to influence the conflict using patronage. In terms of influencing the conflict dynamics, the *mahaz* system represents a dominance of tribalism over jihadism, and the latter vice versa.[113]

The Quetta Shura's plan for a centralized structure was laid out in 2009 and 2010. New *mahazes* were banned and a clear command hierarchy was articulated with more detail provided on the rules and responsibilities of the district and provincial military commissions.[114] The *nezami* system was mainly funded by charitable donations from individuals in the Middle East,[115] which were routed through Pakistani intelligence officers who sat on the Quetta Shura.

Outside Helmand and some other southern provinces, the implementation of the *nezami* system has been successful. Helmand, however, has managed to resist its implementation.[116] This is due to two factors specific to Helmand. First, Helmand generated vast sources of income through drugs and co-opted or stolen development funding. The *mahaz* system, which is better integrated with society, was better able to use this income to maintain a degree of independence. Second, Helmand's social structure—the *rutbavi* (hierarchical) Pushtun tribal system—is highly commensurate with the *mahaz* system. The *rutbavi* tribal system is based upon land ownership and a cycling of resources up and down a tribal hierarchy to maintain social cohesion.[117] This is mediated by key individuals, who usually pass on their position through family links. The *mahaz* system works in a similar way.

The resilience of the Helmandi *mahaz* system has led to a strange hybrid that is neither *mahaz* nor *nezami*.[118] This hybrid situation has created a confused Taliban command system in Helmand. As the Quetta Taliban have attempted to centralize their supplies, and hence the fighting, the *mahaz* commanders have attempted to co-opt that system. Moreover, if an order comes down through either the *mahaz* or *nezami* systems, it must be checked with the other system before it is carried out.[119] The greater levels of conflict due to the presence of US and UK forces meant that the information requirement to understand the conflict dynamics on the ground has increased. The difficulty for the Talban in Quetta of knowing what exactly is happening on the ground in Helmand has meant that they have been unable to dictate the conflict dynamics in the way that they could in 1994–2001, or even in 2006.

Interestingly, Zakir, the head of the *nezami* system and an Alizai from northern Helmand, felt the need to create his own *mahaz* in order to enforce the *nezami* centralized structure. Zakir's men consistently pointed out that they followed him in his *mahaz* capacity rather than his *nezami* capacity (contrary to what the Taliban in Quetta desire). Either the Taliban Quetta Shura did not have a good enough knowledge of Helmandi politics to enact a *nezami* system of control, or the *mahaz* system was too strong and ingrained in the Taliban organization in Helmand, or both. This confused situation was not resolved before

Western troops left Helmand in 2014 and, for unrelated reasons, the Taliban began to route funding through Peshawar and away from Helmand. Both of these factors caused a massive reduction in the intensity of the conflict during 2012–14 in Helmand.[120]

The year 2015 saw new developments in the cyclical Helmandi conflict. These started with reports of the rise of Islamic State (IS), a jihadi organization from Iraq and Syria, in Helmand and elsewhere in Afghanistan. Rauf, a protégé of the aforementioned Rais Baghrani (from the same clan of the Alizai) and a previous member of Harakat, Jamiat and the Taliban as well as an ex-Guantanamo prisoner, was denounced by Afghan government officials as being the IS Deputy Commander for Afghanistan. According to them, he had defected from the Taliban some weeks before causing bitter fighting between Rauf's Taliban faction and his erstwhile colleagues. He was then killed in a US drone strike in February 2015.[121]

In the middle of the year, there were reports in the media of heavy fighting between the Taliban and government troops around the district centres in the north of the province. By August, Sangin, Now Zad, Kajaki and Musa Qala had all fallen from government control. Tribal elders in Helmand indicated that Musa Qala may have been taken by Taliban linked to Baghrani in an attempt to limit the now-ill Sher Mohammad Akhundzada's influence in the opium growing area. This family feud—discussed above as that between 'Harakat' and 'Hizb' during the jihad—still continues. The same sources also discussed whether the Afghan government might recognize Baghrani's de facto control by making him governor of Helmand.[122]

By October 2015, media reports indicated that the Taliban were threatening the capital of Helmand, Lashkar Gah.[123] Again, initial reports from contacts in Helmand indicated that these Taliban were Alizai from the north of Helmand. This latest phase of the conflict is still unfolding and it is difficult to assess what is causing the fighting. Has there been a massive influx of Taliban interest and funding, or are local factors driving this latest round of fighting? Is this latest assault on Lashkar Gah, for example, representative of the centuries-old competition for government patronage between the largely Alizai north of the province and the largely Barakzai centre of the province? Time will help us draw conclusions, but it is clear that both tribalism and jihadism are alive and well in Helmand.

Conclusion

This chapter set out to demonstrate that jihadi movements are only able to impose their will—that is, unity amongst factions—when they understand tribal factionalism and use it to achieve their aims. Jihadi ideology is important for cultivating unity, but it is not sufficient. There is also an absolute requirement for local political intelligence on tribal factions. This requirement becomes very difficult (if not impossible) to fulfil in the presence of conflict because of other ideological, or legitimacy-giving, powers that are competing for the allegiance of the same tribal factions. This creates a natural advantage for on-the-ground tribal factions, as they are the source of the political intelligence that outside powers need to enact their ideological programme.

The Helmandi conflict offers a useful example due to the sheer numbers of tribal groupings and jihadi groups which live and operate there. During 1994–2001, the Taliban were able to impose peace and law and order when they carefully manipulated the tribal politics and propagated their ideology: their very entrance into Helmand was on the back of a tribal betrayal. By contrast, during the 1980s the mujahidin groups had not been able to impose their will on Helmand. The ongoing conflict meant that the parties in Peshawar were unable to understand the local dynamics, which, coupled with outside competition for tribal allegiance, meant that they were constantly manipulated by local tribal and military actors. There was a similar dynamic during the post-2001 era, when many tribal leaders balanced between the government and the Taliban, or switched between the two. Critically for them, the Taliban were not able to impose their preferred command structure on the fighting groups, which were rooted in their (tribal-structure mirroring) *mahaz* command system.

What remains to be seen is whether these dynamics are occurring in other areas of the world where tribalism and jihadism coexist. Circumstantial evidence suggests that this is the case. For example, in the most prominent current example, Abu Bakr al-Baghdadi, the leader of Islamic State in Iraq and Syria and the self-declared caliph, is Qurayshi—that is, from the Prophet Mohammed's tribe. This is not a coincidence: Sunni Muslim religious law states that all caliphs should be Qurayshi, and the fact that Baghdadi is a Qurayshi contributes to his ability to maintain his position.[124] If this dynamic is shown to be true elsewhere, then scholarship that attempts to understand jihadi groups will fall short without a deeper study of the tribal groups with which they coexist and extensively interact. This warning extends to those countries and organizations which seek to combat jihadism: take a leaf out of the jihadis' book and understand the tribes.

3

TRIBES AND POLITICAL ISLAM IN THE BORDERLAND BETWEEN EGYPT AND LIBYA

A (TRANS-) LOCAL PERSPECTIVE

Thomas Hüsken[1]

Destroyed tombs and the reserve of a friend

My first visit to the borderland between Egypt and Libya took place in 1993. I was a young student of Social Anthropology at the Freie Universität in Berlin then, and I had just received an internship as scientific research assistant at the German Agency for Technical Cooperation's Al-Qasr Rural Development Project (QRDP).[2] The project was engaged in introducing sustainable desert agriculture to the Bedouin population. The measures implemented and training programmes were based on water harvesting with cisterns and dam building in the *wadis* of the coastal zone.[3] The task for me and my fellow student Olin Roenpage was to conduct a study of the Bedouin economy in order to inform the project's development experts. After seven months of training in modern standard Arabic and Egyptian colloquial Arabic in Cairo, I was eager to prove myself in the field of development in general and as an ethnographer among the *Awlad 'Ali* Bedouin of the borderland in particular. In the first weeks of the field studies we roved around the coastal road between Marsa Matrouh and Ras Abu Lahu and along the desert highway to the Siwa oasis in our pick-up truck trying to understand the landscape, documenting settlement patterns and surveying the modes of agriculture and farming. Since we were particularly interested in the Bedouin customary law—'*Urf*—we were also looking for the tombs of renowned *shuyukh* (sg. *sheikh*, tribal leaders or holy men). As particular places filled with spiritual aura and the *baraka* (blessing) of the *sheikh*, these tombs were important for sacrificial offerings in popular Bedouin Islam. They also served as holy places for the resolution of conflicts among and between kinship associations and for the oath-taking of the *'Urf* councils.[4] All we could find, however, were ruins: tombs with collapsed domes that looked as if they had been exploded. Seemingly abandoned by people, the tombs appeared like hollow teeth in the desert. We were irritated and puzzled by these signs of destruction and neglect and at first could not make sense of them. When I asked my Bedouin mentor and key informant, Abd Al-Malik, he claimed that the destruction of the tombs had been committed by Egyptian Islamists from the Nile valley: 'They come here to trouble us with their radicalism. Among the *Awlad 'Ali* there are no such people,' he said.[5]

In the following months Abd Al-Malik became a fatherly friend of mine, tirelessly answering questions and helping me to pursue my studies, but he subtly avoided talking about the issue of radical Islamism among the *Awlad 'Ali* and the real happenings around the tombs. Abd Al-Malik had good reasons for his reserve. The early 1990s were the time in which *Al-Gama'a al-Islamiyya* (the Islamic Group) challenged the Egyptian state with a number of assassinations and severe attacks on foreign tourists, which seriously harmed the Egyptian tourism sector. The Egyptian state responded with fierce measures. Thousands of alleged or de facto Islamists were detained, tortured and executed. Even in the peripheral borderland between Egypt and Libya, the security forces were on the alert and eager to investigate potential interconnections between Egyptian Islamists and the Libyan Islamic Fighting

Group. Therefore, even talking about the issue of radical and violent Islamism to a foreign researcher was a sensitive matter and Abd Al-Malik wanted to avoid trouble both for himself and for me. But there were also more personal reasons. The influence of Saudi-Arabian Wahhabism and Salafism in Egypt also became apparent in a number of mosques in the borderland, and in Marsa Matrouh, the capital of the Matrouh governorate, in particular. Salafist preachers agitated against everything that they identified as conflicting with the pure doctrine. Besides criticizing the hostile foreign forces of the West and Israel (a common subject all over Egypt), much of the criticism was also directed at alleged heresies within Islam such as Sufism. As a member of a small *Sufi-Tariqa* (Sufi order) in Marsa Matrouh, my mentor Abd Al-Malik was directly affected by this and he was going through hard times. It could be that he did not want to involve me in this, or that he did not want to disenchant my enthusiasm for the *Awlad 'Ali*, but in his statements the Islamists appeared as an outside force, not as a part of *Awlad 'Ali* society.

Other informants and friends were less reserved or less involved in potential trouble. During Ramadan 1993, my friend Miftah Riziq revealed to me who was behind the destruction of the tombs: 'The tombs were exploded by Bedouin members of the Masgid al-Salam in Marsa Matrouh. They are followers of Sheikh Mohammad, a Salafist imam. Everybody knows them. They are *Awlad 'Ali* like me'.[6]

Since I did not want to offend Abd Al-Malik, and because our study was dealing with the economy of the *Awlad 'Ali* and not with politicized Islam, I did not confront him with my knowledge. It was only several years later when I returned to the *Awlad 'Ali* in 1998 for my doctoral thesis that we started to have an open discussion on the issue. It became clear that a highly politicized and even radical violent Islam had been virulent among the *Awlad 'Ali* for quite some time, and it was obvious that the *Awlad 'Ali* were no exception to the rest of Egyptian society.

Introduction

The current crisis of the post-colonial state in the Arab world and the ongoing violent reformulation of the post-colonial order (in the aftermath of the Arab Spring) in countries like Iraq, Syria, Yemen and Libya have redirected public, political and academic interest to non-state forms of socio-political organization, and to tribes in particular.[7] Studies of tribes and their socio-political organization once belonged to the core of anthropology of the Middle East, and great names and works are linked to this field.[8] However, some lines of anthropological theorizing have (intentionally or otherwise) exoticized Bedouin as nomads and essentialized them as examples of segmentary lineage organization and tribalism.[9] Within the context of the post-colonial critique, *homo segmentarius* was qualified as a construct of orientalism, and as an unintended effect tribes were neglected (by scholars and students) or portrayed as insignificant.[10]

Among those who kept in touch, the debate moved beyond an understanding of tribes as collective actors, bound by blood and honour and trapped in some sort of balanced opposition game.[11] Instead, processes of innovation, vitality and persistence have been emphasized in the analysis of tribal socio-political organization. In this perspective, tribal traditions serve as resources for the formation of 'we-group' identities and are used to understand and organize the social, political and economic world.[12] Tribes offer a social and cognitive system of reference in which a wide range of corporative networks of different scales and depths can be arranged. As in any form of human social organization, flexibility and innovation are as important as the continuing 'invention of tradition'.[13]

The recent rediscovery of tribes in the Arab Muslim world, however, is predominantly driven by political, military and security considerations that revolve around the alleged link between tribalism and jihadist terrorism.[14] In contrast to this, I will argue that politicized Islam and jihadism among the *Awlad 'Ali* in the borderland between Egypt and Libya have very little to do with their particular form of social organization as a tribal confederation. It is true that there are jihadist networks within tribes in a number of societies in the Middle East, and it is also apparent that some factions of certain tribes have forged political and military alliances with jihadist movements, but the same could be said about any other social group, class or milieu in the Arab Middle East.[15]

Instead, I will deal with certain political, social, economic and cultural patterns that are involved in the development of Islamism among the *Awlad 'Ali*. It will become clear that these developments are in concordance with non-tribal populations in the Middle East. In this respect, this chapter will not contribute to any sort of exceptionalism about tribal people. This chapter deals with the practice of Islamism in the borderland between Egypt and Libya from an empirical and local perspective. This means that I will focus on 'concerns, practice and experience in everyday life'[16] rather than on grand schemes or on Islam(ism) as a discursive tradition.[17]

At this point, a clarification in terminology concerning the meaning of definitions such as Islamism, political Islam and jihadism might be useful. As indicated above, I focus on the local and trans-local level. When I speak of Islamism I basically follow Oliver Roy's definition of neo-fundamentalism and thus refer to individual actors and groups in the borderland who promote a conservative re-orientation of Islam revolving around the evocation of piety, ethics and tradition that has developed throughout the Middle East since the 1970s.[18] In addition, I refer to individual or collective actors who have an explicit politico-religious agenda that demands the erection of a just Islamic societal and political order. In the borderland, these groups mostly refer to Salafist lines of politico-religious thought and the population also qualifies them as *Salafiyya*. Some of these actors use violence or have been instigating their followers to do so, while others confine themselves to political rhetoric and preaching. When I talk about jihadism, I refer to groups who intend to pursue their object of an Islamic caliphate by revolutionary means, including the use of excessive violence and the deliberate extinction of supposed adversaries.

The chapter will start with a short introduction to the people and their place: the borderland between Egypt and Libya. I will proceed with portraits of two Salafist preachers based on my fieldwork and participant observation. Next, an analysis of the audiences, followers and disciples of the preachers and of Salafist Islam will be offered. In the following section, I will discuss Islamism as a critique and as an evocation of a just order. I will then deal with processes of radicalization among the Islamists in the borderland and I will also direct attention to the role of Islamism during and after the Arab revolutions in Egypt and Libya. I will argue strictly on the basis of my research at the local and trans-local level. It will become apparent, however, that many currents at the local level are interlaced with broader national and global currents. The events discussed in this chapter cover a timespan of roughly twenty years, from my first fieldwork in 1993 to my last stay in the region in 2013.

Awlad 'Ali *in the borderland between Egypt and Libya*

The *Awlad 'Ali* Bedouin are a transnational tribal confederation that dominates the borderland between Egypt and Libya. The confederation consists of five sub-tribes and sixty-four clans. The sub-tribes are the *Abiad* (subdivided in *Kharuf* and *Sanaqra*), the *Ahmar*, the *Sinina*, the *Qutuan* and the *Gimi'at*.[19] The *watan*[20] (territory) of the *Awlad 'Ali* tribes in Egypt as it is today stretches along the Mediterranean coast for around 500 kilometres from Al-Hamam to Saloum. Inland, it reaches the Siwa Oasis[21] in the Qatarra depression. The port city of Marsa Matrouh is the capital of the Matrouh governorate and the seat of the governor, the governorate administration and the *Maglis Mahall* (governorate assembly/parliament). Marsa Matrouh has around 150,000 inhabitants, of which 85 per cent belong to the *Awlad 'Ali*. Matrouh is the second largest governorate in Egypt (in terms of size) at 212,112 square kilometres. Between half a million and a million[22] fully sedentarized[23] *Awlad 'Ali* live in the governorate and represent the majority (85 per cent) of the entire population.[24] At the Egyptian border town Saloum, the *watan* of the *Awlad 'Ali* transgresses into Libya. Its nucleus is the port city of Tobruk in the very east of Cyrenaica. Some lineages and extended families (mainly of the *Samalus*, the *Asheibat* and the *Quinishat* sub-tribes) reside in the cities of Derna and Al-Bayda. Apart from that, nuclear families and single men live and work all across Libya. All together, around 15,000[25] *Awlad 'Ali* reside in Libya. Among other tribes such as the *Obaidat*[26] and the population of Cyrenaica, the *Awlad 'Ali* became known as *Saad Shiin*, which stands for *Sahara Sharqiyya* (Eastern Desert). The Libyans use the term *Saad Shiin* to signify smuggling and other (illicit) trans-border activities that are attributed to *Awlad 'Ali*. It is used in an ironic but also a morally disqualifying way. It is therefore not surprising that *Awlad 'Ali* reject the term as dishonourable and discriminating.

The economic possibilities of the borderland are accompanied by certain political advantages. In the past, the existence of two radically different state systems in Egypt and Libya increased the number of political settings and chances of appropriation that the Bedouin could use to pursue their ends. Therefore, willingness to be subordinate under one state system and to be obedient citizens was replaced by the opportunity of choice. Any claims on the part of the states could be rejected by crossing the border. Political problems or conflicts with state authorities were avoided by disappearing into the tribal context. Thus, the Leviathan lost a significant amount of its domination over the Bedouin citizen. Unlike other tribal groups such as the Bedouin of the Sinai Peninsula, who have been confronted and affected by the changing policies of two competing states (Egypt and Israel), the *Awlad 'Ali* could and can live as part of a transnational social, political and economic connectivity.[27] The political order in the borderland can be characterized as a form of 'heterarchy' that combines and intertwines tribal socio-political organization with elements of statehood, party politics, development cooperation and entrepreneurial rationales.[28] The principal architects of this order are local Bedouin politicians and their kinship associations, which have achieved a genuine political sovereignty beside the state.[29]

However, the borderland economy between Marsa Matrouh (Egypt) and Tobruk (Libya) suffers from several structural deficits: a weak labour market with a high rate of unemployment among the youth and the limited potential of desert agriculture.[30] Tourism is predominantly in the hands of Egyptian investors from the Nile valley (private and state-owned) and often operates with non-Bedouin employees, or in the case of eastern Libya is literally non-existent. The construction sector basically employs cheap seasonal workers from Upper Egypt. Both states have failed to enact comprehensive measures for the education and vocational training of the Bedouin population (or left it to international development agencies in the case of Egypt), and there is an almost total ignorance of the development of the local and regional cross-border economy. In a setting like this, it is not surprising that smuggling becomes a principal economic alternative.[31] The political economy is shaped by competition among different kinship associations.[32] This competition involves a necessity to mobilize a maximum amount of economic resources to gain wealth and turn it into political influence and social status. In contrast to the tribal ideology of equality and solidarity, *Awlad 'Ali* society is shaped by a growing inequality in the distribution of wealth and an uneven political participation that favours the already powerful.

Preachers

According to my informants, the first pronounced Islamist preachers appeared in the mid 1980s in Marsa Matrouh, Saloum, Sidi Barani and Al-Alamein. The local population still addresses them as *Salafiyya* (Salafism) or *Haraka Salafiyya* (Salafist movement) without much differentiation. The *Ikhwan Muslimin*, the Muslim Brothers, on the other hand, had their difficulties in the borderland. Some of the local tribal population perceives the Muslim Brothers with some suspicion because most of their activists do not belong to the *Awlad 'Ali* and are thus associated with the Nile valley and the big Egyptian cities. This also applies to the *Awlad 'Ali* in Libya, but not to other tribes in Libya where the *Ikhwan* gained much influence. In the following, I will discuss two preachers as representative example cases: Sheikh Mohammad, the non-Bedouin imam of the Mesjid As-Salam (the Peace Mosque) in Marsa Matrouh, and Sheikh Osman, a preacher and activist from one of the leading *Awlad 'Ali* clans in the borderland. Both preachers are representative of many others,[33] but not, of course, in a statistical sense.

Sheikh Mohammad is a Nile valley Egyptian from Alexandria. He is around seventy years old, claims to have an Al-Azhar University education and became imam in a medium-sized mosque in the city of Marsa Matrouh in around 1989. Although lacking in tribal affiliation, he gathered an audience among the urban Bedouin population that gradually turned into devoted followers and made him a prominent figure in the religious and social world in Marsa Matrouh. Among his devoted audiences at Friday sermons he was also able to attract unmarried young urban Bedouin men in significant numbers, who became his committed disciples and saw him as their *sheikh*, their spiritual leader and mentor. For these young men, the mosque became an important factor not only in their religious life but also in their social, political and cultural world. Sheikh Mohammad gained his position through a combination of genuine skills, like charisma and the gift of preaching, but he also showed talent as an organizer of a growing community and a successful conflict mediator. I personally got to know him during the research for my doctoral thesis in 1998. At the beginning of our relationship he presented himself to me as a pious man whose thoughts and deeds revolved around the questions of how to be a good Muslim and the renaissance of the true Islamic tradition.[34] After our first meetings, which resembled a sort of classical student–religious adviser situation, he started to lay out his politico-religious agenda quite openly. This agenda, which appeared in his sermons, in his religious advice, his teaching at the religious school and also in his role as head of the *sharia* court, was similar to Salafist 'neofundamentalism'.[35] This was virulent in Egypt at the time and it appeared in Salafist publications, audio cassettes and the teachings of the emerging satellite TV preachers. However, Sheikh Mohammad added pronounced references to the specific local settings in and around Marsa Matrouh and the society of the *Awlad 'Ali*. He openly articulated his distance from the *Ikhwan*, the Muslim Brothers, whom he considered to be collaborators of the Mubarak regime. This did not prevent him from making use of the tactical support for the Salafist camp of the Mubarak regime. In order to weaken the Muslim Brothers, the government allowed Salafist groups to open *madrasahs*, religious schools, without formal registration. Sheikh Mohammad took advantage of the opportunity in Marsa Matrouh and thereby extended his influence to the younger generation and their families. By the mid 1990s, Sheikh Mohammad had established his mosque as a busy *sharia* court, which gained a reputation as a place for conflict resolution agreeable to the principles of Islam.

The second prominent figure is Sheikh Osman.[36] He is around fifty years old and belongs to a well-known *Saadi* clan (a clan with a noble origin) of the *Awlad 'Ali*, but comes from an extended family with only average property and wealth. Osman was born as his father's second son, and was therefore unlikely to become head of his kinship association, a position reserved for the first-born. Since the family had little fertile land, it moved into the city of Marsa Matrouh in the late 1970s and opened up a shop for kitchen equipment and a market stall for vegetables. Piety and religious tradition became a fascination for Osman during the late 1980s, and when he became acquainted with a Salafist circle in Marsa Matrouh his attention and thinking were directed to political questions and the idea of a more just moral and political order based on Islam. He went to Alexandria to receive advice and training as a preacher. From the 1990s on, Osman regularly travelled to Saudi Arabia for the same reason. Because of the cost, these trips were exceptional for someone from the lower middle class of the Bedouin population in Marsa Matrouh, and Osman gained a reputation as someone with *Da'am min Sa'udia* (support from Saudi Arabia).

The training gave Osman advanced rhetorical skills and enhanced his motivation to preach and spread his ideas. When I first met him in 2007, he appeared to me to be a strongly committed man and a deep believer in his cause who could hardly wait to start a lecture. Osman presented himself as part of a politico-religious movement that was bigger and more important than the daily conduct of politics in the borderland. This self-perception was habitually supported by a monkish display of faith and modesty, a neatly ironed *jellabiya* (robe), a white *samada* (head scarf) and a heavily perfumed beard. Faith, modesty and cleanliness signifying moral purity, however, could quickly turn into fierce agitation if someone (in this case an anthropologist) challenged or questioned his teachings. Osman established an unregistered mosque in Marsa Matrouh in 2004, which quickly became known as a Salafist centre, and he also started to travel the borderland from Al-Alamein to Tobruk. Osman not only preached and agitated but also founded a *sharia* court, which offered conflict resolution to the population. Among his followers, mostly young urban Bedouin from the lower middle class, he became Sheikh Osman, a sign of his spiritual, social and political leadership.

Since he had vital kinship connections with Libya, Osman became involved with the Islamist movement in Tobruk, Derna and Al-Baida, but under clandestine conditions since the Libyan Islamists were strongly oppressed and persecuted by Qaddafi. In Cyrenaica (the eastern province of Libya), a significant proportion of the Islamists came from the families of former tribal counsels to King Idris (1890–1983), the monarch of Libya in the years 1951–61. Many of these representatives of the tribal elite lost their political office and societal relevance in the course of Qaddafi's revolution, and some eventually became part of the covert Islamist opposition. This opposition comprised a wide spectrum of different Islamists. Some were solely concerned with piety, tradition and being good Muslims in the face of Qaddafi's impositions. Others positioned Islamism as a politico-religious alternative to Qaddafi's regime. Things changed dramatically with the return of the Libyan fighters from the battlefields of Afghanistan in the 1990s.[37] Now, men with experience in fighting, conspiracy and a determination to replace Qaddafi with a just Islamic order entered the arena. The *Gama'a al-Islamiyya al-Muqatila bi Libya* (the Libyan Islamic Fighting Group, LIFG) emerged and over the years developed into a jihadist formation. Osman did not join the LIFG and neither did he have contacts with any other jihadist group in Libya until the Arab revolutions in Egypt and Libya. However, he did benefit from exchange and mutual support with the moderate Islamist opposition in Tobruk. Some of these men were at the same time kinship allies of Osman's clan, and thus were linked by a double bind of Islamism and tribal affiliation. Others came from different kinship associations of the *Awlad 'Ali* and were not bound by the obligations of close *qaraba* (kinship).

At first sight, the main difference between these two preachers seems to be rooted in their different degree of social attachment to tribal society. Sheikh Osman is a Bedouin of a *Saadi* clan (of noble descent) of the *Awlad 'Ali*, whereas Sheikh Mohammad is an Egyptian from the Nile valley. The *Awlad 'Ali* actively produce their ethnic uniqueness in symbolic and practical ethno-policies that draw clear lines of origin, status and morals between them and what they call the *Masriyyin* (Egyptians) or the *Naas min Wadi Nil* (people from the Nile valley).[38] However, Sheikh Mohammad's popularity and influence were not affected by his ethnic and regional background. His lack of activity in Libya was above all a result of a deliberate choice and not of a lack of social connections based on tribal kinship associations. Although Sheikh Osman could rely and capitalize on his tribal affiliation in Libya (documented by his transnational activities and his access to the spectrum of Libyan Islamism), this kinship connectivity also had its particularities. His obligations within the tribal system subordinate him under the authority of non-Islamist politicians and the leading figures of his kinship association. In addition, his position as head of a mobile *sharia* court (operating in the borderland) was restricted by the claims of Bedouin customary law, and in particular by those of his kinship association, which enacted it. Furthermore, his status and reputation were compromised by the strong social, political and economic competition among different kinship associations in the borderland, where adversaries could always portray his role as part of tribal clientelism—*Siassat al-Ailat* (politics of families).[39] In this respect, tribal affiliation was an obstacle rather than an asset for Sheikh Osman's cause.

For both preachers, Islamism opened the way for a religious, social and political mobilization of the borderland population beyond the tribe. The evocation of Islamism as a 'pan-tribal' religious and social movement enabled Sheikh Osman to distance himself from the antagonisms of tribal politics. It also allowed him to address audiences and followers from a broader tribal range. This is particularly true for the multi-tribal population of Marsa Matrouh, where the integrative power of kinship has been altered by more complex urban identities.[40] In addition, he could capitalize on his connection with fellow preachers and Islamist networks in Egypt and Libya (who pursued similar pan-tribal strategies) and present himself as part of a transnational Islamist ecumene through his connections with Saudi Arabia. All together, this stands for a globalization of Islamist thought and practice that reaches into the peripheries and changes religious, political and cultural modes. Sheikh Mohammad, free of any tribal involvement, could even go a little further by promoting Islamism as a post-tribal alternative, and thus be able to attract not only the urban Bedouin but also the Egyptian population[41] of Marsa Matrouh. In this respect, both preachers represent processes of overarching integration on the basis of religion, which were essential in the early days of Islam[42] and were also typical of the confederation of Cyrenaica tribes under the *Senussia* order (1837–1969) in Libya.[43] Knowledge of these historical legacies and continuities, however, was and is quite limited among the Salafist preachers in the borderland.

Followers and disciples

It is difficult to make precise empirically grounded statements about the number and character of the followers and audiences of these two preachers. However, some patterns can be identified on the basis of my qualitative research. Islamism has often been seen as particularly successful among the urban poor, and indeed many followers, not only the poor, belong to the growing urban Bedouin population in cities like Marsa Matrouh, Al-Alamein, Saloum and Tobruk.[44] On the Libyan side of the border, almost 90 per cent of the population live in or near cities and this development is also taking place in cities like Marsa Matrouh, where multi-tribal quarters along the Matrouh–Siwa road have doubled their inhabitants in the past six years.[45] However, one should not confuse these cities with metropolitan spaces like Cairo or Benghazi. The organization of the urban space in Tobruk and Marsa Matrouh is shaped by tribal and kinship patterns. There are quarters for the *Quinishat*, the *Samalus* and other tribal segments, and even in the above-mentioned multi-tribal quarters people try to organize streets under a common kinship umbrella. In addition, the distinction between rural and urban is not so easily made in the borderland. People in the cities are very much connected to rural communities. They own shares of land and orchards on the *watan* (territory) of their tribes and are involved in the marketing of the agricultural products of their rural kinship association. From the perspective of rural groups, the relatives in the cities serve as docking points in urban life with access to markets, job opportunities, public services and political arenas. Thus, not only wealthy kinship associations possess shops and small hotels or maintain offices for their political representatives in the cities. People circulate between the countryside and the city rather than being separated into two different realms.

The urban poor (mostly landless Bedouin) certainly benefited from the social activities of the preachers. At the mosques they received money for hospitals or doctor's bills or were otherwise supported. In addition, the *sharia* court offered them a chance to resolve conflicts or at least to be heard. In this way, the mosques became places where issues of poverty and inequality were addressed and could be expressed instead of being left in the hands of kinship solidarity alone or treated with ignorance by the state. In terms of agency and mobilization, the most important followers of the preachers were not the poor but the urban Bedouin middle and lower middle classes, who combined their own goals with those of the Islamists. These goals were largely about ensuring or enlarging their social, political and economic status. The social critique (see below) of the Islamists offered these upward social climbers (or potential losers) an attractive socio-political platform beside the kinship association and beyond the tribe. In this respect, the kinship association of Sheikh Osman is a good example of a lower-middle-class family that enhanced its social status by joining the Islamist cause. However, the character of this allegiance has not been visible in activism, but materialized in a growing common Salafist view of religious, social and political questions. Activism and discipleship were and are a domain of the younger Bedouin men between 18 and 35 years old, who are either just married or not yet married. Due to the strict segregation of sexes among the *Awlad 'Ali*, young women do not play any visible role here. This does not mean that young Bedouin women have no specific religious or political standpoints, but since their lives are limited to the household, these standpoints remain in the families and kinship associations and do not become public. Unlike in the Nile valley and cities like Benghazi in Libya, organized female Islamist groups do not exist among the *Awlad 'Ali*.[46]

The young male disciples have adopted a dress style similar to Sheikh Osman and they can be easily recognized by their white *jellabiya* and their long wild beards. Non-Salafist Bedouin often use an ironic gesture to identify these young men: they imitate the grabbing and shaking of a long beard beneath their chin. During my studies at Sheikh Mohammad's mosque, there were usually about twenty young men from various tribal backgrounds around involved in lively debates about religion and politics. For these young men, the mosque and its community served as a platform for self-expression and empowerment in a society that is dominated by the principle of seniority. Authority and power among the *Awlad 'Ali* lie in the hands of senior men, and the male (and female) youth has to obey. During discussions held in the *marbu'a* (the men's and guest room in the Bedouin house), young men have to keep silent and follow the arguments of the senior men. However, the demographic development of the *Awlad 'Ali* corresponds with general trends in the Middle East, which means that around 30 per cent of the population are under twenty-five years old.[47] Although there is no visible clash of generations so far, preachers are among the few actors who explicitly address the male youth. Young male activists have been active in loading public discourses and practices with Salafist ideas about piety and morals, and also with political ideas about a just Islamic order. For example, regarding private family life, Sheikh Osman's disciples started with campaigns against smoking and continued with the promotion of a strict morality that particularly referred to women. Since it is not so easy to reject religious claims based on the teachings of a popular sheikh, the status and influence of pious young men in their families and kinship associations grew, or at least gave the disciples the means to gain importance.

Islamism as critique and evocation of a just order

Despite the persistence and inventiveness of tribal politicians in ensuring local and trans-local tribal sovereignty, a critical public discourse on religion, social problems and the question of a just political order never really developed in the borderland.[48] Preachers like Sheikh Mohammad and Sheikh Osman established such a discourse and gave religious, social and political criticism a place for articulation and exchange at their mosques and among their audiences, followers and disciples. In addition, they have been promoting the idea of a just Islamic alternative. In this respect, preachers differ fundamentally from non-religious public figures, entrepreneurs, businessmen and tribal politicians, who are instead pragmatic and involved in local power games. Preachers go beyond the world of interest-driven power politics that focuses on the welfare of specific kinship associations and into a sphere of religious morality that focuses on the common good and the vision of a just Islamic order.

The religious critique articulated by preachers like Sheikh Mohammad is clearly aimed at a Salafist reorientation of Islam and Islamic practices. This refers to popular Bedouin Islam with its belief in *baraka* (blessing) but also concerns magic (protection against evil and the evil eye with amulets), traditional healing and a number of tribal customs like dance and music at wedding parties. These beliefs and practices were systematically rendered as *'Aib* (shameful, sinful) and subsequently disappeared or are nowadays mostly practised secretly. The promotion of strict veiling rules (*niqab* or *burka*) enhanced the power of men over women to a significant degree. It was accompanied with a growing concern about the need to discipline and control ('to protect') women and the female body. Particularly young male disciples took this discourse into their families and positioned themselves as guardians of morality. Even in remote desert settlements where women used to move freely among their kin wearing a *hijab* (loose head scarf) men started to ask for a *niqab*. In the multi-tribal setting of Marsa Matrouh and Tobruk, women were forced to wear a *niqab* or *burka* in public. Since Friday services started being transmitted into the streets of Marsa Matrouh (in 1992), and in smaller villages too, it has not been easy to avoid them, and their teachings have become influential to the point that even non-Salafist Bedouin have started to look at their very own traditional legacies with a critical eye. The verdict of something or someone being *'Aib* (shameful) or *didd al-Islam* (anti or un-Islamic) became a common denominator. As indicated above, this was particularly true for alleged heresies within Islam, such as Sufism, and it also changed significantly the interrelations with the Coptic community in Marsa Matrouh.[49] In the latter case, Sheikh Mohammad started to question the status of the Copts as *Ahl al-Kitab* or *Ahl al-Dhima* (people of the book, people covered by Islamic law) and thus broke with the conventions of the *sharia*.[50] This inconsistency did not prevent him (nor his fellow preachers) from promoting the authority, sovereignty and rulings of *sharia* over public life. Although the preachers in Marsa Matrouh, Saloum and Tobruk did not turn the population of the borderland into *Mutatarrifin* (radicals), they certainly dominated the setting of the religious agenda and they successfully established a more or less unquestioned Salafist common sense of religious belief and practice. This success is not only the result of their efforts, but also arises from the fact that the majority of the population in the borderland do not have a (religious) education. In fact, many of my informants and hosts cannot read the Quran properly and neither do they have a differentiated knowledge of *sharia*. Oral tradition not literacy, religious practice not theological discourse, and in particular the teachings of the imam or *sheikh* based on their evocation of the 'unquestionable authority of Islam' are the fundamental parameters for religious orientation. In addition, Salafist publications, audio cassettes (in the 1990s), YouTube clips and the teachings of satellite TV preachers like Hazem Abu Ismail have consolidated the impression (among audiences) that Salafism is true Islam.

The social and political critique of the preachers has layers that refer to specific local or regional questions, as well as to national (Egyptian and Libyan) issues. Calls for *'Adala* (justice) and *Gadiyya* (earnestness) and criticism of *Fasad* (corruption) are among the more general issues that were addressed to the regimes of Mubarak in Egypt and Qaddafi in Libya, and they have continued in the post-revolutionary phase after 2011. This general critique went along with an assertion that only a truly Islamic order (or state) would guarantee social justice for all. At the local and regional levels, the preachers avoided direct confrontation with tribal politicians and influential kinship associations but turned the mosques into places where people could express their discomfort with the dealings of the powerful kinship associations. The notion of *Siassa taht al-Tarabeeza* (politics under the table) targets the financing of election campaigns (or the buying of votes) with smuggling revenues, and *Siassat al-Ailat* refers to the distortion of equal chances in politics through clientelism.[51]

The social critique defines winners and losers, and emphasizes that inequality should not be legitimized by tribal tradition or tolerated because of tribal relations of authority. The idea of the common good is positioned against the tribal *'Asabiyya* (we-group feeling based on agnatic kinship). As a result, many followers of the preachers perceive *'Asabiyya* principally as tribal sectionalism and not as affiliation or closeness among kin. Nowadays, even non-Salafist Bedouin avoid the term *'Asabiyya* and replace it with *Takaful* (solidarity), which has no tribal connotation. In providing a pan- or post-tribal social space where people from various kinship backgrounds can meet and exchange (and where the male youth can experience an alternative mode of social integration), the preachers have certainly reproduced the historical role of Islam (and spiritual leadership) within tribal or segmentary societies as discussed by Evans-Pritchard (1949) and Gellner (1969). However, the contemporary activism of the preachers is connected with a broader Islamist reform movement that reaches beyond the tribal society of the borderland and is not a functional element of segmentation but part of the ongoing globalization of neo-fundamentalist Islamism.

Beside their social and political critique, the preachers in the borderland are active in the field of conflict resolution. Conflict resolution in the borderland is characterized by a form of legal pluralism[52] that consists of the codified state law, the Bedouin customary law—*'Urf*[53]—

and the *sharia* courts of the preachers. Beside the phenomenon of 'forum shopping'[54] as a form of choice between different opportunities for conflict resolution for the parties involved, legal pluralism also involves competition among different providers. The preachers attack '*Urf* and its protagonists as well as the state law and justice system from an 'Islamic perspective'. At the same time, they present themselves as a legal and legitimate Islamic alternative based on *sharia*. This legitimacy of the *sharia* that they invoke plays a major role in their legal practice, with the religious legitimacy positioned against '*Urf* and the state law. The manifold interlacings between *sharia* and '*Urf* are therefore denied and rejected by the preachers, even if they are Bedouin, as in the case of Sheikh Osman.[55] For their Bedouin clients, the religious and moral authority of the preachers' claims are quite significant, and so a growing number of Bedouin feel obliged to consult a *sharia* court instead of an '*Urf* one because they want to follow an orderly Islamic way of life.

On the other hand, the *sharia* courts have gained a reputation for reliability of conduct and a comparatively high durability of their judgements. This is not only related to their own practice but also to the weaknesses of the competing '*Urf* and state law. The latter is not necessarily corrupt, but it is ineffective. Lawsuits in Egypt and Libya usually take a long time and involve costly legal experts. Although the customary law of '*Urf* was a central contributor to the integrity of tribal society and the stability of order before, during and after the Arab revolutions, it also has its shortcomings and problems.[56] Customary law has been dragged into the social, political and economic competitions among kinship associations. Postponement of the '*Urf* procedure by changing the mediators, disobeying arbitration and entanglements of legal and political quarrels are common features of the contemporary legal culture in the borderland. In addition, a frequent overpowering of '*Urf* by mighty kinship associations is also a feature. This overpowering takes the form of manipulation, such as the bribing of the *Maradi* (conflict mediators on the basis of '*Urf*) or political pressure on inferior associations linked to 'financial compensation'. For weak associations, the quest for justice often leads to a fundamental lack of legal security. Thus the management of conflict resolution and its financial dimension is both challenging and politically delicate, as it becomes a domain of the wealthy and powerful, who can afford the costs and the potential political frictions. This is the context in which the preachers have established the *sharia* courts as custodians of justice, with the result that many people feel that real justice can only be achieved in a *sharia* court.

Pitfalls of radicalization

In spring 2010, Marsa Matrouh witnessed riots against the Coptic community that lasted for a day.[57] The incident received international attention and was intensively discussed on Coptic websites.[58] Hostility, discrimination, riots and even pogroms against Copts are nothing unusual in Egypt, but the borderland had not been a hotspot of anti-Coptic resentment and action. On the contrary, the Copts have been under the protection of the *'Amira*, a clan of the *Kharuf* sub-tribe of the *Awlad 'Ali*. *Sharia* defines and protects the status of Christians and Jews as *Ahl al-Kitab* (people of the book) or *Ahl al-Dhima* (protected people) and the *Awlad 'Ali* have been following this rule for many centuries. However, with the rise of the Salafist preachers, reservation towards and discrimination against Copts among the *Awlad 'Ali* has steadily grown over the years, and, as I have indicated above, actors like Sheikh Mohammad were actively involved in this. When Sheikh Mohammad started to question the status of the Copts as *Ahl al-Kitab* or *Ahl al-Dhima* in his Friday sermons (to my knowledge, around 2008), the Copts were turned into some sort of evil religious other. His previous preaching had not only developed a consciousness of inequality and injustice among his audiences and followers, but also inflamed unrest and anger. Some of the available press reports say that the trigger for the riots was the attempt to enlarge a Coptic church site in Marsa Matrouh, but according to my informants the main reason was the constant agitation against the Copts that had been taking place for several months.

That particular day was *Yom al-Gumm'a* (Friday) when Sheikh Mohammad started to attack the Copts as enemies of Islam and called for jihad against them during a sermon that was broadcast into the streets. Since land rights and land ownership are sensitive issues in the borderland,[59] the alleged enlargement of the church site was a welcome cause for anger. Sheikh Mohammad succeeded in inflaming the audience and he urged them to use force against the Christians. From late afternoon to night, mostly young Bedouin men (followers and disciples of his) protested and then started to destroy, loot and burn down Coptic shops, houses and cars, and seriously injured more than twenty people. The local police arrived late and were ineffective, but eventually managed to end the turmoil late at night. Some parts of the tumult were documented on mobile phone videos filmed by Bedouin protesters or people who were just watching. These videos still circulate in the borderland carrying titles like *Yom al-'Ar* (day of shame) or *Yom al-Intiqam* (day of revenge), depending on the position of the filmmakers. I arrived in Marsa Matrouh a month after the incident and started to research the riots. At this time, non-Salafist tribal politicians and conflict mediators of the *'Amira* clan were busy with resolution of the conflict. Compensation payments were arranged and handed over, and at least some form of apology was expressed. The Salafist preachers fell silent or denied any involvement. It was tribal custom and the commitment of the tribal leaders to their obligation as protectors of the Copts (rooted in *sharia*) that took over the responsibility. The preachers, on the other hand, had demonstrated a willingness for radicalism and a use of instigation to violence that was formerly unknown in the borderland. This process accelerated during and after the Arab revolutions in Egypt and Libya.

Islamism, tribes and the Arab revolutions

Although the Salafist preachers and their followers were not among the protagonists of the revolution in Egypt, they tried to capitalize on it.[60] In the first months after the revolution, Sheikh Osman's disciples started to take over the duties and sovereignty rights of the Egyptian state. They policed the streets, erected checkpoints on the international highway to Libya and presented themselves as guardians of order in the absence of the state. This conduct, however, provoked a strong reaction from the established (non-Salafist) tribal politicians, who felt that their authority was compromised. After a gathering of the leading men of Sheikh Osman's clan, he was ordered to stop the policing and leave the question of public order to the tribes and the state security forces.

Sheikh Osman obeyed. When I asked Sheikh 'Aissa (tribal leader and local politician of Osman's clan) about the issue, he replied, 'They are *Haraka Salafiyya* (Salafist Movement), but they are also of my tribe. That is why they have to obey me and the *Awaqil* (wise men)'.[61] In the case of the Libyan revolution, the situation was a little different. There, the tribal Salafists from the Egyptian side of the border were the first organized actors to supply the Libyan population (kin and non-kin) of Tobruk with food and medicine.[62] At the same time, the turmoil of the revolutions (with an almost total absence of border control) allowed them to reconnect with their Salafist fellows in Libya.[63] These connections quickly included radical Islamist and jihadist militia like the *Gama'a al-Islamiyya al-Muqatila bi Libya* (the Libyan Islamic Fighting Group, LIFG) and the *Ansar al-Shari'a* (Followers of *Sharia*). Thus, Sheikh Osman and his fellows were dragged into, or at least became connected with, radical and violent jihadist groups which aimed to turn Libya into an Islamic state.[64] The subsequent internationalization (or globalization) of jihadism in Libya and the rise of Islamic State (IS) in cities like Darna (with jihadists from all over the Middle East) developed far beyond the reach of the Salafists in the borderland and certainly go beyond the scope of *Awlad 'Ali* society.[65] However, in the political arena of Tobruk the pragmatism of local *Awlad 'Ali* politicians (and their voters) prevented a successful translation of the Salafist connections into formal politics. In the election of 2012, the population articulated a clear anti-Salafist and anti-jihadist position by voting for Mahmud Jebril's *Tahaluf al-Quwat al-Wataniyya* (Alliance of the National Forces). Even those politicians with a legacy in the Islamist opposition against Qaddafi (see above), like Sheikh Faraj Yasin Al-Mabri, head of the local council of Tobruk, supported a pragmatic approach in politics that would guarantee a continuation of intermediary local sovereignty but exclude religious extremism.[66]

When *Hizb al-Nour* (Party of the Light), the Salafist party founded in the course of the Egyptian revolution, won the quota of seats reserved for the *Awlad 'Ali* in the governorate of Matrouh in the 2011 election, the *Haraka Salafiyya* (Salafist Movement) entered party politics and the parliament. The fact that powerful tribal politicians of the Mubarak era were defeated by the Bedouin candidates of *Hizb al-Nour* was a serious blow for these intermediary[67] tribal elites. To some extent, this success was also a result of the religious, social and political mobilization of the preachers, and it seemed that a new political setting featuring Salafism as a political movement (and party) and certain tribal actors was emerging in the borderland. However, things developed in a different direction and these developments were clearly beyond the agency of the *Awlad 'Ali*. With the re-emerging authoritarian Egyptian state under military rule and the subsequent presidency of Abdel Fattah as-Sisi, the division of labour between the central state and local non-Salafist Bedouin politicians has been renewed. When the above-mentioned Sheikh 'Aissa was promoted from *Sheikh al-Qabila* (tribal leader) to '*Umda* (higher-ranking tribal leader)[68] in December 2015, the social media networks of his clan applauded it as a triumph over *Hizb al-Nour*.

Conclusion

Twenty-eight years ago, Lila Abu Lughod argued against an alleged nexus of tribalism and terrorism.[69] On the basis of the empirical facts discussed in this paper, I can only add that, despite the dramatizations in the global media or the assertions of certain experts, there is no empirical evidence for a systematic link between tribal social and political organization, Islamism or jihadism. This does not mean that Islamism or jihadism do not occur among tribes. Like any other social group, class or milieu, in the Arab Middle East the *Awlad 'Ali* have also been affected, influenced and actively involved in the rise of neo-fundamentalist Islamism and its violent branches. However, this process has not followed some sort of teleology and neither is it in any case part of an inevitable development enrooted in tribes. Salafist neo-fundamental preachers (and their followers and disciples) have pluralized and changed the religious, social, juridical and political discourses and practices in the borderland. They have also initiated different forms of radicalization commonly associated with political Islam. Nevertheless, these preachers were also confronted with clear contradiction and rejection. The radicalism and the violence they instigated against the Coptic community were moderated and compensated for by responsible tribal leaders who know and respect the rulings of *sharia* and the obligations of their tribes. When Sheikh Osman and his disciples started to take over the sovereign rights of the state, tribal politicians stopped and disciplined them. The Salafist political party *Hizb al-Nour* in Egypt has been confronted with the opposition of the tribal establishment of the Mubarak era. This intermediary tribal elite has lately found a strong ally in the new Egyptian president, Abd Al-Fattah al-Si. In Libya, the majority of the *Awlad 'Ali* favour the elected government seated in Tobruk. Moderate politics, not extremism, seems to be their credo. What we see here are complex and sometimes contradictory processes at the trans-local, national and global levels. In any case, the *Awlad 'Ali* themselves will decide the ways in which religion, social relations and politics in the borderland will develop in the future.

⊛ Note to be posted on the first page:

The initial draft of this chapter was the author's contribution in ____ workshop on ____. He presented it via Skype as he couldn't obtain the required Schengen Visa in appropiate time because of his Middle Eastern (Egyptian) passport, the consular officer frankly told him at the Italian Embassy in Washington, D.C. where he was conducting a short-term fellowship at Woodrow Wilson Center for International Scholars. The final draft had been submitted before he returned to his home country and being arrested in the airport. Pre-printing review was done while he was detained for more than 16 months, without trial or even official charges, but only for his field research and investigative journalism in Sinai.

He sent this note on a hidden small piece of paper from his prison to tell the readers that he doesn't regret his path to fact- and reality-based knowledge; to remind them that the risks of integirate and independent research are not worse than giving up to the authoritarian propaganda; to ask them to spread the word that has costed a lot; and, finally, to say that if there is neither justice nor equal opportunities in this unfair world, we have no choice except fighting. The weapon is HOPE!

4

SUFI JIHAD AND SALAFI JIHADISM IN EGYPT'S SINAI

TRIBAL GENERATIONAL CONFLICT

Ismail Alexandrani

Egyptian jihadists and their relation to the desert and tribes

The expansion of new jihadist organizations which are influenced by or support the al-Qaeda organization and Islamic State (*Daesh*) has been linked to the tribal communities and clans in the Bedouin environment, either in the barren deserts or in the mountains. These organizations spread in Afghanistan, Pakistan, Yemen, Iraq, Nigeria and East Africa, and then arrived in Libya, Mali, Syria and other locations where small outposts of the head organizations are situated, or where new groups inspired by their principles and general strategy have emerged, and later declared their allegiance to the heads of the transnational organizations.

In the Egyptian case, three jihadist surges can be observed which are outwardly similar in their reliance on the desert and mountain environments but differ in their relation to the tribe as a social Bedouin or semi-Bedouin component. The first wave of the first generation of jihadists formed their ideas in the prisons of President Gamal Abdel Nasser (who ruled from 1954 to 1970) under the pressure of severe torture and defamation of their ideological and religious beliefs. Among them was Shukri Mustafa, the leader of a group called the Muslim Community (*Jamaat al-Muslimin*) by its members, but known in the media as *al-Takfir wa-l-Hijra* (Excommunication and Emigration). The ideology of this group, as its name implies, was to represent true Islam to its members and it excommunicated whoever did not join and pledge allegiance to the emir, whether they were part of the regime or members of society. They felt a need to migrate from the infidel society to a faithful society governed by *sharia*. As this hypothetical society did not exist, they settled for a temporary and symbolic migration through a kind of worship, a retreat from the society which they saw as infidel, and joined mountain or desert camps where they could wield authority. The group only used deserted and mountainous surroundings as isolated and secret retreats and campsites. This connection evolved with the rise of the two major Egyptian jihadist organizations in the first Egyptian jihadist surge, namely the Islamic Group (*al-Jamaa al-Islamiyya*) and the Jihad Movement (*Harakat al-Jihad*), as the central Egyptian mountains (northern Upper Egypt) again provided refuge and a suitable location for training camps in preparation for armed fighting.

At the intellectual and social levels, there were no significant differences between the migration of the Muslim Community from the society which they considered infidel and the establishment of the Islamic Group and their training to fight outside the authority of a state which they considered infidel. It is true that the Islamic Group and the Jihad Movement did not reject society, as the Muslim Community did, for infidelity was strictly related to the ruling system. However, they agreed on the idea of surviving on their own, and trained to use weapons in safe areas in preparation for their operation.

The first jihadi organization members separated from their nuclear and extended families to restructure the hierarchy of their allegiance within their ideological organizations. The behaviour of the young groups which settled under the wings of the jihadi and Islamic groups was characterized by aggression and hostility towards those around them who did not obey them. Their isolation and wanderings among the rugged mountains were considered proof of a lack of concordance between these organizations and the societies and villages of the Nile valley. However long they stayed with their wives and children, their settlements were deliberate, not authentic. This means that they physically moved with their belongings, equipped with small- or medium-sized arms, to form socially marginal and fragile communities. It should be noted that the jihadist organizations were based in northern Upper Egypt and could not invade the south, which is Bedouin and agricultural with Sufi tendencies.

The first jihadi surge in Egypt came to a peak with a local alliance between the Islamic Group and the Jihad Movement in 1981, which aimed jointly to carry out the assassination of Anwar Al Sadat (who ruled from 1970 until he was killed in 1981). They managed to complete this mission by penetrating the military intelligence services. This was despite the fact that Sadat had since 1979 given a green light to the Egyptian jihadists to travel and fight in Afghanistan against the Soviet Union in cooperation with the United States of America and Saudi Arabia.

The experiences accumulated abroad by the Egyptian jihadists led them to take different paths. Local jihadists, especially members of the Islamic Group, whose alliance with the Jihad Movement collapsed after the latter became weak and backed down, continued to wage war against Hosni Mubarak's regime for a decade and a half until the declaration renouncing violence from inside the prisons in 1996. Until that time, the Egyptian jihadists' connection to the mountains and deserts was principally a question of security; later it became one of social disconnection. The desert and mountainous environments with their tribal society were never natural havens for them.

The jihadi relation to the Egyptian deserts and mountains became different in the second jihadi surge. The first officially ended in 1996 in Mubarak's jails, when the historical jihadist leaders formally declared that they renounced their attempt to make changes through violence. It ended both practically and on the field after the extended crackdown that followed the terrorist attack in Luxor in 1997, the last operation carried out by the rebellious wing against the change in policy of the

Islamic Group. This led to a security crackdown, which was received with popularity and solidarity by local communities, disregarding the severe violations that accompanied it. After a geographical and organizational separation from the first surge, in the late 1990s the second surge started to grow in the Sinai Peninsula, which had been insulated from the first surge in the Nile valley.

Rumours about Khaled Mosaed establishing *al-Tawhid wa-l-Jihad* and its precise timing were spread by the security forces and locals in northern Sinai. However, what is certain is that Mosaed, a dentist from the Sawarka tribe who lived in the outskirts of Al-Arish city, had met in Mubarak's prisons some senior jihadists who did not go along with the renunciation of violence. He then connected with the ethics of the global Salafi jihadist movement and was affected by the second Palestinian intifada (2000), the invasion of Afghanistan following the events of 11 September (2001), and then the invasion of Iraq (2003).

As a result, *al-Tawhid wa-l-Jihad* inspired the name of the 'Platform Tawhid and Jihad' website, which is supervised by the global Salafi jihadist theorist Abu Muhammad al-Maqdisi, the same name that Abu Musaab al-Zarqawi gave his nascent jihadist group in Iraq after the fall of Saddam Hussein before it was changed to *Qa'idat al-Jihad fi bilad al rafidayn* (or al-Qaeda in Iraq), and then to the 'Islamic State of Iraq' and finally to the 'Islamic State of Iraq and the Levant', known simply as *Daesh*/ISIS.[1]

The second Egyptian jihadist surge started in Sinai and was the first Salafi jihadist surge in the peninsula, which had always considered jihad to be in conjunction with Sufism or led by the Egyptian military intelligence against the Israeli occupation. This surge was new to Sinai in terms of its Salafism and ideology, but not in terms of the discourses considering Israel a religious enemy. It was also new in that it stepped outside the field of Egyptian state power and had a religious and hostile attitude towards it.

This time, the desert was not only a refuge or a haven, and the rough grounds in the middle of Sinai were not only secure training camps away from security threats. They were regular environments for organization leaders and members, not just the destinations of an ideological migration resulting from withdrawal from society. The second jihadist surge was accompanied by aggression against the population living in the northern Sinai borderlands. However, it did not last for long since it was hit by the security forces after its operations on the southern Sinai resorts (2004–6). In fact, it ended with the death of the leader and helpers. However, the connection between the Salafi jihadists and tribal entities as a local social nest was born.

Tewfik Freij (murdered in February 2014), who led the revival of the Salafi jihad in Sinai at the end of the Mubarak era, was one of the remaining *al-Tawhid wa-l-Jihad* members. He then formed the first core organization of what was known afterwards as *Ansar Beit al-Maqdis*. Later, he declared allegiance to ISIS in November 2014 and changed his organization's name to 'Sinai State'. This modern surge was the second in Sinai and the third in Egypt. The locals also called it the 'new jihadist phenomenon'.

It is 'new' in two ways: its members are new jihadists with a different ideology from the previous Egyptian jihadists of the Nile valley; and because they are different from the Sufi mujahidin, who had been allies of the Egyptian state and had fought with it again the Israeli occupation years before. All that remains of the Sufi mujahidin are memories and jihadist speech absorbed by the tribal community in Sinai since childhood. This modern surge creates strong social bonds between the organizations loyal to *Daesh* and the local tribal environment. It is radically different from the first long surge in the Nile valley and is considered a developed extension of the short second surge briefly represented by *al-Tawhid wa-l-Jihad*.

The second jihadi surge strategy was to hide and seek shelter in the rough grounds in the middle of Sinai. By contrast, the proponents of the third surge were hiding among the locals by the end of 2009. This may be the main reason why the organization is only present in the north-east of the Sinai Peninsula, along the coastline between the border at Rafah and Al-Arish. The population there is not as dense as in other areas of the peninsula, separated by the western deserts and the rough southern grounds. Consequently, the Sinai State organization (previously *Ansar Beit al-Maqdis*) spread into the Sawarka and Rmaylat tribal lands and among some small clans in the city of Sheikh Zuweid. It also gathered followers and leaders from non-tribal urban families in Al-Arish.

This chapter focuses on the Sawarka tribe to study the relationship between the main jihadist organization in Sinai and the tribes and local environment in northern Sinai. Most of the reasons for choosing the Sawarka are objective, but some are subjective. The Sawarka tribe is one of the biggest Sinai tribes in terms of population (even though it is not as widespread as the Turabain tribe); the Sinai State central organization is situated on its land; and the most important organization leaders belong to the Sawarka. It constitutes a case study of the ideological conflict between the Salafi jihadists led by the tribe's youth and the Sufi jihadists connected to its elders.

The subjective reason is that I lived and bonded with them, developing strong connections and friends among the community's youth and elders. I was sad to see the Egyptian media affected by the Israeli campaign that classified Sawarka as a terrorist organization, together with its many peaceful unarmed tribe members. This classification from the Israeli point of view was no surprise to me, since the tribe's attitudes had always been against the Israelis. However, it is intriguing that in the Egyptian context the Salafi jihadists, rebels against the regime and infidels to military officers and the police, can be equalled to the jihadi Sufis who fought against the Israeli occupation in complete cooperation with the Egyptian military intelligence and later were honoured with certificates of appreciation, medals and badges.

Consequently, this study investigates jihadi trends and conflicts between ancient Sufism and contemporary Salafism, conflicts whose dimensions I consider related to generational and social differences within the tribe under study. They are inseparable from the sensitivities and tribal conflicts between the Sawarka and their Bedouin neighbours. For reasons of security I could not conduct field research in order to complete this study properly. Therefore I have relied on my observations from over three years living with the tribe before embarking on this research. During those three years, I conducted hundreds of individual and group interviews with members of the Sawarka and other local residents of the Sinai, some of which were for research and documentary purposes and some for journalism, while many others were informal and improvised.

Jihad and jihadism—background

The religious and ideological use of the term jihad does not have a single meaning in Egypt's modern history in general, and in the Sinai

Peninsula in particular. Not only at the linguistic level but also socio-culturally, the word jihad sounds, or used to sound, more broadly positive than at the narrow ideologically coloured level.

As a part of Sayed Darwish's (1892–1923) living legacy, the Egyptians still sing '*Aho dah illī sar*' (This is what happened), the lyrics of which say *Wi badal ma yeshmat fina hased/īdak fī idī ne'oum negahid* (Before envious gloating/ Hand in hand, let's stand and fight together [launch jihad]). Darwish was the composer of the current Egyptian national anthem, and he lived in Alexandria under the Ottoman Empire before any of the recently known Islamist groups had appeared. His lifestyle, romantic relationships and the rest of his legacy, including a song praising cannabis, contradict the expected stereotypical image created by the recent use of the word 'jihad'.

In 1923, the same year as that of Darwish's death, Egypt ratified its independence constitution and held a contest to choose a new national anthem. The poem by Mustafa Sadeq El-Rafie (1880–1937) entitled '*Eslamy ya Misr*' (Stay safe, Egypt!) won the contest and became the official anthem until 1936. It supported the liberal Al-Wafd party's leader, Saad Zaghloul Pasha, and contained the word jihad twice: *Wa ma'i qalbī wa 'azmī lil-Jihad/Wa li-qalbī antī ba'd eddini dīn* (And I have my heart and my honest will to jihad/ For my heart, you (Egypt) are a faith second to my faith); and later, *Fi difa'ī wa Jihadī li-bilad/ La amīlo, la amallo la alīn* (In my defence and jihad for my country/ I never bend, am weary or soft).

Al-Jihad was also the name of the influential partisan Al-Wafd newspaper, founded by Tawfiq Diyab (1888–1967) and inspired by the poem of Ahmad Shawqi (the 'Prince of Poets', 1868–1932) that says *Qif dona ra'yaka fi el-hayatī Mujahidan/ Inna Al-hayata 'aqīdaton wa Jihad* (Stand for your opinion in life as mujahid/ Life is faith and jihad).[2] Furthermore, the word jihad was not used exclusively by Muslims. The last line of the poem is the slogan of the *Al-Hayat* daily newspaper, which is currently owned by the Saudi Prince Khaled bin Sultan but was initially founded by Kamel Merewah in Lebanon in 1946. Merewah was a Christian, and jihad at that time had a broad meaning of making efforts and sincere sacrifices for a noble cause.

Three decades earlier, another non-Muslim military and intellectual figure, Noam Shoqeir, had used the word jihad in the introduction to his comprehensive reference work on the history of Sinai, to explain how much he had suffered and how persistent he had needed to be to edit the book and revise it for printing in 1916. It had a similar socio-linguistic meaning in Shoqeir's history of the Al-Obeidiya Orthodox School in Cairo, which was founded as a Greek Orthodox endowment under the supervision of the Saint Catherine Monastery in southern Sinai. The school board of trustees' oath included the verb from the noun jihad.[3]

Since Muhammad Ali Pasha's reign (1805–48), military conscription had been called *jihadiyyah*. This name continued until it was documented in twentieth-century cinema productions featuring Egypt under British colonialism. Jihad did not have any specific local significance, but only meant, in its narrowest sense, a holy fight against the foreign enemy of the nation. However, the 'nation' had several meanings among Egyptian nationalists, pan-Arab nationalists and political Islamists, who did not emerge as organizations until after the fall of the Ottoman Caliphate.

In this context, it was not strange for the Egyptian public when the Muslim Brotherhood (MB) movement, founded in 1928 on the west bank of the Suez Canal close to the Sinai Peninsula, used the word jihad in its slogan: 'Allah is our cause, the Messenger/Prophet (Mohammed) is our leader, the Quran is our constitution, jihad is our way, and dying for the sake of Allah is our noblest ambition'.[4] The call for voluntary jihad in 1948 to fight the Zionist occupation of Palestine was also perceived in this context. Therefore, brigades of MB's volunteer mujahidin were led by Egyptian military officers with no sensitivity to using the word jihad. Christian volunteers fought shoulder-to-shoulder with Muslims under MB leadership.[5]

The MB was officially dissolved in December 1948 while its fighters were still on the front lines in Palestine. A ceasefire was agreed between the Arab League and the Zionist armed groups (the new-born state of Israel was not yet recognized by the Arab countries) under the supervision of Britain. The returning mujahidin awaited jail.[6] A story accusing Egyptian Prime Minister Mahmoud Fahmy Al-Noqrashy Pasha of conspiracy and treason was created, and revenge quickly took place in Cairo with his assassination in the same month. This was the shifting point when the weapons assigned to fighting the foreign enemy were used to shoot a local political foe in religion-based activism.

The MB's Special Organization (SO) was redirected along another path. Before the assassination of Hassan El-Banna, the MB's founding father, he released a statement entitled 'Not Brothers, Not Muslims' condemning and denying responsibility for the SO recklessness. After his death in February 1949, the MB entered a completely new era, allying with the Free Officers Movement (FOM), which led the coup against King Farouk on 23 July 1952 and established the Egyptian Republic in 1953. In 1954, MB's first ordeal began and Sayed Qutb started his conversion from being an Islamic-socialist writer and thinker to the main theorizer for the upcoming jihadist and Takfiri groups (groups which practise excommunication). Starting with Sayed Qutb (who was executed in 1966 during the second ordeal), jihad has been ideologically modified into jihadism in sophisticated arguments. In a post-colonial republic, there was no foreign enemy in Egypt's mainland that would attract ideological hostile mobilization. Thus, the ruling authoritarian regime was the only available alternative and was provocative enough to invite accusations of blasphemy. The transformation of jihad began with a paradigm and then evolved into various sorts of action over the following decades.

Patriotic Sufi jihad in Sinai

Despite a lack of sociological and anthropological references to Sinai society(ies) in the first half of the twentieth century, both the available published literature and the locals' oral history testify an absence of fundamentalist religiosity. Noam Shoqeir's pioneering book *Tarīkh Sinaa al-Qadīm wa-l-Hadīth* (The Ancient and Modern History of Sinai), first published in 1916, discusses the status of religion in Sinai's society:

> Sinai Bedouins recognize Islam as a religion, but none of them knows the basics of Islam or how to pray. I socialized with them for several years and found only a few who might sometimes pray. Even these, who are mostly connected with the cities, do not pray regularly but only when they remember. If Sinai Bedouins did not celebrate Eid al-Adha (the Feast of Sacrificing), mention the Prophet [Mohammed], and swear in his name and bless him, I would not know they are Muslims.

This ethnographic observation written a century ago is supported by the oral and written narratives of tribal elders in both the north-east and west of Sinai. In September 2011, I interviewed a tribal veteran (domestically called 'mujahid') in Ras Sadr, a coastal town on the Gulf of Suez in the south-west of Sinai, and he told me about a relative of his family from the Tarabin tribe who had until recently been called *Al-Mussally* (Prayer Performer) because he was almost the only person who prayed regularly in his whole extended family.[7] Anthropological research on Sinai's local communities produces a completely different image from the stereotype of Sinai as 'the incubator of the most dangerous jihadist groups'.

The status of religion in Sinai in the first half of the twentieth century is documented by Arafat Khedhr Salman, a Sufi sheikh and author of a biography of the late Sheikh Khalaf Al-Khalafat (1930–2009) of the Sawarka tribe. In an interview on Al-Khalafat in November 2013, Salman praised his teacher, who used to travel to Al-Jura and back on foot for two days just to join Friday prayers in Al-Arish. 'He, may Allah bless his soul, used to travel on Thursdays straddling a camel or even on foot to join Friday prayers in Al-Abbasi Mosque in Al-Arish. At sunset, he started his trip back to Al-Joura, where he arrived on the Saturday.' According to Salman, the eastern area of northern Sinai, where nomads were continually following the seasonal rains and trade, was empty of any mosques until Sufi preachers arrived.

Al-Khalafat was eighteen years old when the 1948 war broke out in Palestine. He joined the local volunteer fighters coordinated and supervised by General Mustafa Hafez, director of the Egyptian Military Intelligence in Sinai and Gaza, and participated in several operations.[8] He was the target of repeated failed assassination attempts by Israeli commandos and local spies in 1952 and 1953. Three years later, he survived another assassination operation and left Al-Jura to hide in Al-Ajraa, south of Rafah, during the short Israeli occupation of 1956–7. He moved out of Sinai into the Palestinian lands and then to Jordan, searching for religious guidance. In Amman, he found himself comfortable with a sheikh who lectured in the Al-Husseiny Mosque, who supported him in joining the Sufi Order (Tariqa) of Sheikh Abu Ahmad Al-Falugy,[9] who had recently moved from Gaza to Sinai.

Early in 1957, Al-Khalafat went to Al-Thuma village, where Abu Ahmad's Sufi School (Zawiya) was located, and officially joined the Order. A new alliance between national jihad and the Sufi Order

Alawiya Daruqwiya Shatheliya started with a union between the tribal leadership and Sufi chiefdom. Al-Khalafat was not the only Sufi tribal leader. Indeed, he was the second tribal leader to combine religious leadership with socio-political stature. Sheikh Eid Abu Jerir, sheikh of the Jerarat curia, was a close friend, student and comrade of Sheikh Al-Falugy.[10] Al-Khalafat supervised two-thirds of the Sufi schools (Zawaya) in Sinai, which were hubs of community service as well as of religious education and advocacy. Thus, Al-Khalafat became the semi-elected successor after Al-Falugy died in early 1967.

Unlike the common stereotype of un-politicized Sufism, Al-Khalafat resumed his political struggle against the Israeli occupation in 1967 when he could no longer continue as an armed mujahid. He was arrested twice, in 1968 and 1973, for his activism against the Israeli policy of displacing the indigenous people, particularly the plan to build Al-Jura airport and an attached settlement on more than 8,500 acres of inhabited fertile land. His activism extended to participation in a public conference held by the leftist opposition in Israel. On 1 October 1973, he spoke in public in Sheikh Nuran village, south of Gaza, demanding that a fact-finding committee should investigate Israeli violations against his people in Al-Jura and the surrounding villages. This was after repeated correspondence with the Israeli government and the international community. On 6 October, a fact-finding committee including two ministers visited Al-Jura and left at noon, just two hours before the October War started.[11]

From 1973 to 1979, Al-Khalafat continued non-violent resistance to Israeli policies in secret coordination with Egyptian intelligence. His main strategy was to stay inland and not to move whatever the punitive military policy was, even if people were to die 'under the treads of tanks'.[12] After five months under arrest in Al-Arish, Al-Khalafat returned to Al-Jura on 3 March 1974 and won the battle over the airport. He then started another battle against rigging land sale contracts in 1975. In the same year he was interviewed by the international media and became an icon of community leadership. The Sufi Order followers responded positively to a call to establish a domestic clinic (1976) and a primary school (1977–8) in Al-Jura.

All of these tactics, which in the recent terminology of peace and conflict studies might be considered non-violent resistance, were planned as part of 'unarmed jihad'.[13] Al-Khalafat neither abandoned the lifestyle of mujahid resistance nor the discourse of jihad. In a meeting with a group of Israeli intelligence officers, Al-Khalafat answered a question from Abu Assad (codename of the director for the Sinai area) on his situation regarding jihad against disbelievers (*kuffar*):

> I know what you mean by this question. You want to know what I feel deep down about Israel and if I have an intention, or we have a plan, to run armed resistance against Israel. Well, I will be frank and clear. I swear if I could erase Israel from Sinai and Palestine with two hundred of my men, I would never hesitate.[14]

In parallel with the spirit of unarmed jihad, his students and younger companions were involved in an armed struggle, participating in many military operations shoulder to shoulder with the Special Forces of the Egyptian army. When Sinai was partially liberated and President Anwar El-Sadat raised the Egyptian flag in Al-Arish on 25 October 1979, official recognition was given to both the armed and unarmed locals who had cooperated with Egyptian intelligence during the occupation. Sadat insisted on holding parliamentary elections in the still-occupied border area, and Khalaf Al-Khalafat became Sinai's first elected representative in the Egyptian People's Assembly.

Importantly, the men and women involved in the struggle were all officially recognized as 'mujahidin' and 'mujahidat'. Later, an association was registered under the name 'The Association of Sinai Mujahidin'. The administrative authority registered it using the word derived from jihad, even under Mubarak's rule. Of the approximately 750 officially honoured mujahidin, I met seven men and three women. I saw the charms, medals and certificates of appreciation that were awarded to them. Some of them welcomed the opportunity to tell some of their stories, while others were depressed and disappointed with government neglect. I heard many stories of mujahidin who are not officially listed for various reasons, among which, for instance, their achievements were attributed to the supervising officers while the real heroes and heroines were ignored. Apart from the facts and narratives that I investigated, I noticed that the only word used to mention the local veterans (who were not officially affiliated to the army) was mujahidin (a masculine plural word, referring to both males and females, mujahidin and mujahidat). The majority of them are, or were, moderately religious with a Sufi tendency, and many of them are, or were, from the Sawarka tribe.

Another Sufi mujahidin figure and exceptional veteran hero is Haj Hassan Khalaf, a sheikh in the Ziyadat curia from the Sawarka tribe. Khalaf does not play an official role in the Association of Sinai Mujahidin but he is informally called 'the Sheikh of the Sinai Mujahidin'. He does not speak much about his doctrine, but his turban roll and some decorations in his guest room indicate that he converted to moderate Shiism. This was confirmed by some of his relatives, who insist that it was an individual choice as there is no collective Shiite existence in Sinai. In spite of his support for the Syrian regime, which he expressed in one of his rare TV appearances, he acts in a very statesmanlike way, showing complete loyalty to the Egyptian army against the Salafi jihadists and Takfiri groups. In several interviews he repeatedly urged patience with the military's mistakes rather than accepting the alternative possibility.[15] Khalaf's son was accidentally killed by military shooting at the gate of his house less than a month before his wedding in autumn 2013, but it did not affect the father's support for the army. Because of Khalaf's remarkable record with the army and the military intelligence apparatus, an exceptional statement of condolence was released by a military spokesman on an official Facebook page, in addition to an official private apology. As I write this study, Khalaf is outside Sinai at the request of his young relatives, the Sawarka leaders of ISIL-affiliated Sinai Province (SP).

The sociological context of Salafi jihadism in Sinai

According to my ethnographic observations, it is common in Sinai to consider an absence of war to be an exception. Both Bedouin and urban locals in Sinai, in both the north and the south, are convinced or at least afraid that the Israeli occupation might be repeated at any time. Abandoning local partnerships and even consultation, anger at President Sadat's unilateral reconciliation with the former common enemy has erupted. It should be remembered that the people of Sinai have experienced Israeli invasions and armed occupation three times: in 1948, 1956 and 1967. Each occasion affected a larger area and lasted longer than its predecessor. Hostility and mistrust are still the dominant feelings among the locals towards Israel. This is not difficult to understand in the light of Sinai demographics, with approximately 25,000 Palestinian refugees living in Al-Arish, ten Bedouin tribes and dozens of urban families divided across the borders and distributed across Sinai, Gaza and Israel.[16]

This incubation of hatred towards Israel, which is supported by both nationalist and religious discourses, was the soil in which Islamist jihadist seeds could be planted in Sinai. The earliest spark of Sufi jihadist activism after the October 1973 war was in 1976, when Salah Shehada (1953–2002) returned to Sinai after graduating from Alexandria University. In Alexandria, he had joined the Islamic Group (*al-Jamaa al-Islamiyya*), which used to be an extensive umbrella organization encompassing all activist Islamic students before it split into Salafis and MB revivalist leaders. From 1976 to 1979, besides his new job in Al-Arish specializing in social services, Shehada peacefully mobilized and recruited young members with jihadist motivations to his group in Al-Abbasy Mosque.[17] When Al-Arish was liberated in May 1979, Shehada moved with his family to his birthplace of Beit Hanoun in the north to Gaza. Later, he founded the Palestinian mujahidin group (*al-Mujahidun al-Falastiniyun*), the nucleus of the Izz al-Din al-Qassam Brigades, or the armed wing of the Hamas movement. Shehada's local students and companions quickly converted to other non-jihadist ideological and religious groups. One of them, former Member of Parliament Abdulrahman El-Shorbagy, became a leading figure and a founder of the MB revival in Sinai.[18]

In this environment, the Sawarka Khaled Mosaed (1977–2005) was brought up among stories of heroes and veteran mujahidin, social fears towards Israel, a community ideology of 'national jihad', economic and socio-political marginalization, underdevelopment, and mistrust of the patriotism of the ruling power, the new friend of the old enemy. His thinking crystallized during a dentistry studentship in Zagazig University in the Nile delta. Returning to live in Al-Arish in 1999, Mosaed began to establish the first local jihadist group in Sinai history, together with Nasr Khamis and Salem El-Shenub.[19] In 2003, three years after the second Palestinian Intifada and a few months after the invasion of Iraq, *al-Tawhid wa-l-Jihad* was founded in north-eastern and central Sinai, based on prevalent global Salafi jihadist ideas, especially the *al-Tawhid wa-l-Jihad* platform run by Abu Muhammad Al-Maqdisi. A strongly influential impulse was given to the new-born group by the punitive security 'revolving heel' policy, which was applied to randomly arrested suspects.[20] 'Revolving heel' is the practice of continually moving prisoners from one jail to another further away in a non-stop moving process. This procedure not only aims to debase the detainees but also to overstrain their families and make it harder for them to find their relatives in the restricted visits. However, the result was a jihadist guided educational tour where the beginners, and even irreligious young men, learned much from the expert jihadist and Takfiri leaders in Egypt's various high-security prisons.

The first terrorist attack in Sinai took place in Taba and Nuweiba on 7 October 2004, on the Aqaba Gulf close to the border with Israel. It mainly targeted Israeli tourists, who are perceived as reserve officers and soldiers in the Israeli army. Twenty-four Israeli and seven Egyptian deaths, in addition to 135 injuries, were the outcome of three synchronized car bombings implemented by *al-Tawhid wa-l-Jihad*. A second operation, on 23 July 2005, which also included three simultaneous car bombings, targeted the Sharm El-Sheikh resort 200 kilometres south-west of Nuweiba. There are some doubts about the organizational identity and affiliation of the bombers in this operation, which left eighty dead and 200 injured; while a third (and the last under Mubarak's rule) which took place on 24 April 2006 in Dahab, between Sharm El-Sheikh and Nuweiba, was undoubtedly committed by *al-Tawhid wa-l-Jihad*. It left twenty-three dead, twenty of whom were Egyptians.

The timing of these attacks was carefully chosen to coincide with national days: 6 October is the anniversary of the October War (1973), 23 July is the Day of the Revolution (1952) and 25 April is the Day of the Liberation of Sinai (1982). They were meant as a radical desecration of national symbolism and rejection of the claims of liberation and victory as long as Israel still existed. Mosaed was killed in August 2005 during a tough security campaign that involved committing many violations and abuses against tens of thousands of the local population in northern and central Sinai. *Al-Tawhid wa-l-Jihad* was almost defeated after the last such operation. Many members and non-members were killed and thousands of locals were randomly arrested and tortured.

The group was dissolved; the remaining members disappeared in the border area's remote villages or crossed the border through tunnels and escaped to Gaza for a while. The escaping beginner fighters enhanced their skills and built up their fighting abilities during the Israeli War on Gaza (2008–9). Some of these new experts secretly returned to Sinai to revive Salafi jihadism. They became the core constituents of *Ansar Beit al-Maqdis* (ABM), which did not claim its responsibility for bombing a natural gas pipeline until summer 2012.

The first attack on the gas pipeline was anonymously implemented in June 2010. Seven months later, a peaceful revolution erupted in Cairo's Tahrir Square, the streets of Alexandria, Suez and several cities and towns including Al-Arish. The killing of one peaceful protester, Muhammad Atef, by the police forces in Sheik Zuwayyid's main square on 26 January 2011 was enough to make the north-eastern area of Sinai the only violent exception in the first wave of the revolution (25 January–11 February 2011). Revolutionaries protested and peacefully demonstrated nationwide, including in Al-Arish, although in Rafah and Sheikh Zuwayyid, Kalashnikovs and RPJs replaced banners and chants. In several interviews with local activists, including anti-Islamists, the community explained this exception of Sheikh Zuwayyid and Rafah by referring to serious violations by state security, especially against Bedouin women.[21] No one claimed it was an Islamist revolution or even a jihadist one in north-east Sinai. However, Sinai followed the post-revolutionary political division, and polarization dominated the centralized scene in Cairo, with a kindling of jihadism.

It would be helpful to map the Sinai religious groups, categorizing which are armed, which unarmed, and the varieties of their weapons, their locations, types and different uses. However, that is beyond the scope of this chapter and too complicated to be included here. It would be similarly complicated and space-consuming to identify the Takfiri groups, categorize them as peaceful or violent, and illustrate the dilemma of the jihadi–Takfiri intersections and interactions in Sinai. However, I might generally argue that ideologically-armed groups which may include some non-locals differ from tribally-armed persons and families who do not use their weapons in religious or ideological activities, even if their personal and family weapons are in some cases heavy and advanced. Neither national jihad nor ideological jihadism in

Sinai are always armed, but are actually concerned with timing and conditions. After the 3 July 2013 coup and the start of the open war on 7 September, personal and family arms have gradually disappeared in the border area, where weapons are exclusively held and used by the army and ideological jihadist insurgents.

After the January 2011 revolution, the small number of faithful Salafi jihadists had the opportunity for free advocacy, mobilization and recruitment. Corruption and the collapse of security facilitated all kinds of smuggling, including human trafficking. New arms and vehicles came to Sinai from Libya in huge quantities, many more than had been kept in Sinai and not smuggled to Gaza before the revolution. Becoming a political Islamist in Al-Arish seemed to be closer to the new emerging political power, while becoming an armed Islamist in Sheikh Zuwayyid and Rafah, whether named jihadist or not, seemed to be fashionable and more powerful locally. Many human traffickers and smugglers grew beards, established a new class of warlords with the title of sheikh, and were able to gain the desired prestige which criminals would never normally be granted by society or the government. The generation gap widened more and more, and a tribal polarization between older Sufi mujahidin and younger Salafi jihadists became clearer. Regional news attracted faithful jihadists to fight in Syria and Libya. Many of these did not return. Jihadist ideology and amended versions of it were growing not in a vacuum or a purely mental arena but in hard socio-economic circumstances, in an underdeveloped community that had a terrible record of rights violations and political marginalization.

Unofficial al-Qaeda affiliate ABM started to release both written and audio-visual statements and propaganda materials, and so did another Salafi jihadist group called *Majlis Shura al-Mujahidin–Aknaf Beit al-Maqdis* (MSM–ABM) or the Mujahidin Consultation Council in the Jerusalem Area. In other studies, I have followed the developments and transformations of ABM and MSM–ABM. They abided by a previous strategy of not being involved in any bloody clashes with Egyptian or Palestinian parties.[22] Here, it is most important to view the retreat of MSM–ABM to Gaza and the strategy-shifting of ABM in Sinai and Egypt's mainland in their local socio-political context before looking at the regional context. On the one hand, former President Muhammad

Morsi and the MB were being sharply attacked in Sinai-based Salafi jihadist propaganda. The main criticism was that MB had followed the democratic electoral path, which was not that followed by the Prophet Mohammed to establish the Islamic state and apply *sharia*. However, when the military coup ousted Morsi on 3 July 2013, jihadists received the message as war on all Islamists, and not only political ones. The immediate reaction in Sinai was hysterical: armed demonstrations in Al-Arish (3 July) and then in Sheikh Zuwayyid (5 July). Local MB members in Al-Arish did not tolerate the violent discourse of the jihadists and stopped participating in any joint events.

War broke out in September 2013. The jihadists increasingly stiffened their resolve, and the rapidly changing Arab world has since been feeding ABM with manpower and moral justifications. In November 2014, ABM officially announced a pledge of loyalty to the Islamic State in Iraq and the Levant (ISIL) and changed its name to Sinai Province (SP). The older Sufi mujahidin are currently watching their tribes' younger generation fight the successors of older officers who used to supervise national jihad in Sinai and who are unable to interfere. Some of them are silent, some escaped because they were wanted by the jihadists/terrorists, and the rest were lucky enough to die before this combat began.

Generational conflict and anti-marginalization rebellion

In arguing against the ideological and culturalist approach to the current jihadist scene in Sinai, I refer to a previous study in which I analyzed the jihadi discourse of the Egyptian army. The official military discourse and its internal rhetoric not only utilize the word jihad in its old socio-linguistic sense, but also motivate junior officers and conscripts with jihadist language, setting Israel as the enemy of God, not the nation.[23] The old socio-cultural meaning of the term jihad can be traced in the early literature of the Free Officers Movement, the founding organization of the officers' republic, which used 'jihad' in several historical documents and statements. Nasser's daughter, Huda Abdel Nasser, uses 'jihad' in the same way in her biographical article on her father on the Bibliotheca Alexandrina website. She writes:

> Until that time [1939], the Egyptian army was non-combatant. It was in the interests of the British to keep it so. But a new class of officers emerged in the army. These officers saw their future careers as part of greater Jihad to liberate their people. Gamal went to Manqabad filled with ideals, but he and his companions became disappointed. Most of the officers were incompetent and corrupt. Hence, it turned his thinking to reforming the army and clearing its corruption.[24]

Interviews with ex-conscripts who served in the Egyptian army during the 1960s and 1970s, as well as some rare written diaries, show that the army did not welcome religiosity and religious practice. Ahmad Heggi, an ex-conscript who served in the War of Attrition (1969–71), remembers a conversation between two young officers, a captain and a major, in which the latter complained that his office did not have a refrigerator to cool his beer.[25] At least until the mid-1970s the main training camp had not a single mosque.[26]

Later, many things changed. Every smallest military unit or camp anywhere in the country must include a mosque; many noticeboards, mottos and slogans, both within the army and its administration and in civil projects implemented by the military business entities, are full of religious discourse and use the word jihad; and the official statements released by military spokesmen use religious and jihadi vocabulary to announce claimed achievements in the war on jihadists and Takfiris in Sinai. Furthermore, it is interesting to see how similar the main slogan of MB is to the slogan of the Arab Authority of Manufacturing (AAM), the main industrial entity of the Egyptian army. Both are quotations of Quranic verse. Ironically, the AAM slogan is a longer quote than the MB's. This applies to many branches of the military, where many of the official slogans are Quranic and Hadith quotations (sayings of the Prophet Mohammed). Samples of military anthems show the pivotal position of Sinai in Egyptian military doctrine, which formulates religious jihadi discourse on an ideological state-oriented jihadist template, chanting the name of Allah and enthusing the soldiers against Israel as the enemy of Allah. Interviewees testify that Moral Affairs officers motivate soldiers in the ongoing war in Sinai by accusing ABM/Sinai Province of being Israeli agents. The Second Field Army, which runs the operations in Sinai, pays great attention to inviting sheikhs and imams from Al-Azhar to motivate the troops with jihadi/jihadist discourse. The military propaganda depends on Islamic praise of the Egyptian soldiers as 'the best soldiers on earth', as is mentioned in some historical Islamic references. Both the graphics and the language of current military propaganda use jihadi/jihadist symbols and vocabulary. The state-owned *Al-Akhbar* newspaper had as its front-page headline on 3 April 2015: '35 infidels killed', referring to alleged jihadists killed by the army.[27]

The above-mentioned examples, in addition to the personal and family religious profiles of recent and former senior officers, reaffirm the inability of the ideological and culturalist approach to comprehend and explain the jihadist complexes in Sinai. Instead, ethnographic observations, interviews and informal talks with the local Bedouin community in northern Sinai may give a clearer picture of the sociological and socio-political dynamics that have shaped the jihadist scene, both ideologically and organizationally. The tribal sensitivities between the Sawarka and Rmaylat, for instance, explain why the majority of SP leaders are from Sawarka and why they cannot easily accept Rmaylat members among the SP leadership. Inter-tribal and urban–Bedouin relations in Sinai, however, are too complex to include in this study, which focuses in particular on the Sawarka tribe in order to illustrate the intra-tribal interactions.

In three years of research and socialization with the Sawarka elders and youth, I found it domestically quite clear that the ideological debate is a superficial mask covering a hidden socio-economic, ethical and political generational conflict. The elders have gained ethical and social capital from their historical patriotic jihadi glory and official recognition. This might not be widely understood, but it is well-known in the local community. Sawarka elders obtained the title of sheikh on the basis of tribal selection or government ratification, or at least as a sign of respect for their age. They make money in the hardest ways, living on the basics without financial ambition, and have clear criminal records. Many of them are good speakers; some of them deliver speeches at tribal and government meetings and conventions, even though their Sufi background only gave them minimal levels of education.

On the other hand, some young men in the most marginalized and oppressed zones in Sinai have found no way to make money other than through smuggling. They smuggle everything from cigarettes, food, essential and luxury goods, construction materials and weapons to humans. The common feature among them is a low educational level. Security policies and corruption push more and more of them to join leagues and interest networks. The previous smuggling boom made them rich in a short time. Thus, they had alternative sorts of ambitions and aspirations, quite different from their predecessors. The criminal and unethical profiles of some of them, especially the human traffickers, made them more despised, socially in general and tribally in particular. Some of them were jailed under Mubarak, and it was in jail that they met the few individuals who were honestly committed to jihadist ideology.

A revolution of rage was violently set off in Sheikh Zuwayyid and Rafah in January 2011 as an exception to the peacefulness of the protest in the rest of Egypt. A demonstration of power after seven years of abuse and abasement was a logical reaction. The smugglers had already understood the situation and found that the jihadist path was the perfect way to kill two birds with one stone. On the one hand it was a shortcut to cleansing their reputation as fighters for the noble cause that the elder Sufi mujahidin had supported. This jihadi, not jihadist, flirtation may explain the huge funeral held for four jihadists who were killed by an Israeli drone in August 2013. Such popularity and solidarity were never seen when jihadists were killed by the Egyptian forces. Among the locals, even those who did not participate in the funeral, there was much appreciation and respect for those killed fighting the Israelis, with their black history in Sinai and continuing attacks on civilians in Gaza. Fighting jihad against Israel was the shortest way to challenge the glory of the retired veteran Sufi mujahidin, the loyal alliance of the army of Camp David. On the other hand, Salafi jihadist groups and organizations offered an alternative leadership to excluded young men who would never get the title sheikh with their criminal records, unethical profiles and low education, but could easily be sheikhs in the religious/ideological sense.

Before the coup in July 2013, Salafi jihadism was a choice to manoeuvre across the deep generational and socio-economic gap. Relations between the jihadists and the state, represented by the military regime under both the Supreme Council of Armed Forces (February 2011–June 2012) and Morsi (June 2012–July 2013), were tense. However, it was an extension of what had existed before the revolution rather than a founding point or the start of a new era. The personal and commercial histories of many of the post-revolutionary jihadists were full of brushes with the security apparatuses, even though many officers and soldiers were involved in illegal activities together with the smugglers, who were to become the new jihadists. The new phase came when the coup ended doubts about a potential open war on all Islamists with no differentiation between politicians and armed fighters. Shifting the combat targets coincided with a rapid regional escalation. The ISIL-leaning wing inside ABM led the transformation and it officially became SP, a branch of the jihadist organization serious enough to implement its imagined project and to rule. Late in summer 2015, it was testified that SP was ruling the remnants of seven villages south of Sheikh Zuwayyid. The seven 'liberated' villages are all in Sawarka lands. The majority of the residents have been displaced, forcibly disappeared, detained, killed, injured or moved to Al-Arish or out of Sinai. The remaining people who live in the debris of these villages are practically under SP rule. It does not require male conscription but also does not tolerate cooperation with the army. When young Sawarka men go masked on motorcycle patrols monitoring prices in the local markets, challenging and threatening drug dealers, and serving the community as representatives of the Caliphate, a sociological and anthropological perspective may penetrate the khaki uniforms and see a local generational takeover of rule from the elders.

5

THE GLOBAL AND THE LOCAL

AL-QAEDA AND YEMEN'S TRIBES

Marieke Brandt[1]

Introduction

Much has been written on the global strategies and objectives of al-Qaeda. We also have an idea of which regional agendas various branches of al-Qaeda pursue and these agendas may be quite different from the organization's global goals. However, we still know little about what happens when al-Qaeda affiliates encounter local scenes, how their relationships with locals are negotiated and shaped, and which motives ultimately lead to cooperation or rejection between these groups. Above all, we know little about how locals exploit and utilize the ideology of jihadism, or at least its militant zeal, for the assertion of their own goals and objectives. The aim of this chapter is to shed light on this issue by taking the example of al-Qaeda and the tribes in Yemen.

Jihadism in Yemen in general, and al-Qaeda in particular, are tremendously complex issues. This chapter is limited to consideration of just one aspect of them. It aims to explore the mutual, very variable, relationship between al-Qaeda and Yemen's tribes and how al-Qaeda operates among them at the local level. In doing so, it builds on recent socio-cultural anthropological approaches which emphasize the importance of local people—rather than authorities such as religious scholars, states, etc.—in the implementation of policies, ideologies and religious hermeneutics. It is the locals who invoke the symbols of these policies to reconfigure the boundaries of civic debate, public life and conflict.[2] Local actors do not lead the expert debates, but they formulate the local agendas, shape the reality of political practice and implement policies on the ground. Rather than adopting a more centralized view, this chapter focuses on these local and 'peripheral' views and perceptions.

Discussion of Yemen's tribes is challenging because 'tribe' is a particularly ambiguous concept. On the one hand, in Yemen 'tribe' is an emic concept of social representation. On the other hand, the concept of tribe remains disputed among scientists.[3] The term is hard to define, and Yemen's tribal societies are diverse and function through different mechanisms.[4] Moreover, critics of the concept rightly say that 'tribe' is only one of many models of social representation in Yemen as Yemeni society is composed of different social strata.[5] Furthermore, many citizens of Yemen's growing urban and peri-urban areas, large parts of central and southern Yemen, and even parts of the rural peasant north do not consider themselves tribal (any more). However, many remote areas in the country's extreme north, north-east and east are still dominated by strong tribal customs and traditions. It is therefore no coincidence that al-Qaeda came into contact with Yemen's tribes early on, since jihadis favour precisely such remote areas decoupled from direct state influence as 'safe havens' and refuges: areas which are seldom the central focus of researchers' interest.

The interplay between tribalism and jihadism, in this case the complex relation between al-Qaeda and Yemen's tribes, can be divided into two distinct phases. In the first phase, from 1990 until the late 2000s, the tribes' readiness to cooperate with al-Qaeda's jihadis was often regulated by tribal customary law and motivated by the tribes' desire to strengthen their status and bargaining power in their power struggles with other tribes and the Yemeni (and Saudi) government.

Al-Qaeda, in contrast, adhered to a global strategy and was little or not at all attuned to the local situation in Yemen. As a result, the presence of al-Qaeda remained an isolated phenomenon. Al-Qaeda's position among the tribes was vulnerable and precarious, and ultimately tied to the goodwill and tolerance of powerful actors among these tribes.

From the late 2000s, al-Qaeda in Yemen began to undergo an internal change that enormously contributed to its expansion. After 2009, when it united with al-Qaeda's Saudi branch into a group that called itself al-Qaeda in the Arabian Peninsula (AQAP), both the political situation in Yemen and jihadi strategy underwent profound changes. The power and security vacuum caused by Yemen's political upheavals, which commenced in 2011, and the subsequent military expansion of the Shia Ḥūthī group into territories that were majority Sunni became an opportunity for al-Qaeda to earn de facto acceptance in some tribal areas because of the fighting capabilities its jihadis were able to bring to bear against the Ḥūthīs. Moreover, from 2011 AQAP pursued a strategy change and began to focus systematically on local agendas and 'soft approaches' in order to secure the acceptance and support of the local population. AQAP's strategic turnaround from the exogenous to the indigenous, from the global to the local, was reinforced by a grievance narrative in which AQAP blurred long-standing local discontent with transnational aims. Interestingly, their arch-enemies, the Shia Ḥūthīs, operate in a similar fashion in Yemen's Zaydi-dominated areas.

Yemen's diverse sectarian environment

Islamic identities in Yemen are historically divided into three main orientations: Shia Zaydism, Sunni Shāfiʿism, and a numerically much smaller group of Ismāʿīlīs. Roughly speaking, the main settlement area of the Zaydis covers Yemen's highlands north of Sana'a. Lower Yemen south of Sana'a and its eastern regions are mainly dominated by Sunnis. Ismāʿīlī communities are present in the eastern part of Ṣaʿdah governorate near the Saudi border city of Najrān and in the Ḥarāz mountains west of Sana'a.

The Zaydis are a sect of Shia Islam who trace their name back to their eponym Zayd b. ʿAlī, the great-grandson of ʿAlī b. Abī Ṭālib.[6] The first Zaydi imam in Yemen, Yaḥyā b. al-Ḥusayn, managed to establish a

Zaydi community in Yemen in 897 and laid the foundations for the Zaydi imamate. Throughout its existence, the Zaydi imamate has been in a state of varying influence and often intermittent authority. The legal teachings and judgements of Yaḥyā b. al-Ḥusayn became the basis for the so-called Zaydi Hādawī school of law, the main emphasis of which is its insistence on righteous rule through the *sādah*, i.e. the descendants of the Prophet through his grandsons Ḥusayn and Ḥasan. *Sādah* occupied the position of imam (the spiritual and secular leader of the Zaydi community) and also the leadership positions in government, administration and the military apparatus of the imamic state. The imamate existed for almost a millennium until the revolution of 26 September 1962, which led to the overthrow of the imamic system and the establishment of the Yemeni republic.

The majority of Yemeni Sunnis adhere to the teachings of the Muslim Arab scholar of jurisprudence, Muḥammad b. Idrīs al-Shāfiʿī (d.820). In matters of jurisprudence the Zaydi and Shāfiʿī schools of law are not far apart. Their main difference comes down to the question of the supremacy of the *sādah*. Historically, this disagreement between Yemen's Sunnis and Zaydis has not always been one of antagonism. The Zaydis are generally considered a moderate Shia sect, so moderate indeed that the Zaydi community has at times described itself as the 'fifth school' (*al-madhhab al-khāmis*) after the four orthodox Sunni schools of Islam.[7]

Since the fifteenth century, for reasons of dynastic retention of power some Zaydi imams have promoted a gradual convergence between the Zaydi and Shāfiʿi doctrines. This 'Sunnization of Zaydism' or 'Traditionist Project' to bridge the jurisprudential gap between the two doctrines is closely associated with the scholar-jurist Muḥammad al-Shawkānī (d.1834).[8] Traditionist doctrine advocated the development of a non-*madhhab* identity. During the September 1962 revolution, which led to the abolition of the imamate, the project of non-*madhhab* identity was taken up by republican ideologues whose goal was to create a republic as an enduring ideological form through the merger of Sunni and Zaydi doctrines, and a 'unified' Islam based primarily on the Quran and Sunna.[9]

During recent decades, Yemen's process of doctrinal convergence has become increasingly derailed by the spread of radical Sunnism and

Zaydi revivalism. Sunni Islamists, financed by Saudi Arabia, intensified their activities in Yemen after the 1962 revolution. The Yemeni branch of the Muslim Brotherhood was founded in the 1960s. From the early 1980s, a brand of Yemeni Salafism developed which was associated with Muqbil al-Wādiʿī (d.2001) and his Salafi teaching centre *Dār al-Ḥadīth al-Khayriyyah* in Dammāj near Ṣaʿdah city.[10] Among ordinary people, Salafism was able to develop a certain attraction, mainly because of its egalitarian doctrine which aimed at the elimination of social divisions, especially Zaydi-Hādawī principles such as the *sādah*'s enduring claim to religious authority and social superiority on the grounds of religious descent.[11]

The increasing Sunnization of the Zaydi doctrine and, above all, the spread of Salafism led to the emergence of a Zaydi revival movement. Zaydi revivalism began as a defensive movement to counter the Salafi onslaught and the continuing government policy of neglect towards the Zaydis. In the late 1990s, factional disputes within the Zaydi revival movement escalated and ultimately led to a schism and the emergence of a group led by members of the al-Ḥūthī family, which from 2001 onwards became known as 'Ḥūthīs' (*al-Ḥūthiyyūn*). Between 2004 and 2010 the Yemeni government pursued six military campaigns against the Ḥūthīs, which went down in Yemen's recent history as the Ṣaʿdah wars (*ḥurūb Ṣaʿdah*).[12] In the north of Yemen, in particular, the Ḥūthīs received growing support from the local population as their movement managed to embrace a powerful social revolutionary and political agenda. In the extreme north, riven by socio-political and economic imbalances, the Ḥūthī movement ultimately became a focus which served to unite the interests of many of those who felt economically neglected, politically ostracized and religiously marginalized.

Hidden roles: al-Qaeda's first generation

Although inspired and influenced by external debates and developments, the Yemeni forms of Salafism and Shia revivalism mainly emerged out of the domestic context. Their home-grown programmes and objectives were embedded in the local and national context, gave answers and solutions to the problems of individuals and communities, and therefore found overt and covert agreement among considerable sections of the Yemeni population. In contrast, until the late 2000s, al-Qaeda's jihadis in Yemen, who adhered to the mother organization's transnational agenda and objectives, remained alien to Yemeni society. This only changed in the late 2000s when both the profound transformations of Yemen's political landscape and the strategy changes within al-Qaeda's Yemen branch led to the emergence of a new generation of al-Qaeda in Yemen.

Jihadi groups have been active in Yemen since the end of the Afghan war against Soviet occupation in the 1980s. During the Soviet–Afghan war, al-Qaeda was created in response to the Soviet invasion. After the war, many jihadis from Arab countries—the so-called Afghan Arabs—were not allowed to return to their home countries and settled in Yemen along with Yemeni veterans of the Afghan war. The Ṣāliḥ government repatriated many of these foreign and domestic Afghan Arabs and dispatched them to fight the Soviet-backed Marxist government of South Yemen in a successful bid for unification, and subsequently to crush southern secessionists.[13] During the 1990s, various jihadi groups emerged in Yemen. Two early militant jihadi groups who claimed to maintain ties with Osama bin Laden were the Islamic Jihad in Yemen (active 1990–94) and the Aden–Abyan Islamic Army (1994–8). Furthermore, many Afghan Arabs were inducted into the regular Yemeni army after they had battled against the southern socialists for former President Ṣāliḥ in the 1994 civil war.

It is unclear when the Yemeni branch of al-Qaeda officially coalesced as a cohesive group. Al-Qaeda in Yemen did not carry out large-scale attacks until it first emerged with the 12 October 2000 bombing of the USS *Cole* in Aden harbour. One year later, the mother organization of al-Qaeda, which had solidified its position as an international militant and terrorist organization with a wide-reaching leadership structure and a powerful global network of cells, orchestrated the 9/11 attacks against the US, killing nearly 3,000 people. In the US and its allies, the combined effect of these attacks caused outrage against al-Qaeda, eventually contributing to the initiation of the US-led global War on Terror.

The relation of the Yemeni government to jihadism and al-Qaeda was (as was its relation to Salafism and Zaydi revivalism) always an ambiguous one, with jihadis moving in and out of government favour depending on the political climate. Following the 9/11 attacks in 2001, the US and Yemeni governments cooperated to carry out counter-terrorism initiatives against al-Qaeda in Yemen, in particular by using drones, despite Ṣāliḥ's earlier dealings with militant Islamists. Since Ṣāliḥ had his fingers painfully burnt during the first Gulf War (Desert Storm) when he sided with Saddam Hussein, after 9/11 he came out in support of the US. Under international pressure, the government began to combat al-Qaeda. Quietist Salafis, in contrast, were spared overt repression despite international pressure because they helped theologically to delegitimize the recourse to violence on the part of groups linked to al-Qaeda.[14]

A few years later, Ṣāliḥ's position vis-à-vis al-Qaeda changed again. Instead of being rewarded for his efforts in the fight against terrorism, during a visit to the US in 2005 he was confronted with the news that Yemen was suspended from the USAID programme for inadequate successes in the fight against corruption. The World Bank, too, told him that it was slashing aid, from $420 million a year to $280 million.[15] Following this, Ṣāliḥ's position towards al-Qaeda changed again and he secretly began to facilitate its expansion. By causing chaos and disorder he hoped to distinguish himself as the only anchor of stability and saviour of Yemen, in particular in the eyes of foreign countries. Phillips has dubbed this informal ruling system used by the Ṣāliḥ regime, which is based on the sponsorship and exploitation of conflict, the 'politics of permanent crisis'.[16]

Because of their rugged terrain, geostrategic location, proximity to Saudi Arabia, the weak state and their famously independent tribes, in the late 1990s Osama bin Laden, whose father had Yemeni roots, saw Yemen's remote hinterlands as an ideal retreat and operation platform for al-Qaeda. In 1996 in an interview with *al-Quds al-ʿArabī*, Osama bin Laden optimistically described the remote borderlands of Yemen as areas in which 'the writ of the national government barely reaches, and whose people allow one to breathe the clear air unblemished by humiliation'.[17]

Osama bin Laden's assumptions about the Yemeni tribes and the operating conditions in Yemen, however, remained in the realms of utopia. The reality on the ground was different and revealed his blatant ignorance of the situation in Yemen. Until the late 2000s, the attitude of Yemen's tribes towards al-Qaeda was often self-serving and ambiguous. Although some tribes in the predominantly Sunni areas granted refuge and collective protection to jihadis, their room for action and manoeuvre among their host communities remained limited by tribal interests and calculations.

In Yemen's far north and north-east, which were dominated by strong tribal traditions, the reception of the jihadis was usually governed by the provisions of *ḥaqq al-rabāʿ* or *ṣaḥb* according to tribal customary law (*ʿurf*). *Ḥaqq al-rabāʿ* is a legal option which allows a tribe to grant refuge or political asylum (*lujūʾ sīyāsī*) to external persons.[18] It is a versatile mechanism for protecting a wide range of external persons, from aid agencies to those fleeing tribal revenge (*thaʾr*) or arrest by security organs. It assigns the asylum seeker or refugee temporary reversible membership of the tribal community, which includes protection and non-surrender to official authorities or other tribes. The regulations of *ḥaqq al-rabāʿ* provide that both the sheikh and the asylum seeker sign a formal contract defining the tribe's responsibility to protect him in exchange for an undertaking to abstain from unilateral actions. For the time of his asylum, the refugee is instead expected to participate in the tribe's own conflicts as any of the other tribesmen would. The visitor is neither exactly a guest nor a member of the tribal community. At no point is the arrangement intended to be a permanent one, and the asylum seeker remains at something of a disadvantage, being denied both the responsibilities and legitimacy afforded to native members of the host tribe. A second option for the tribal protection of outsiders is *ṣaḥb*, which is a permanent integration of the asylum seeker into the host tribe.[19] The less restrictive and temporary solutions of *ḥaqq al-rabāʿ*, however, appear to have been the method of choice for securing the protection of asylum seekers who were members of al-Qaeda and other jihadi organizations by host tribes in the areas dominated by strong tribal customs and traditions, particularly because a portion of al-Qaeda's membership base was actually from Saudi Arabia.

It also happened that the jihadis were linked by common descent and kinship ties to the tribal community whose protection and shelter they were seeking. In this case, the imperatives of *ʿaṣabiyya*—'spirit of tribal solidarity' or 'cohesive drive against others'—took effect.[20] *ʿAṣabiyya* implies that whoever commits a wrong or a disgrace against a member of a tribe is reckoned to have insulted the whole tribal community. These jihadis were provided with support and protection because of their tribal affiliation, and members of the related tribal group protected their kin against intrusion. But here, too, the jihadis were subordinated to the policy of the tribe, not vice versa. It is therefore questionable whether such tribal communities were proper operation platforms for jihadi activities.

Providing shelter for jihadis—through either the regulations of *ḥaqq al-rabāʿ*, *ṣaḥb* or *ʿaṣabiyya*—implied that at times tribal authority and state authority collided, especially in cases when asylum seekers were related to terrorism and/or wanted by the security services. In these cases, the state attempted to subvert the tribal practice of *ḥaqq al-rabāʿ* in various ways or even to use it for its own purposes. In accordance with Yemen's political system, which was based on co-option and patronage of its rivals and adversaries, enormous amounts of money were channelled to the sheikhs of the areas and tribes concerned. Selznick defines co-option as a strategy of absorbing adverse elements into the state's policy-determining structure in order to avert threats to its stability or existence.[21] Financial co-option was usually the government's method of choice to impose its will on a tribe. The purpose was to prevent the tribe from granting shelter to those who were seeking its protection. Financial co-option was also used as a lever to force tribes to extradite certain persons to the state's security organs. Depending on the situation, these cash flows could also ensure that the tribes monitored and controlled these persons instead of extraditing them to the state. In a few cases—often due to enormous foreign pressure—military coercion was also applied when the state had a vital interest in the extradition of certain individuals and it could not be achieved by means of financial co-option.

Why did tribes provide refuge for jihadis? What advantages did this offer them? It is possible that one member of a tribe or another sympathized with the global ideology of al-Qaeda. In the Yemeni context of this period, however, these cases seem to have been the exception rather than the rule. To understand a sheikh's or a tribe's incentives to grant refuge to jihadis and to offer them their protection, the mechanisms of tribe–state relations need to be taken into consideration. From the point of view of a tribe, patronage and co-option as the state's means of neutralizing threats meant the following: the more risk and threat emanating from a tribe, the greater its bargaining power over benefits in cash and in kind, state posts, etc. In other words, by granting refuge to jihadis (the more dangerous the better), lamentably neglected and marginalized tribes on the periphery of the state's interest seized the chance to move finally into the government's central focus of attention. The government responded to the 'growing importance' and the increased bargaining potential of the tribe with the distribution of financial resources, etc. in order to secure its influence in unruly and risky areas. These are the imperatives of co-option and in the power play between the tribes and the government the jihadis were often merely the pawns with whom the tribes boosted their importance in order to extort attention, resources and other benefits from the government. In a nutshell, the politics of co-option necessarily produced the risks which the government was simultaneously trying to contain.

In Yemen's border areas these bargains not only took place between the tribes and the government in Sana'a, but also between tribes and Saudi Arabia. The patronage politics of the Saudi Kingdom in the Yemeni borderlands goes back even further to the end of the 1934 Saudi–Yemeni War.[22] The bargains and power plays between the tribes and the Yemeni and Saudi states did not remain unnoticed by al-Qaeda's local leadership. In 2009, Qāsim al-Raymī (then leader of al-Qaeda's Yemen branch) noted with displeasure in regard to Yemen's tribes that 'those hirelings do not represent anyone but themselves'.[23]

The jihadis were aware of the limitations which the provisions of both *ḥaqq al-rabāʿ* and the policy of co-option imposed on them. In the late 2000s they started their first attempts to break down the barriers between them and the tribes. However, only anecdotal evidence of these endeavours exists for this period and some reports indicate that certain members of al-Qaeda married into local tribes.[24] Furthermore, to some extent jihadis began to frame their operations in the language of *qabyalah*.[25] These constitute conscious attempts to become constituents, rather than just refugees and asylum seekers, among the tribes. The success of these actions at that time, however, seems to have been limited.

The failed negotiations between a group of sheikhs from eastern Ṣaʿdah (Wāʾilah), al-Jawf (Dahm) and Maʾrib (Murād) and Afghan emissaries from Osama bin Laden, who in 1997 considered taking sanctuary somewhere in these sheikhs' domains, are a good example of the role of the jihadis as pawns in tribe–state bargains over power and resources. These negotiations also demonstrate the lack of awareness by al-Qaeda's top leadership vis-à-vis the situation in Yemen's tribal peripheries.

Muḥammad b. Shājiaʿ, sheikh of Āl Ḥusayn, was central to these negotiations. The Āl Ḥusayn, a segment of the Wāʾilah, dwell in a vast and remote area in eastern Ṣaʿdah governorate where the international frontier between Yemen and Saudi Arabia turns into the poorly demarcated territory of the Empty Quarter. They are *badū*, former nomads who periodically straddled the boundary. In the past, their settlement area was of only symbolic significance, but after the beginning of oil and gas exploration in Yemen it gained supreme strategic importance in the struggle for fossil energy resources. Despite being a Bedouin tribe from one of the remotest regions in Yemen, Muḥammad b. Shājiaʿ and his tribe were quite adapted to globalization. Smuggling and trans-border trade were an important pillar of their activities. They operated large-scale illegal trade flows from Yemen across the vast space of the Empty Quarter to Riyadh and the Gulf states in the north, using their borderland territories as a hub for contraband. Members of the tribe and the Shājiaʿ clan itself were also settled in Qatar. The emigration of some of them, coupled with family and tribal solidarity, provided the Āl Ḥusayn with ways to connect with international networks.

Historically, and for reasons of bilateral border protection, the Āl Ḥusayn were close allies of the Saudi Kingdom. In return for their services, Saudi Arabia turned a blind eye to their illegal trade activities. Nevertheless, in the early 1990s the alliance between the Āl Ḥusayn and the Saudi Kingdom began to deteriorate. There were several reasons for this. The uncontrolled influx of arms, drugs, human trafficking and, not least, the Gulf crisis in 1990 clearly showed the Saudis the vulnerability of their borders. When the Kingdom began to demarcate these sections of its south-western boundaries in the 1990s and to erect border fortifications there, Muḥammad b. Shājiaʿ perceived it as a threat to his tribe's territorial integrity and economic prosperity, which depended on smuggling. Moreover, he suspected that pasture lands which the Wāʾilah had a right to use would fall to the Saudi Yām tribe. In consequence, his tribe blocked the Saudi demarcation and fortification works through fierce resistance, which led to a temporary suspension of the project.

To build an additional threat and greater bargaining power against the Saudi government and the Yemeni state (which he suspected of collusion), Muḥammad b. Shājiaʿ did not hesitate to receive in 1997 the Afghan delegation from Osama bin Laden, who at the time was considering taking refuge somewhere in the remote domain of Muḥammad b. Shājiaʿ. In the end, however, the negotiations between Muḥammad b. Shājiaʿ and Osama bin Laden's envoys failed to yield any results. To put it bluntly, Muḥammad b. Shājiaʿ welcomed al-Qaeda's jihadis, but following the rules of *ḥaqq al-rabāʿ* he imposed the condition that they surrender their military might to the tribe's command, which simply implied that on his territory Muḥammad b. Shājiaʿ demanded control and sovereignty over the activities of al-Qaeda's jihadis. Sectarian conformity between them was impossible anyway since the Āl Ḥusayn are of Ismāʿīlī denomination, and Ismāʿīlīs and al-Qaeda can hardly harmonize. What counted were the tribe's political goals. The negotiations thus proved fruitless. Osama bin Laden's envoys were no fools and realized that Muḥammad b. Shājiaʿ intended to utilize the presence of al-Qaeda as leverage in his power struggles with the Saudi and Yemeni governments concerning the demarcation of the international boundary. During these negotiations, the Afghan envoys may have realized that Osama bin Laden's assumption that one could 'breathe freely' in the remote Yemeni borderlands was profoundly naïve.

Another example of the local complexities is the tribal setting of the so-called Kitāf camp. Unlike in Muḥammad b. Shājiaʿ's case, in Kitāf cooperation between local tribes and al-Qaeda did materialize and led to the emergence of a highly complex political and tribal situation. In the early 1990s, a camp for Afghan Arabs was set up in the Āl Abū Jabārah wādī (valley) in Ṣaʿdah's Kitāf region. Āl Abū Jabārah is both an ethnonym and a toponym, i.e. it designates both a tribal group and its area of settlement. The Āl Abū Jabārah, too, are a segment of the Wāʾilah, the predominant tribe in Ṣaʿdah's Kitāf region. Just like the Āl Ḥusayn further to the east, the settlement area of Āl Abū Jabārah is also situated in close proximity to the Saudi border.

Officially, the Kitāf camp carried the designation of a Salafī teaching institute. However, it hosted activities different to those of the other well-known Salafi teaching centre Dār al-Ḥadīth, located in Dammāj near Ṣaʿdah city. In Dammāj the teaching aspect was stronger, and the leadership of Dammāj was trying hard to emphasize that it was not in any way connected to al-Qaeda.[26] In contrast, the Kitāf camp had distinct military features. Local sources indicate that it hosted al-Qaeda operatives and backed their activities. In fact, the Kitāf camp had multiple allegiances and its trajectories kept oscillating. The armed men of Kitāf have at times been labelled jihadis, militant Salafis, Wahhabis, mercenaries (*murtaziqah*) and al-Qaeda, and the distinctions between them appear to have been somewhat fluid and blurred. As so often in Yemen, people were wearing more than one turban, so to say. 'They met on paper' (*yajtamʿūna ʿalā l-warqah*), as locals characterized the jihadi conglomerate of the Kitāf camp.

The history of the Kitāf camp is murky. Sources from the area suggest that it was originally a military base of the Yemeni army which in the early 1990s fell under the stewardship of Afghan Arabs. Later on, jihadis of various shades and al-Qaeda operatives joined them in Kitāf.[27] Just as he had done during the 1994 civil war, in which he had used the Afghan Arabs against the socialist south, from 2004 Ṣāliḥ used the jihadis of the Kitāf camp as mercenaries in the Ḥūthī conflict, declaring their struggle against their Shia opponents a 'Holy War'. Inspired by the situation in Syria, its fighters temporarily adopted the name *ḥilf al-nuṣrah*. For the Yemeni branch of al-Qaeda, this camp in the close vicinity of the Saudi border was of supreme strategic importance as an outpost and relay station, since the group drew many of its operatives from Saudi Arabia.

The situation among the Āl Abū Jabārah was similar to that of the Āl Ḥusayn regarding the proximity and importance of the Yemeni–Saudi frontier in the local tribal environment. It differed, however, from the Āl Ḥusayn case in other aspects. Since the Treaty of Ṭāʾif, which defined the border between Yemen (then the Mutawakkilite Kingdom) and the Kingdom of Saudi Arabia after the brief Saudi–Yemeni War of 1934, the Saudi government had patronized the Āl Abū Jabārah (along with most of the other Yemeni borderland tribes) in order to secure and stabilize the tribally and politically disputed border. To this end, Saudi Arabia established a network of patronage in the area with the purpose of turning the borderland tribes into a bulwark against any possible overspill of conflict from Yemen. Moreover, after the 1970s the Saudi 'Wahhabization' campaign, made possible by the Kingdom's sudden oil wealth, seems to have been particularly successful with the Āl Abū Jabārah tribe. Many residents of the area abandoned their fathers' Shia Zaydi faith in favour of the Wahhabi faith.

Ultimately, the willingness of some Āl Abū Jabārah to cooperate with militant jihadis seems to have been driven by mundane interests and the political power benefits they could derive from the massive presence of jihadi warriors on their territories. Through the presence of the militants, certain segments of the Āl Abū Jabārah tribe acquired the military might, weapons and financial benefits which they needed to pursue their grey, dark-grey and black trans-border trade activities (the smuggling of weapons, ammunition, *qāt*, liquor, drugs, and also human trafficking were a central part of the area's economic profile) and their intra- and inter-tribal infightings. With militant jihadis on their side, certain segments of Āl Abū Jabārah were able to assert their interests successfully against other segments of the tribe with whom they were in historic competition over influence and hegemony, and thus to settle old tribal accounts.

Not all the sheikhs and tribal segments of Āl Abū Jabārah cooperated with the jihadis. Notably, their senior sheikh Ibn Dāyil b. Fayṣal kept his distance from them. Three minor sheikhly clans of Āl Abū Jabārah and the tribal segments they represented were considered jihadi-affine: the sheikhly clans of al-T., al-I. and ʿU.[28] Nāṣir Masʿūd ʿU. took a particularly prominent role: he was called the 'warrior prince' (*amīr al-muqātilīn*) of Kitāf, the 'arm' (*dhirāʿ*) of al-Qaeda in the Ṣaʿdah region. The three families were simultaneously heavily involved in the licit and illicit trans-border trade and were considered extremely wealthy.

After 9/11, Yemeni honey companies, notably the honey chain stores *al-Shifāʾ li-l-ʿAsl* and *al-Nūr li-l-ʿAsl*, were put on US terror lists. This was because of the involvement of people considered close to al-Qaeda in the honey trade. *Al-Nūr* is affiliated to the al-Ahdal clan, one member of which, Muḥammad Ḥamdī al-Ahdal, was one of al-Qaeda's leaders in Yemen in the early 2000s. The owner of *al-Shifāʾ* was Ṣāliḥ al-T. of Āl Abū Jabārah. Honey from Yemen is among the most expensive in the world and is legally exported in large quantities to Saudi Arabia, which has a high demand for honey but relatively little production. Besides the astronomic revenues generated by the Yemeni honey business, the shops allowed the owners involvement in money laundering and the shipping of contraband like weapons, explosives and drugs. In 2001 the *New York Times* cited a US official saying that 'the smell and consistency of the honey makes it easy to hide weapons and drugs in the shipments. Inspectors don't want to inspect that product. It's too messy.'[29]

One naturally wonders how it can be that such a large camp with ties to al-Qaeda was so close to the Saudi border, in the territory of a tribe that was known for its close ties with the Kingdom. In fact, the Saudi influence in Wādī Āl Abu Jabārah was enormous. The ideology of al-Qaeda is directed *inter alia* against the Saudi royal family, the House of Saʿūd, and Saudi responses to terrorist activity on Saudi soil are merciless. However, there is a set of answers to this puzzle. The senior sheikh of the Āl Abū Jabārah tribe, along with many of its segments, was first and foremost an ally of the Saudi Kingdom, a key partner in the bilateral protection of the vulnerable boundary, and the presence of al-Qaeda in his area certainly was a lesser evil because the Kingdom knew that al-Qaeda was 'in good hands', so to speak, and under the surveillance of a close tribal ally. The decentralized and unpredictable command structures of al-Qaeda, however, remained a problem in this setting, particularly after the 2009 merger of the Yemeni and Saudi branches of al-Qaeda into a group which henceforth became known as al-Qaeda in the Arabian Peninsula (AQAP). One of the ways that the security threat emanating from AQAP manifested itself was AQAP's failed assassination attempt in 2009 on Saudi Deputy Minister of the Interior Emir Muḥammad b. Nāyif, the prince who ran Saudi Arabia's counter-terrorism efforts. It is also very likely that the jihadis of the Kitāf camp were involved in the abduction of foreign aid workers in Ṣaʿdah in June 2009.[30]

Despite these incidents, Saudi Arabia did not take any action against the jihadis in the border region because since 2004 the jihadis of the Kitāf camp had been deeply involved in the fight against the Shia Ḥūthīs, i.e. they served the interests of both the Yemeni and the Saudi governments. During the Ṣaʿdah wars (2004–10) Nāṣir Masʿūd ʿU., the 'warrior prince' of Āl Abū Jabārah, led the jihadis' fight against the Ḥūthīs. Nāṣir Masʿūd ʿU. was said to have had a close relationship with General ʿAlī Muḥsin al-Aḥmar, then commander of military forces in northern Yemen and in charge of the campaign against the Ḥūthīs since its inception in 2004. General ʿAlī Muḥsin is a relative of President Ṣāliḥ. Some suspect that one of his sisters was married to Ṭāriq al-Faḍlī, a prominent Islamist and 'Afghan Arab' of southern elite background. ʿAlī Muḥsin played a prominent role in recruiting Afghan Arabs against southern secessionists and defeating the southern forces during the 1994 civil war. He has been accused of supporting al-Qaeda and the spread of Salafi Islam in the Ṣaʿdah area and beyond.[31] A local source described the entanglement of jihadis, the military and the state in the following words:

> Despite their pretentious rhetoric, Quranic citations and photo-shopped internet magazines, al-Qaeda in Yemen was just as corrupt as the Ṣāliḥ regime itself. The enmeshment of al-Qaeda with Yemen's subverted military and intelligence services was a product of long-standing relationships that stretched from the caves of Afghanistan to the presidential palace in Sana'a.[32]

From 2011 onwards, Yemen's transition process generated a vacuum which strengthened the Ḥūthīs in northern Yemen and enabled them—now allied with their former enemy ex-president Ṣāliḥ, who had been forced to resign in late 2011—to begin their march on Sana'a, which they eventually seized in September 2014. A landmark event in the consolidation of their power was the demolition of the Kitāf camp. In December 2013, the Kitāf camp faced a true 'clash of fundamentalisms'. Led by their military field leaders, ʿAbdullah al-Ḥākim and Yūsuf al-Madānī, the Ḥūthīs blew up the camp's military compound and expelled the jihadis and their tribal allies from the Āl Abū Jabārah. Al-Qaeda's 'warrior prince', Nāṣir Masʿūd ʿU., was killed. While the heads of the three jihad-supporting families from among the Āl Abū Jabārah reportedly fled to the Saudi city of Najrān (where they owned extensive real estate), the external jihadis fled towards the south and east. Following the demolition of the Kitāf camp, the Salafi Dār al-Ḥadīth in Dammāj was also left unprotected. On the recommendation of Interim President ʿAbd Rabbuh Manṣūr Hādī, it was evacuated in January 2014. The word is that many tribal inhabitants of Wādī Āl Abū Jabārah have since refocused on their original Zaydi faith, although this may be Ḥūthī propaganda. Ultimately, though, Wahhabism and Salafism have a history of only forty years in the region, whereas the roots of Zaydism reach back to the ninth century. In particular, the Zaydi segments of the Wāʾilah tribe often played a significant part in the politics of Zaydi affairs.[33]

Both of the above cases—the consultation meeting between al-Qaeda envoys and Muḥammad b. Shājiaʿ and the fate of the Kitāf camp—show that during the phase prior to 2011 tribal groups who at one time or another were at least partially affiliated with jihadi groups can hardly be portrayed as local proxies for a transnational terrorist movement. Their readiness to cooperate with jihadis can instead be explained by their desire to boost their status and ability in their own local and national power struggles. In other words, the ties between the tribes and the jihadis were often the outcome of political horse-trading, unequal power relations, financial and commercial interests, tribal infighting, turf wars, and the changing ability of actors to control, steer and resist other actors. The rationale that lay at the bottom of these power plays was pre-defined by contests over the still-controversial border question between Yemen and the Saudi Kingdom. In their shady deals with the jihadis, the tribes mostly had the upper hand: it was they who determined who was allowed to stay in their territories, and they used the jihadis to assert their interests. Jihadi groups have seldom been able to build a broader popular support base and have never been able to seize territories in this area. At least among the Wāʾilah tribe, the presence of jihadism has instead remained a somewhat isolated phenomenon and has ultimately been tied to the goodwill and tolerance of powerful actors among the local tribes.

Strategy changes: al-Qaeda's second generation

In Yemen's extreme north, AQAP has suffered a disastrous defeat from which it has not yet recovered. However, in the southern and eastern regions—notably Abyan, Shabwah and Ḥaḍramawt—al-Qaeda has managed to expand enormously. This has mainly been for two reasons: after 2011 both the political situation in Yemen and al-Qaeda's strategic approach underwent fundamental changes. AQAP has been able to expand its support among the population through the military threat emanating from the Ḥūthīs' expansion and its increasing use of 'soft approaches' in Yemen's tribal and non-tribal areas.

After 2011, Yemen's 'Change' Revolution led to profound transformations in the country's political landscape. A range of complex issues merged at the national level: the Ḥūthī conflict in the north; the secessionist Ḥirāk movement in the south; the fight against corruption; and partisan, sectarian, civil society, gender and youth movements. The political turmoil caused mass defections and the resignations of politicians and military officers formerly loyal to the Ṣāliḥ regime. Among the defectors was General ʿAlī Muḥsin, who in March 2011 joined the revolution and change axis.[34] In November 2011, after much prevarication, President Ṣāliḥ agreed to leave office under the terms of a 'transition agreement' mediated by the Gulf Cooperation Council. This so-called GCC initiative forced Ṣāliḥ to resign and regulated the transfer of the presidency to former vice president ʿAbdrabbuh Manṣūr Hādī in return for domestic immunity for Ṣāliḥ. A UN-sponsored transition roadmap included three principal tasks: holding a National Dialogue Conference (NDC), addressing issues of transitional justice, and both unifying and reforming the security sector. However, after the conclusion of the NDC in January 2014 the political transition process slowed down and political decision-making again began to follow the old exclusive patterns rather than the new required inclusive patterns.[35] The confrontation between the Ḥūthīs and the interim government hardened as the Ḥūthīs accused the government of purposefully delaying the transition process. Meanwhile, the Ḥūthīs—now allied with their former nemesis Ṣāliḥ against interim President Hādī—continuously expanded their military dominance. In September 2014 they seized the capital. While continuing to expand their dominion southwards and eastwards, they began to press forcefully into the Sunni-dominated areas of lower and eastern Yemen.

The expansion of the Ḥūthīs into territories that were predominantly Sunni created a new threat situation and pushed some of their adversaries into the arms of jihadi groups like AQAP and, later on, the Islamic State (we will return to this). The majority of Yemen's population, including its tribal strata, remained opposed to all forms of extremism, and many tribes and tribal militias remained opposed to AQAP.[36] Nevertheless, the front line of the anti-Ḥūthī fight combined with the power vacuum left by the failing Yemeni state became the opportunity for AQAP to earn de facto acceptance in some tribal areas because of the fighting capabilities that jihadis were able to bring to bear against the Ḥūthīs. The Ḥūthī expansion helped AQAP to join with and integrate into some tribes, as both had a common goal: the fight against the Ḥūthīs. It is within this space that AQAP seems to have been able to expand its base and dominion in some of Yemen's Sunni areas, particularly in the south and east, where groups affiliated with al-Qaeda had demonstrated their presence since the early 1990s. As Zimmerman argues, the alignment of AQAP's objectives with those of the various—tribal and popular—resistance militias created alliances where they might not otherwise have existed, especially since AQAP's translocal ideology was foreign to most Yemenis.[37]

A second reason for the increasing acceptance of AQAP in some Sunni areas was a clever strategy change by AQAP. AQAP's record of bank robberies, prison breaks, kidnapping, extortion, smuggling and lethal operations against both domestic and foreign targets is well known. But AQAP is an adaptive organization. It appears to have learned from the strategic errors which prevented its expansion in Yemen and even led to a popular uprising against it. Whereas before 2011 AQAP and its predecessors had adhered to the mother organization's transnational agenda and its pursuit of global goals, from 2011 AQAP began to focus systematically on local agendas in order to strengthen its hitherto often insufficient support among the population.

This strategy change did not happen overnight. Even before the beginning of Yemen's political upheavals, there had been evidence that al-Qaeda was beginning to focus on regional issues, because the jihadis—then isolated and restricted by the rules of *ḥaqq al-rabāʿ*—had become aware of the importance of local acceptance. Signs of this increasing attention to the local situation became evident as early as 2007–8 when al-Qaeda's Yemen branch began to try to balance local, regional and international interests.[38] AQAP began to avoid attacks on Yemeni civilians and instead projected itself as a protective force dedicated to fighting government corruption and repressive security raids. Although there was already evidence in the late 2000s that AQAP had begun to plug into local complaints and to develop certain 'soft touches', a coordinated programme only emerged after 2011. As Kendall argues, before 2011 AQAP tried to display empathy with populations suffering from marginalization, corrupt authorities and sheikhs, and under-investment, but it did not try to do anything tangible about these things other than attack the authorities.[39] AQAP's governance and public project model and its strategic turnaround towards 'soft power', she argues, only evolved in a more coherent form after its initial aggressive attempt to control territories and construct an Islamic 'emirate' in central southern Yemen—notably in the areas of Zinjibār, Lawdar and Jaʿār in Abyan in 2011/2012—ultimately failed. Cigar sees the opposition of local tribes as a reason for AQAP's failure to hold these seized territories, as many tribes feared retaliation by the Yemeni military and by US airstrikes for any AQAP presence in their areas, a factor towards which AQAP was acutely sensitive. One reason why AQAP felt it was unable to spread further into Yemen was because the local population was afraid that it would attract drone strikes.[40]

Since 2011 the desire to make common cause with local groups on the battlefield has become central to AQAP strategy. Kendall shows that by that time AQAP had begun to speak to local audiences at both practical and emotional levels, rather than through religious ideology: practically, by latching onto community problems such as corruption, poverty and marginalization, and positioning itself as saviour-defender; and emotionally, by deploying traditional cultural materials such as poetry and song.[41] These AQAP narratives strongly resonated with local tribal codes of honour and revenge.

This strategy change included an increasing AQAP tolerance towards local forms of law and government. Despite the mother organization's strong emphasis on *sharia* law, the legal code of Islam, AQAP began to follow a different route, building ties with local groups and refraining from strict application of *sharia* when faced with local resistance.[42] Although it still carried out periodic *sharia* punishments, such as execution for adultery or sorcery and amputation for theft, its primary emphasis shifted towards local power-sharing models accompanied by an energetic programme of community development. To help fund this, it robbed the rich in the name of the poor, an approach which Kendall calls AQAP's evolving 'Robin Hood' tactics.[43] Positive 'good' works and strategies of administrating public life became part of their plan to help fill the vacuum left by the failed Yemeni state, or to correct the failures of the national system. Given the importance of charitable work in Islam, it is therefore not surprising to see AQAP fill this need in order to win broader 'street credibility' by portraying themselves as community protectors. This strategic turnaround was reinforced by a grievance narrative in which AQAP blurred long-standing local discontent with transnational aims. This shift from the exogenous to the indigenous, from the global to the local, suggests that such approaches do succeed in building tolerance for extremist groups in Yemen and beyond, if not outright support.

AQAP's rapprochement with the local communities and their needs, however, was not a smooth process and it also suffered setbacks. An example is the 2013 attack on the Yemeni Ministry of Defence in Sana'a, which killed at least fifty-six people and wounded 162. Anṣār al-Sharīʿah, a militant group linked to al-Qaeda, claimed responsibility for the attack. After footage of the attack was aired on Yemeni television and caused public outrage, the head of AQAP released a video message publicly apologizing for the attack.[44] This apology suggests that AQAP did not have full command and control of all the groups and persons affiliated with al-Qaeda in Yemen, and that not all jihadis equally endorsed the strategy shift towards soft approaches.

On the other hand, AQAP's seizure of Mukallā, a southern port in Ḥaḍramawt, is an example of the success of the new approach. In March 2015, AQAP exploited the governance and security vacuum in the area to seize Mukallā. After taking the city, AQAP entered into a cooperative agreement with the local tribes. This campaign involved astute local rebranding with friendly names, such as the 'Sons of Ḥaḍramawt', and handing over the day-to-day running of the port to a council made up of local leaders.[45] By emphasizing the development, stability and security that it had brought to coastal Ḥaḍramawt, AQAP managed to convince the locals by drawing on its track record of good governance, rather than by relying on religious arguments or aggression. This approach enabled AQAP to pose as a local protector-saviour rather than an overlord in Mukallā. The alliance between local tribes and AQAP, however, proved uneasy. In April 2015, after a particularly brazen series of prison breaks, occupation of government facilities and lootings executed by AQAP, local tribes and militiamen loyal to embattled president Hādī positioned themselves against the jihadis, who withdrew without a fight from Mukallā's centre. Their withdrawal, rather than willingness to fight, suggests local disenfranchisement with AQAP after all and despite its 'soft' strategies.

The Islamic State in Yemen

Whereas AQAP proved to be an adaptive organization capable of learning from the experiences of the past, the Islamic State (IS) in Yemen is still in its infancy. In the three years that have passed since the establishment of the Yemeni branch of IS, it has repeated the early mistakes of al-Qaeda: neither is it attuned to the local setting, nor does it pursue a local agenda (except battling the Ḥūthīs). Instead, it scares off potential supporters with excessive violence. Moreover, the IS land-grabbing model of jihad antagonizes the Yemeni tribes.

In the summer of 2014, the self-proclaimed Islamic State swept through large swathes of north-western Iraq and eastern Syria, where it endeavoured to establish an Islamic 'caliphate' with 'Caliph' Ibrahim Abu Bakr al-Baghdadi acting as its head. In November 2014, IS officially announced the expansion of the Caliphate into Yemen, and al-Baghdadi accepted the oath of allegiance sworn to him by 'Yemen's mujahidin'.[46] Significantly, al-Baghdadi at the same time announced the nullification of all other jihadi groups in Yemen. Hence AQAP ceased to have any legitimacy in the eyes of IS. In turn, AQAP reconfirmed allegiance to al-Qaeda leader Aymān al-Zawāhirī, rejecting the legitimacy of the Islamic Caliphate.[47] With the emergence of IS in Yemen, AQAP thus began to face a triple threat: American drone strikes, the Ḥūthīs, and IS's competing model of jihad.

The IS narrative of violence appears to have found approval mainly among those jihadis who were already radicalized to the extreme. Most of the initial supporters of IS in Yemen seem to have defected from Anṣār al-Sharīʿah and AQAP. The gruesome beheading of up to fourteen Yemeni soldiers by AQAP in Ḥaḍramawt in August 2014, for example, already bore the hallmarks of an IS operation rather than one by AQAP's second generation in Yemen.[48] This suggests that AQAP's leaders were not in full control of their movement, and that some jihadis did not support the change in strategy and ideology of AQAP's second generation in Yemen. Although these movements are distinct from each other, in many cases their adherents cannot be clearly distinguished, as the groups can overlap and change quickly due to shifting alliances.

Whereas AQAP's second generation leadership has clearly tried to steer away from the alienating effects of extreme brutality in a bid to achieve and maintain broader support, among IS the jihadist horror genre has gained full momentum. The formal debut of IS was a suicide attack on two Sana'a mosques linked to the Ḥūthīs in March 2015, which killed 142 people and injured more than 350, making it the deadliest terrorist attack in Yemen's history. Ever since, IS has continued its modus operandi of rule through fear. In Aden, IS has been particularly active and able to gain a foothold following an uneasy alliance with southern separatist groups who pursued the same goal: to stop the advance of the Ḥūthīs.[49] Here, the IS militants conducted a series of brutal attacks, such as the beheading of Ḥūthī militants in March–April 2015, the destruction of Christian sites, and the targeting of the temporary government headquarters and a coalition base in Aden in October 2015. It assassinated the governor of Aden in December 2015 and has made numerous attempts on his successor and Aden's police chief.[50]

Despite many spectacular and bloody actions, the followers of IS in Yemen were not numerous. In 2015, the number of active IS fighters in Yemen was estimated at a few hundred.[51] Its spread in Yemen has been hampered by several factors. First, the land-grabbing model of jihad typical of IS proved to be particularly problematic in Yemen's rural and tribal areas. In Yemen, tribal borders are remarkably stable and often remain unchanged over centuries. In its tribal society the concept of territory (*arḍ*) is closely related to the concept of personal and tribal honour (*sharaf*), and the protected space on which this honour depends is often identified with physical space; that is, with territory.[52] This honour can be impugned by attacks on any component of the tribesmen's honourable selves, and landholdings have an iconic status and significance for a tribesman's honour. The territories and borders of tribes are therefore considered sacrosanct. Any insult to territory seriously threatens a man's and his tribe's honour. Hence, it is not surprising that IS's land-grabbing model generated violent opposition and proved to have a particularly negative effect on the recruitment of new supporters from among the Yemeni tribes.

Second, IS has not yet paid attention to the development of local 'soft approaches', which have become the hallmark of AQAP's second generation in Yemen since 2011. Interestingly, governance activities did become a trademark of IS in Iraq and Syria, where it pursued a kind of *ummah* project offered to local and foreign supporters. In contrast, by 2016 the *wilāyahs* (provinces) of the Yemeni IS branch were still establishing themselves and have seldom, if ever, pursued coherent governance activities.[53] The only contribution of IS to the local context in Yemen has been its narrative of savaging the Ḥūthīs. Beyond the anti-Ḥūthī narrative, the Yemeni branch of IS remains unattuned to the local context and instead continues to focus on the religious ideology of global jihad. Being largely alien to local culture and showing no intention of becoming a 'good guest', although IS may have gained support among the most radical of Yemen's jihadis, it appears to have achieved little traction within Yemen's local communities and tribes.

Conclusion

The rise of al-Qaeda's Yemen branch is an instructive story which underlines the importance of local narratives for the success of any movement in Yemen. After AQAP's profound internal transformations of the late 2000s, its strategy today in many respects resembles that of the Shia Ḥūthīs, whose rise and expansion was also much more strongly facilitated by their local agenda than by their regional and global rallying calls (as mirrored in their slogan 'Death to America, Death to Israel...').

Initially, the rapprochement between al-Qaeda and Yemen's tribes was ponderous and marked by misunderstandings. No sweeping generalization can be made, but there is considerable evidence that during the first phase from 1990 to 2011 the tribes' readiness to cooperate with al-Qaeda's jihadis was in many instances motivated by the desire to boost their status and their ability in their power struggles with other tribes and the Yemeni (and occasionally the Saudi) government. Al-Qaeda, in contrast, mainly adhered to the mother organization's global strategy and was little or not at all attuned to the local conditions in Yemen. In the case of a partnership between al-Qaeda and tribes, the jihadis were embedded in the local tribal communities according to the provisions of *ḥaqq al-rabāʿ* or *ṣaḥb*, which subjected the jihadis to the sovereignty of the tribes. In their shady deals with the jihadis, the tribes usually retained the upper hand: it was they who determined who could stay in their territories, and many of them used the jihadis as bargaining chips and pawns for the assertion of their interests. The jihadi groups were seldom able to build a broader popular support base and never were they able to seize large territories in Yemen's tribal areas. The presence of the jihadis was ultimately tied to the goodwill and tolerance of powerful actors among the local tribes.

Starting from the late 2000s, al-Qaeda in Yemen began to undergo an internal change that enormously contributed to its expansion. In 2009 it united with al-Qaeda's Saudi branch into a group that called itself al-Qaeda in the Arabian Peninsula (AQAP), and both the political situation in Yemen and jihadi strategy underwent profound changes. Two factors began to encourage al-Qaeda's recent success in Yemen. On the one hand, the expansion of the Ḥūthīs into territories that were predominantly Sunni created a new military threat situation and pushed some of their adversaries into the arms of jihadi groups like AQAP. Although the majority of the population in Yemen, including its tribal strata, remained opposed to all forms of extremism, the frontline of the anti-Ḥūthī fight combined with the power vacuum left by the failing Yemeni state became the opportunity for AQAP to earn de facto acceptance in some tribal areas because of the fighting capabilities that jihadis were able to bring to bear against the Ḥūthīs.

The second reason for the increasing acceptance of AQAP in some Sunni areas was a clever strategy change. From 2011, AQAP began to focus systematically on local agendas in order to secure the acceptance and support of the local population, and especially among the tribes which controlled the remote areas which al-Qaeda preferred as regions of retreat and safe haven. By positioning itself as saviour-defender, AQAP successfully plugged into local complaints and developed certain 'soft touches' by latching onto community problems such as conflict resolution, corruption, poverty and marginalization. As Ḥūthī-opposed tribes and the jihadis of al-Qaeda became partners and brothers in arms facing common enemies, formerly vital tribal legal regulations such as *ḥaqq al-rabāʿ* or *ṣaḥb* hardly played a role any more. This lack of restraints granted the jihadis much more room for action and manoeuvre.

It is precisely the absence of a local agenda which has so far prevented Islamic State from achieving success in Yemen. Since the establishment of the IS Yemen branch in January 2014, it has neither been attuned to the local settings, nor has it pursued a local agenda (except that of savaging the Ḥūthīs). Moreover, its acts of horrific violence scare off potential supporters. In addition, the IS land-grabbing model generates violent opposition among the Yemeni tribes. While AQAP remains strong in Yemen and is set to expand, without adaptations to the local context IS has little chance of success.

In Yemen's Sunni areas, AQAP now increasingly pursues a similar approach to that employed by the Ḥūthīs in Yemen's Zaydi heartland. The Ḥūthīs, too, embrace a somewhat global agenda as mirrored in their slogan, yet have pursued a local agenda at the grass-roots level since their founding days, which aims at addressing the prevalent political, economic and sectarian imbalances and injustices in Upper Yemen's Zaydi-dominated areas. Today, both groups display a notable ability to create safe havens in which extremism can flourish by establishing relationships and common agendas with local populations.

It is the Ḥūthī case which probably provides a glimpse into AQAP's future. The Ḥūthī example shows that local agendas and soft approaches enable groups to lay the groundwork for eventually imposing their will on local populations. Since their de facto takeover of the capital in 2014, the Ḥūthīs have evolved from a credible political alternative to Sana'a's political establishment into an increasingly oppressive and authoritarian militia. It is likely that in the medium term AQAP, despite its soft approach, will use its newly gained acceptance among local communities and tribes to switch from indirect to direct rule and to impose its model on them.

6

BETWEEN THE 'KANURI' AND OTHERS

GIVING A FACE TO A JIHAD WITH NEITHER BORDERS NOR TRIBES IN THE LAKE CHAD BASIN

Claude Mbowou[1]

Introduction

How did the insurrection of the jihadist movement Boko Haram (*Jama'at ahl al-sunna li'l-da'wa wa'l-jihad*), which was originally limited to the Nigerian territory, manage to diffuse itself throughout the countries bordering Lake Chad, thus imposing itself as a mobilizing transnational army?

The dynamic of violent mobilizations and armed protests against the state that had begun as an Islamist insurrection in the state of Borno in the north-east of Nigeria strongly intensified from 2009 onwards.[2] In three years, this army expanded into three countries bordering Lake Chad: Niger, Chad and Cameroon. The repertoire of insurrections in these countries progressed from abductions to targeted assassinations, frontal attacks of varying intensity, suicide bomber attacks and finally anti-personnel mines.

The specificities of this region's geography helped spread the insurrection. It is composed of a landscape of Sahelian plains, barely contained in some areas by the Mandara mountains, or vast areas of fluvial deposits connected to Lake Chad, which makes circulation relatively easy and thus helped the spread of the insurrection. But geography cannot constitute the sole explanation for this phenomenon. The success of the insurrection's actions needed a somewhat favourable basis within the established populations on either side of the border.[3] Its success depended particularly on the creation of a network with the objective of, on the one hand, coordinating actions (whether offensive or defensive) and, on the other hand, recruiting (logisticians as well as fighters). Numerous sources relate that in this manner 10,000 young Cameroonian men, most of whom were inhabitants of bordering villages, joined the insurrection.

In order to understand how the mobilized army expanded across these borders, a close analysis of the sociological mechanisms that allowed it is required. How did the insurrection acquire the support of the populations of the area, enabling it to act? Which actors, speeches, logistics and actions helped legitimize these rebellious acts of violence or made them binding for some categories of locals, thus turning them into support or vehicles of this trans-nationalization? Should the presence of local authorities of a tribal nature, on either side of the borders, be seen as a key element explaining the relatively rapid spread of armed mobilization outside Nigerian territory, especially if we take into account the presumed strength of social solidarities[4] which unify the members of these communities beyond the borders?

In a context strongly marked by the primacy given to ethnic identification by groups and individuals, both from the standpoint of public norms and of private habits of categorizing people, there is a risk that the framework of interpretation[5] used to explain the reasons for the rapid spread of the insurrection is based on a hypothesis of a specific role having been played by community solidarity.[6] This increases the risk of assimilating the insurrection into an ethnicity-based guerrilla war.

As this contribution will show, this is exactly what happened in the north of Cameroon. The Kanuri community[7] has been a victim of this kind of interpretative shortcut, as witnessed by some of the security practices put in place. For example, during road controls or isolation procedures, if in the eyes of the policemen or the military in charge the individual being searched appears to be associated with the Kanuri community, this automatically leads to a thorough check of the individual, which can end with an interrogation. The Kanuri tribal identifiers (particularly face scars) have thus become markers for the profiling of terrorists. Areas which are either Kanuri or Hausa fiefs or are predominantly composed of these ethnicities, as in the region between Bamaré and Maroua (also known as the Kanuri fief), and specifically the area of the central market, where most chechia sellers reside, have become targets of the police and the military.[8]

In the north of Cameroon, associating the Kanuri community with the insurrection has become more common despite a series of elements pleading against it. Indeed, a large portion of the victims of the insurrection attacks (whether killed, held hostage or displaced) have belonged to the Kanuri community,[9] which leads us to believe that the community puts forward a strong resistance against the insurgent. The majority of the community leaders have tried to demonstrate their loyalty to the state.[10] Furthermore, to this day there is also no official evidence showing that neighborhoods considered locally as Kanuri fiefdoms, in towns located in the interior of northern Cameroon such as Garoua or Maroua, where bomb attacks occurred, have played a key role in the propagation of violence. It has been possible to deduce both from close analysis of the areas where the insurrection has been the most active and from the testimonials of former hostages[11] of the insurrection that the composition of the insurrection is trans-ethnic. Far from denying the importance that social relations or community bonds may have had in the diffusion of the insurrection, our argument here is that they only constitute one of the articulations of a wider and far more complex sociological process, created in particular by the existing dynamics of this border space. These dynamics have structured new strongly linked networks, or have redesigned existing networks on the basis of different kinds of social links or representations. These networks have turned out to be stronger than mere community bonds, easier to mobilize, and more suitable for the expansion of the insurrection. For those joining the movement, the price to pay is often a brutal and preliminary rupture with any kind of loyalty to the community, starting with the family bonds that are at the basis of the community. The forms taken by the insurgent violence are based on this logic of rupture. One of the defining ways of proving one's radical engagement with the insurgency, which was a sign of distinction within the insurrection, was the killing of the insurgent's father, sometimes in the ritual form of throat slitting.

The dynamics which structure the relationships with the state in this borderland area, and the more fluid dynamics linked to the progressive start of the war in the Cameroonian territory, appear to be central to understanding the diffusion of the insurrection. The context of the regions where the insurrection was born and flourished has to be studied in depth, going beyond the simple citing of marginalization, which is usually understood solely in economic terms and evaluated using indicators of poverty.[12] More than poverty and criminality, an interesting analytical key is the sociological relationship between lower-class individuals living in border areas, the state and national projects. More precisely, it is important to understand the significance of the relationship with the state for the inhabitants of these areas, while at the same time analysing the different impact which these bonds may have, depending on the social status of individuals, their state of mind or their interests. Our observations show that the network of strong bonds which has been used as fertile soil for the mobilization of Boko Haram more than its nourishment of criminal images is in large part based on a deficit of legitimacy of the state, or on insufficient effort having been put into legitimization of the links to the state. This deficit is particularly marked in the case of the lower social groups in the border regions, as they constitute the dominant and most numerous fringes of Boko Haram mobilization, thanks to which it has been able to establish its current power. Without being completely absent or invisible, and within a context of local crisis of its clientelistic mechanisms, the state often resorts to coercion as its primary means of intervention in these territories. A good illustration of this is provided by the local conflicts regarding agricultural production, which opposed the local peasants to the state prior to the beginning of the war. These have furthermore discredited the local middlemen, who see most of their economic capital as resulting from their privileged bonds with the state. This discredit gradually took new more active shapes as the cleavage deepened within small community groups previously considered tightly knit by tribal bonds. This crisis in the cohesion of communities has played a part in how the insurgents have managed to mobilize help to take action against the state.

The specific ways in which the state is present or absent are characteristics of the political economy of legality in the border areas, which is also characterized by indistinctiveness and fluidity between legality and illegality. This context has consequently given the dominant and subordinate actors of the border region a vision of legal constraints as being essentially arbitrary and lacking any legitimacy. It has resulted in the adoption of work-around techniques and the creation of a universe of social links which were easy to mobilize for the insurrection. In concrete terms, the insurrection made the most not only of the relative lack of differentiation of the area, but also and above all of what we characterize here as a lack of definition and distinction in local timing—especially visible in the difficulty of distinguishing times of war from times of peace—which is a direct consequence of the geopolitical hazards of the region. In other words, the insurrection was present in the Cameroonian territory before the war against 'terrorism' was declared.

The war economy which developed in Cameroon between 2010 and 2014, at a time when the fighting was still limited to the Nigerian territory, was very similar to the 'normal' economy in terms of trafficking, or the usual strategies implemented to get around the state. When the state finally declared war on 17 May 2014, there were many who had one foot, and sometimes two hands, in the insurrection.[13] It was before the war started on Cameroonian soil that the first networks of those depending on the state, the 'little hands', the logisticians and those who 'converted to the insurrection' came about.[14] After the declaration of war, this 'ordinary' networking abruptly became a pretext for a coercive deployment of the state in the area. It started to track the 'local accomplices of Boko Haram'. In this context, the declaration of war constituted a sudden requalification of the local reality, with direct consequences for the norms and perceptions of local collective life, as well as for the meaning of past and present deeds.[15] Transactions which previously took place in total impunity were from then on requalified and used in a different manner in local social games (rumours, resentment, denunciations, finger-pointing, violence, etc.). In some cases, the consequences were dreadful: the 'luck' of some, born from limited relationships to the insurrection, brought the cost of being considered accomplices of the sect, leaving them two choices: to be tracked by the army or actually to join the insurrection.[16] For different reasons, others decided to pursue their track of compromising with the Nigerian jihadists. The insurrection was also capable of using these games and old relationships to pressure any policeman, any local chief, any marabout, any motorcycle driver into giving them information on recruiting. I shall attempt to illustrate these different dynamics and to analyze the ways they have played a part in the transnational extension of this violent mobilization.

Marginal tribes and the unknown faces of the state

Going beyond economic considerations and taking into account the specific historical conditions which helped to build and form the state within the relatively interlocked margins to the south of Lake Chad in Cameroon, one notices some dynamics whose lasting effects have favoured the violent mobilization of a fringe of the local populations against the state. First, the conditions in which these processes came about have kept an important part of the population outside the nation (in the sense of feeling that they belong to or take part in a community) or its production mechanisms. Within this group can be found the majority of the lower ranking participants in the insurrection. Second, even though the insurrection exploited a mobilization based on clientelistic community bonds to gain legitimacy over the whole territory, the state constituted in this manner has contributed to undermining the historical basis of the community's cohesion more than to consolidating it to its own profit, without offering any alternative bond to the nation.

The nation-state in Nigeria and Cameroon, as in Chad and most of the post-colonial African entities, is first of all a state which makes the nation, and in some respects builds it, far away from a romantic unitary vision where the nation precedes the state. In order to establish this nation-state, the post-colonial state used a number of influential institutions, such as schools, the army and the public administration. It also used material and symbolic tools such as flags, civil status—or the ID card—and rituals or state ceremonies, such as the national hymn or a national day, for the creation of citizenship. It was, however, schools that gave the essential tools for actively partaking in the state. The schools are a melting pot of all the types of cultural, linguistic and civil knowledge which are necessary for fully understanding the essential features of the state, such as understanding and recognizing its interests, or occupying, or attempting to occupy, one of its positions. Consequently, these elements aim to create a proper civil religion,[17] based on a feeling of belonging to a common space and a common world. In Cameroon, to be specific, the construction of the state was done in a very unequal manner between the north and the south for historical and geographical reasons. It was in the south, from the Atlantic coast inwards, that the colonial and Western forces which would initiate the building of a modern nation-state put down their roots.

This impetus first went through Christian missionizing, which helped prepare a favourable ground for the diffusion of Western languages, of written culture, and of bureaucratic life in very large segments of society, especially through the networks of schools and churches. It was by means of these languages and practices that the first Cameroonian intellectuals were brought up. It was these languages that would prevail in running the future state.

The capitalist plantation industry (cocoa, coffee, rubber) also played an important role as the violence it caused contributed to triggering collective dynamics of action in which the indigenous elite dominated by the colonialists allied with the exploited subordinates. This alliance created emotional unity around a common interest, around the community feeling of a 'we', which is an essential component of Cameroonian nationalism.[18] In this context, the previous legitimacies that organized local societies were progressively erased. They were absorbed in this forced march towards a modernization and nationalization of society, and the correlated constitution of a nation.

Further from the coast, in the north of Cameroon—which is less accessible, has a more hostile climate and in colonial calculations was deemed to be further away from the more agriculturally exploitable regions—another movement of political and cultural colonization had opposed the building of a nation-state since the eleventh century: that of Peul (or assimilated as such) aristocracies, who were religious zealots practising a Sunni Islam that they used as a hegemonic instrument for the expansion of their power without differentiating between politics and religion. The Quranic school and the Arabic alphabet thus became hegemonic instruments of the political entities or principalities which would succeed one another throughout the wars of conquest.

Two different types of historical experience thus coexist in the same territory, with different and divergent forces opposing the state's movement towards modernization. Within the north itself, the opposition stemming from previous legitimacies affects this movement unequally. The dorsal areas bordering Nigeria, which go from the Mandara mountains to the Logone and Chari rivers, have the particularity of being less open to the influence of the state. From a geographical point of view, because of their size and relative isolation from the administrative centres in the principal agglomerations of the province, this landlocked effect causes economic isolation of these areas. Their survival and prosperity depend on trade with the Nigerian market. This situation has consequences at the cultural and social levels: under the influence of the city of Maiduguri, Islam penetrates and structures the social imaginary more profoundly. It provides a framework on the basis of which the dominating and legitimate norms are defined.

The figures of success which predominate in this universe are the marabout and the storekeeper, not the functionary or the well-read. The first of these, thanks to his spiritual and moral authority, can secure himself a comfortable social base. The second, usually honoured by the title of *alhadji*, sees his wealth considered a sign of divine election, with no link to the written culture of the state.[19] When necessary, by leaning on their wealth to penetrate the state, they can afford education for their offspring and to buy themselves the loyalty of civil servants or political positions. These figures have contributed to diminishing the value of educational institutions significantly in the eyes and the calculations of poor families. Furthermore, the educational system—which has a very limited presence in these communities[20]—has the defect of imposing inappropriate rhythms and costs on the economy of these communities, norms that are not always adapted to the conservatism regulating the social order. It also offers limited horizons and fewer outlets as unemployment has increased exponentially in the last thirty years. However, mastering the language of the state and the writing skills which are indispensable to decode its procedures and interact with civil servants is only possible through access to education. As long as schools fail to create a link between local communities and the state and arouse an interest in it, the two worlds can easily avoid each other.

The post-colonial state would have needed to make more substantial investment to remove these inertias. Furthermore, in addition to these historical factors which caused different degrees of resistance to the implementation of the state-building project, the state did not successfully manage to overcome two great challenges which were imposed by the conditions of its creation. First of all, it was unable to overcome the challenges of distance and to project its infrastructural capabilities effectively from the south towards the borders of northern Cameroon.[21] The state and the people living in the marginal northern areas have thus remained in a relationship of mutual invisibility. The interest that the state took in the territory hid its lack of interest in its inhabitants. By carving out multiple administrative districts, by deploying the army and its officials, and by negotiating the demarcation of its borders with the neighbouring countries, the Cameroonian state essentially implemented a 'politics of the territory', or more precisely of nationalization of the territory.[22] This politic intent did not, however, involve capturing the hearts and minds of the population occupying the territories formally integrated within the nation, or taking care of its rights-holders.

Furthermore, this strategy of affirming sovereignty while not paying attention to the population has allowed vast areas of these marginal territories to be kept in a situation of isolation. Any spatial planning policy has in fact been limited to the distribution of the main rent revenues (cacao, coffee, wood, etc.) on a geographical basis. Cotton, the main cash crop in the north, has made some small areas productive, but the meagre infrastructure created to exploit and transport this cash crop[23]—first along the Benue river to the Niger estuary, then, only since the 1970s, by rail to the port of Duala—have not sufficed to put an end to the isolation of these marginal areas. The more arid zones and the areas where this cash crop is less intensively cultivated—such as the Logone and the Chari—continue to be characterized by an absence of adequate lines of communication allowing regular access. The primary objective of the state-making politics implemented in these conditions has been to give a formal sign—mostly from a perspective based on security and territory—of the presence of the state. This has meant governing from a distance, without linking to the people, with very limited presence in these areas of civil registry and the ID services which are meant to materialize the juridical link to the state and to allow access to essential public services such as justice, or simply the freedom to move around within the national territory.[24]

In order to escape from this situation of invisibility to the state, in these areas the native subordinates must use the specialized state offices. This step presupposes that they have the specific cognitive resources needed to overcome the barriers that the state has installed against this multitude. Indeed, such resources are not accessible to them because of their subordinate status. In the last ten years, free ID registration campaigns (exceptional procedures such as fairground hearings or procedures using testimonial certificates)[25] have only happened on a very ad hoc basis and opportunistically, for instance when elections were scheduled. This shows that the regime in Yaounde has been more concerned with electoral results than by the need to integrate undocumented people. To increase the level of electoral participation, the regime attempted to enrol this subordinate illiterate peasant electorate as 'electoral cattle' who would be easy to manipulate and exploit. The aim of this strategy was also to compensate the clear retreat of the urban electorate, whose estrangement was caused by a sense of elections having no stake, and which appeared less easy to win by bargaining. Nevertheless, the inhabitants of villages such as Léré, Tchatchibali, Karena, Tchokomari and Kuyape had to walk 10–50 kilometres to reach the closest identification post of the fifty-six established in this region in the extreme north of Cameroon in 2013. They generally made this trip on foot or by bicycle without any guarantee of being able to return the same day with the sought-after document. Furthermore, there often existed an important gap between the free access advertised and the reality in practice, when they were faced with corrupt civil servants or the improvised intervention of third parties.

Furthermore, the legitimacy of these operations was seriously affected by the local political elite, who started to bargain the provision of ID papers to those in need in exchange for guarantees of votes.

In fact, it has been reported that some did not hesitate to 'sell off' Cameroonian nationality by strategically arranging for 'Nigerians' and 'Chadians' to be identified as Cameroonians with future national elections in mind. This followed the logic that those who were natives of the border, with either Kanuri or Arab Choa affiliations, among others, could easily be identified as either 'Nigerians' or 'Chadians' because of the ethno-linguistic continuities between Cameroon and neighbouring countries. In the same manner, faced with the congestion of identification centres, sellers of fake papers seem to have found a way to produce IDs cheaper than the official price, or at the same price but with no bureaucratic hassle. The suspicions that arise regarding the authenticity of these documents have managed to reduce any of their value. The results obtained during the last elections, which had limited validity,[26] did not assure the recipients official or definitive recognition of their nationality. When faced with the uncertainty created by their own deficiencies, the security institutions have thus chosen to freeze identification processes and to relegate these populations to the status quo. Strangely, this state strategy thus matched that of the insurgent, who proceeded to burn identity papers in some border-area markets. To counter the effects of this panoptic blindness, traffic checks on the axes of circulation now quarantine these populations deprived of documents.

If there has been no building of a relationship between the state and individuals, it is also mainly because of a government logic which has an essentially community approach to society. As a consequence, the social control of local societies is entrusted to community institutions or to an elite among the elected officials, storekeepers and native civil servants. In this context, characterized by communitarianism and state ethnicism, importance is given to the words spoken by these intermediaries, and their interests are considered to be those of the community or ethnic group whom they claim to speak for by using their resources and their positions within the state. In fact, they also owe their positions to their ability to ensure the cohesion of their community and thereby the persistence of these arrangements of domination. These arrangements built on intermediaries, which utterly obscure the voices and the individual faces of the multitude of subordinates, can last as long as the illusion of consensus is maintained.

Within these border-area communities, the situations which preceded the nationalization process and the divergences within it have made the effects of this form of mediation more extreme than elsewhere in Cameroon. Within the Kanuri community, the fringe of intermediaries is very slim in comparison to the populations that it is meant to represent. These intermediaries are the very limited number of families which laid early bets on education. At Kolofata and Amchidé, for example, this has resulted in strong monopolistic effects in the occupation and reproduction of positions of authority and accumulation in relation to the state. Mayors and their assistants, traditional leaders and deputies are thus former civil servants or former members of the military reconverted into new roles as elected representatives of the community or village. The members of the local elite with governmental positions in Yaounde are also recruited from the same families.

Implosion of the community and the cause of the subordinates

Families who have held state positions for forty years or so continue to monopolize the scene. The religious and economic fields are both characterized by the same logics of monopoly and closure. While the border-area market ensures the survival of most of the population, just a few well-established tradesmen have gained the most from it. The collection of life stories shows the typical shopkeeper to be a man of sixty years or more; he is multilingual but almost or absolutely illiterate, expressing himself in his mother tongue as well as all the other vernacular languages that are useful for trade (Awoussa, Foufoulde) and having an adequate knowledge of French and of Pidgin. These tradesmen invested very early on in long-distance trade with Nigeria, Central Africa, Equatorial Guinea or Gabon. Their intermediary roles in import–export relations have permitted them to accumulate knowledge and important social capital in terms of relationships within the administration. This has allowed them a legal facade for their activities (even though today their affairs often overflow beyond formal or legal circuits). They have also, and above all, accumulated power, influence and the knowledge of transaction games with the state. Thanks to their money and their relations, some have become elected representatives within the party in power, or kingmakers among the candidates.

The 'state capital' thus constituted has allowed them to negotiate special privileges and to consolidate the positions of monopoly they had already built in border-area trade thanks to their fortunes. They have heavily invested in the transport sector and in storage spaces, which has allowed them to control flows and to regulate or limit competition. Furthermore, being major holders of currency, sometimes outside banking channels or spread out among Cameroonian, Nigerian or Chadian banks, they control the flows of monetary exchanges between CFA francs and the naira, which completely avoid the formal channels of financial intermediation. Such financial power has allowed them to become informal moneylenders and to control access to border-area trade. They are the true bankers of the 'bush' and now also regulate the access to land and credit of a large number of peasants deprived of soil and financial resources.

Traditional chiefs, civil servants and wealthy tradesmen find themselves at the heart of compromised businesses which have occupied communal lands or have drained the salaries of peasants.[27] These practices constitute blatant violations of Islamic norms, which are the basis of the moral economy[28] of the subordinates and of the expectations of those in their community who are well-off. They have thus given rise to intense controversies, highlighting the crisis in reproduction of solidarity and of communal cohesion.[29] Other stakes, particularly revolving around *zakat* (obligatory alms), have created some strong tensions. The tradesmen and the elite have thus been accused of mutually granting each other *zakat* or of redistributing it inside the strict confines of family circles, or in the form of trade obligations disguised as donations to a small network of dependent businesses which ensure them an investment return.

In this context, the distress of numerous peasant families has grown greatly in the past five years, as much under the effect of usurious pressures as due to the politics of agricultural product pricing, among other things.[30] Cotton farmers, for example, have always contested the price at which their products are bought by the state company which has the monopoly on buying and exploiting this product in the north of Cameroon.[31] Unable to maintain their debts to moneylenders and businesses from which they have received supply inputs on credit, some of them have simply abandoned cotton production. To get around the rules of the state monopoly, some peasant families use the networks and the know-how of smugglers trading fuel and other illegal products. The legitimacy of the smuggling world has thus widened through a diffusion of its representations and practices among peasants who had previously been the more docile of the subordinates of the established order.

The scope of peasant dissidence led the Cameroonian Cotton Company—a state company—to mobilize multiple means of coercion. Administrative authorities, community leaders, the army and groups of vigilantes were therefore mobilized, almost employing the same repertoire of actions as that implemented today to pursue insurgents. This coalition of forces[32] did not prevent the peasants from continuing their silent disobedience and, very often, displaying great solidarity.[33] They had to organize themselves in networks between the border villages in the Mandara mountains in Kanuri territory and the more isolated inland villages, which are populated by the Mafa community and multiple other communities. The smuggling routes which link the border access points to urban centres such as Mora, Waza and Kousséri underwent further ramification amid this cotton dissidence and the intensification of repression between 2010 and 2012. Cotton smuggling is particular in that it involves entire families: the father of the family owns the production, negotiates the price and determines the quantity to divert; the women (wives and daughters), whose movements attract less attention, carry small quantities of cotton hidden in packages to clandestine pick-up points outside the village; and the young men take care of transport towards the border.[34] All of these practices have had the effect of creating strong bonds between the youth of the border-area villages and that of inland villages.

Repression of cotton dissidence, which is now criminalized, has also provoked tensions within these villages. The collectives of vigilantes established by the administrative authorities and by the Cotton Company were meant to be the tool with which peasants could align themselves in the fight against cotton diversion. In reality, the recruits often happened to be close to the local chief, the mayor, or the most well-off planters, or were the other minor workers used to carry out dirty jobs for the local elite in return for payment. Although these were said to be 'volunteers', the Company paid for food and gas expenses,[35] and each villager who brought a new piece of information was remunerated with 200 CFA francs for a day's work.[36] The members of the vigilante committee had to intercept, check or report any suspicious goods transiting through a village or of unknown origin, and take the transporters to the village chief or the local gendarmerie. They also had to report any accomplice of the traffickers in the village. The measures taken to punish those responsible, the aim of which was to make an example of them, ended up transforming a subordinate dissidence into a criminal or delinquent act, with those found guilty having to bear the stigma of dishonour.[37] At the same time, the vigilante committees offered well-connected planters a resource with which to eliminate minor competitors and take over their production or land by means of founded or unfounded denunciations, or simply to confirm hierarchies of power that provoked a strong feeling of injustice among the rest of the population.

The Cotton Company stopped its activities in the production areas of the Mandara mountains, Nguedjewe, Mozogo, Mayo Moskota, Kuyape and Assighassia, where the dissidence mobilized the largest numbers of peasants. Consequently, many young people from peasant families affected by this decision migrated towards the cities and villages close to Nigeria to find employment in plantations or in other activities, sometimes making the most of the contacts they had established throughout the dissidence campaign. Some peasants, feeling threatened or cornered by their debts and to avoid judicial action by the Company, also fled towards neighbouring Nigeria.[38] In 2013 the border was closed, with the proclamation of the state of emergency in Nigeria and the intensification of violence. However, what put an end to the trans-border market and cotton smuggling was the paralysis of economic activity in the north of Nigeria. A great number of the youth residing in that area, even if they were originally fervent Christians, on their return to Cameroon were considered to be rebels or insurgent recruiters for Boko Haram. Some indeed fulfilled this prejudice by becoming insurgents or recruiters, fed by resentment over their forced migration. The concrete dynamics of the insurgent mobilization were largely based on these dynamics of conflict within the border-area communities.

Jihad with hushed steps: the ambiguous time of Cameroon's entry into war

Almost two years passed between the intensification of violence in the north of Nigeria and the official war announcement by the Cameroonian president. How did the insurrection manage to mobilize supporters on Cameroonian soil during this period? Three main elements deserve to be analyzed here: first, the procrastination of the Cameroonian government in the face of the events which unravelled in Nigeria and their concrete effects on the local politics in the border area; second, the specific dynamics of a war economy on display in the border area, and their concrete effects on further processes of insurgent mobilization; finally, the specific effects caused by the rapid entry into war, the sudden disruptive consequences of which reshaped perceptions and local relationships by offering supplementary margins of manoeuvre to the insurgent mobilization.

What is the extent of the insurgent mobilization in Cameroonian territory, and what is the profile of the recruits? Local newspapers reported an estimated 7,000 individuals. But observations on the ground revealed that village chiefs kept lists of all the young people who joined the insurgency. From the border to almost 60 kilometres towards the interior, almost all the villages in the Mandara mountains as far as the Logone River going through the Mayo Tsanaga produced such lists. In the Kanuri village of Kolofata, for example, the number was around 500 youths. As a general idea, these numbers varied from dozens to a couple of hundred people. On this basis, estimations of about 5,000 insurgents in the Cameroonian territory do not seem like an exaggeration. These numbers for the most part represent children and very young men whose relationship to the family unit could vary between a situation of rupture (as was the case of a good number of homeless beggar teenagers) to a situation of perfect integration. Entire families also joined the insurrection, as well as people who enjoyed the privileges of a comfortable social position, either because they occupied powerful positions on the local political scene or in border trade.

From April 2014 onwards, wide-ranging security measures were implemented by the Cameroonian government in the border areas.[39] These measures included first of all the closure of the border, then a progressive deployment of military operations aimed at securing the border, at first limited to the principal entry points of the corridor (Amichde, Limany, Waza, Dabanga, Kousséri). Subsequently, they moved on to securing the most northern part of the border area close to Lake Chad. It was thus no longer possible to circulate normally between Bangui and Maiguduri (around forty checkpoints interrupted the journey), but circulation continued normally on Cameroonian soil from the border onwards.[40] At the time, the war in Cameroon was considered a purely Nigerian affair. The multiple targeted attacks conducted by Boko Haram, especially that at Kousséri, or even the abduction in February 2014 of French people[41]—who were only freed seven weeks later—did not have an immediate impact on the perception of the threat being limited to Nigeria.[42]

However, the situation revived suspicions between Nigeria and Cameroon, whose relationship has historically been mired by border disputes and armed conflicts (more so in the south, in the Bakassi Peninsula).[43] Effective bilateral mechanisms for the exchange of information did not yet exist, and nor did the possibility of joint action by the armed forces of the two countries. Criminal networks have long profited from these deficiencies. The official closure of the border in 2012 and the state of emergency declared in Nigeria in May 2013 did not interrupt most of the trafficking. Abuja also accuses Cameroon of letting the insurgents use the Cameroonian territory as a supply base.[44] Customs officers, gendarmes and policemen continue to take bribes for the passage of motorbikes, trucks and other cargoes whose content they do not inspect. In this way, the feeling that business continues its normal course is confirmed. The smugglers on Logone River or Lake Chad, however, now carry weapons or ammunition instead of fuel. A war economy has thus developed among the typical networks of trans-border trafficking. In Amchidé, after the release of the French hostages, a large quantity of euros started circulating among petty traffickers who until then were only involved in exchange transactions of CFA francs and the naira.[45] The closure and the increased control of inland routes in Nigeria re-oriented the flows. The smuggling of gas, which now feeds the areas under the control of the insurrection in the State of Borno, only goes through Cameroon via the Yola–Demsa axis (Nigeria) and Demsa–Garoua–Maroua (Cameroon). Prices have increased by up to a hundred times, going from 400 CFA francs to 6,000 CFA francs a litre. New subordinates attracted by this opportunity to make a profit have joined the smuggling activities, beside the typical professionals of the sector.

Other dynamics have also contributed to widening the social basis of the intermediaries of the insurrection. The lucrative food market has attracted young peasants from Cameroonian villages who recently migrated to Nigeria and have become buyers and traders with the peasants in their hometowns or neighbouring villages, under the command of Nigerian bosses. Furthermore, the violence in Nigeria caused a first movement of refugees who settled down for the most part in Cameroonian cities and villages near the border. When they could not establish themselves with relatives in Cameroon, they usually preferred villages in which they already had relationships or which offered them linguistic familiarity. Thus many Kanuri villages or families have hosted refugees. Their presence has not provoked any particular anxiety, especially as some refugees pay generously for their hospitality. A market renting rudimentary homes has rapidly developed in the rural communities of the border area, constituting a great novelty in the area.

An important number of well-off refugees from Borno were among those who joined Boko Haram for ideological reasons. They were often hosted with families, which facilitated their integration with their hosts and the neighbourhood. Their generosity contributed to creating a circle of dependents and admirers around them. They also distinguished themselves by the way they practised religion (the way they pray, or the way they carry out the genuflexion of the five daily prayers). Instead of praying with members of their host community, they withdraw to do it on their own. In everyday life, they exhibit external signs of exclusive attachment to religion (Quranic readings, charitable acts and so on). While these practices could have been seen as sectarian deviances, they were instead received with respectful curiosity because of the favourable reputation of these refugees for generosity. They claimed to have the best knowledge of religion and made their faith appear as the only reason for their persecution by the neighbouring impious state of Nigeria. Neither the imams nor the local marabouts contested these statements. In fact, they were both inclined to confirm them, perhaps less on a religious basis than because of the material relationships they developed with these fugitives and their subsequent dependence on them. These refugees became the people who were consulted and listened to. In some cases, they married into their host families or bore the cost of the wedding of one of their occasional young dependants.[46] Young people followed them in increasing numbers and imitated their way of praying. Through their speeches, they discreetly offered a critique of local morals, standing for example against *zakat* abuse, the obstacles to marriage for youth, the ignorance and illegitimacy of the imams, etc.

Such was the local context when Cameroon officially declared war in May 2014. The security redeployment at the border resulted in increasing pressure on the local populations, who were asked to report any foreign presence. Even though the refugees were for the most part progressively forced to leave Cameroon, when fleeing the proselyte supporters of the insurrection took with them young teenagers, often the children of their previous hosts, or groups of beggars to whom they were occasional benefactors. Other young people were solicited simply to go with them to help carry their goods but were never able to come back home. The stay of the insurrection supporters in border cities and villages had allowed them to acquire good knowledge of their host societies and of their potential divisions and internal conflicts.

The vigilante committees were reactivated, and the village chiefs were summoned by the Senior Divisional Officer and asked to report foreigners and their local accomplices. ('We know that some of your people have relationships with foreigners, or host some of them. Tell us who they are.')[47] Village chiefs were forced to give names. But responding to these orders has resulted in all kinds of score-settling, and also in finger-pointing at young people who were simply absent because they had previously left the village under different circumstances. It equally produced secondary effects, condemning those who were named to either wander or to search for some form of protection or revenge by joining the insurrection. The people who became outcasts against their will have often maintained a relationship with their families and secretly come back home at night to stock up on goods. Surviving whilst being trapped between the army and the insurgents is, however, particularly difficult. Incapable of proving their innocence and knowing that they risk the death penalty if they are caught by the army, these young people generally end up joining the insurgents.[48]

In this context of high security pressure, the sometimes compromising nature of the relationships established between entire villages and some foreigners have encouraged reactions of collective *omertà*. Such has been the case in the Kanuri villages which have hosted numerous refugees. By choosing to remain silent, the inhabitants of these villages have contributed to feeding the suspicions and the violence of the army against them. The villages of Double and Magdeme, for example, have been caught in a spiral of a violence.[49] Mostly populated by Kanuri people and situated only a few kilometres from the border, before the declaration of war these villages naturally welcomed refugees, who later left the country. But this 'evidence', added to attacks that targeted the army in the area, caused entire villages to become the object of general suspicion because of their 'lack of collaboration with the authorities and the army'. As attempts to put in place vigilante committees in these villages turned out to be useless, they were consequently subjected to violent retaliation by the army, which only the local elites, best equipped to understand the situation and negotiate with the authorities, managed to avoid. As a reaction, the victims or the families of the victims who escaped the assaults of the army have become radicalized. Similar processes have happened in other villages following the same logic.

It is, therefore, because of contingent factors and because of the ethnic nature of the repression that the insurgents managed a posteriori to turn community solidarity to their advantage and to use it as an efficient tool. Reciprocally, the tendency of the authorities to consider the insurrection to be a 'Kanuri affair' and to target the community as such has gradually found itself legitimized by the increasing violence, equally resulting in various forms of discrimination against individual Kanuri and the questioning of their national loyalty. In contrast, the involvement of locals from other communities in the insurrection has attracted less attention. This can be explained in part because they are proportionally less numerous, and because before the entry into war their respective communities were relatively less exposed to contacts with foreigners in the border area. Acknowledgment of this phenomenon, however, could have allowed more focus on the trans-community character of the armed mobilization.

Conclusion

What the mobilization led by Boko Haram evidences most is not the strength of community logic (whether it is embodied by the Kanuri or by any other natives of the border area) but rather the entry into crisis in these regions following a certain number of structural modalities. The social and political control of the border areas in the states located south of Lake Chad followed an almost unique model from the beginning of the post-colonial state. The state delegated the political and social control of the local communities to their leaders on the basis of an alliance between major tribal notables, big tradesmen and educated local elites. By doing so, the state followed a communitarian logic in which the government of the community was indirectly exercised through selected private actors. In such a system, the peasants and the subordinates could remain below or outside any link with the state. Clientelistic redistribution and various forms of informal entrepreneurship were meant to ensure the survival of these subordinate groups, whilst providing a basis of legitimacy to this scaffolding of domination of the various groups in the communal space. As long as communal cohesion could be maintained, no contestation of the state could emerge. More particularly, in this area the border worked as a device for externalizing the costs of domination, making it possible to 'feed bellies' when neither the state nor 'the politics of the belly' could provide.[50]

The crisis of this model has become visible in two ways. On the one hand, in a context of demographic growth, the redistribution abilities of the state and clientelistic networks, which had been reduced by dozens of years of economic recession, were no longer able to fulfil the demands of the local populations. On the other hand, the concentration of economic power and of state positions had become too much in these marginal areas, driving a great majority of natives to lose hope in the possibility of social advancement: either start with nothing and become an *alhadji* thanks to trafficking, or become 'a big name' thanks to school. For a long time, the invisibility of these subordinates also kept their conflicts with the state and its local allies invisible. This was no longer true.

The insurrection, through different modalities whether strategic or contingent, managed to capture to its advantage the wrath of these 'no place, no face' people. The neo-jihadists of Boko Haram managed to absorb this wrath symbolically by proposing a makeshift religious language that was both anti-state and anti-elite. It worked all the better because religious language is the only language available and compatible with the system of thoughts and values in these areas where the modernization of the state had only superficially fitted into local societies which had undergone a long process of Islamization. By declaring war on the state, namely on the winners from education and monetarization, the neo-jihadists of Boko Haram managed to clarify the terms of a real cleavage, retranslating it into a language of religious populism which was accessible to the many losers and victims among the border communities of the transformations provoked by the nationalization process. It is therefore only natural that a community such as that of the Kanuri, in which these contradictions have taken extreme forms, finds itself numerically more represented among the insurgents. One should not, however, deduce from this that it corresponds to a phenomenon of mechanical solidarity. Rather, by grounding its policies in a communitarian and culturalist vision of the state and through its policy of repression, it is the state which has tended to favour processes and dynamics of radicalization among communities which feel that they are attacked because of their identity.

7

SIRTE'S TRIBES UNDER THE ISLAMIC STATE

FROM CIVIL WAR TO GLOBAL JIHADISM

Virginie Collombier

On 20 October 2011, anti-Qaddafi forces eventually took control of the coastal city of Sirte, located in the Gulf of Sidra, halfway between Tripoli and Benghazi, and for many Libyans the stronghold of Qaddafi's regime and his Qaddadfa tribe, which had dominated the power system for decades. The fall of the city, and the killing of Mu'amar Qaddafi and his son Mu'tasim by revolutionary fighters, marked the end of a civil war that had pitted pro- and anti-revolutionary forces against one another, with direct foreign military intervention in support of the former.

At the beginning of 2015, the so-called 'Islamic State' (IS) announced its control over the city, which was now to be the capital of its 'Tripoli province' (*wilayat trablus*). The unofficial core of Qaddafi's regime until the 2011 uprising and the civil war, the city would become redefined within a few years as the centre from which the growing global jihadist group would plan its development and expansion in North Africa.

Eastern Libya, and in particular the city of Derna, where the jihadists had historical roots, or the city of Benghazi, where they had significantly increased their influence as a result of the 2011 uprising, at first sight appeared as more favourable locations for IS to establish roots in Libya. Indeed, the first attempt of the jihadist group to consolidate its presence in Libya was made in Derna in October 2014. This was only a few months after Abu Bakr al-Baghdadi announced the establishment of an 'Islamic caliphate' in territories straddling Syria and Iraq and the rebranding of the Islamic State in Iraq and the Levant (ISIL) into Islamic State (IS).

Even though IS found significant support among Derna's jihadist factions and local society, the situation proved less favourable to the establishment of the group than was wished by IS leaders and fighters. Consequently, even before they were militarily confronted and defeated by a coalition of forces from inside and outside the city in April 2016, IS's location and expansion strategy had already shifted focus and moved towards Sirte. What made the local context in the city more favourable to IS?

At the end of 2014, Sirte presented many common features with areas where IS had found fertile ground to root its caliphate, in terms of territory and local people. The parallel with Iraq's Sunni provinces, in particular, looked striking. However, the tribal character of the local society combined with the influence of the Salafist current within the tribes and their search for a channel to regain political influence and military power after the regime change are not the only explanations for why IS could develop and take root in Sirte. While IS could benefit from some support among the local tribes who had been most influential under Qaddafi and opposed to the 2011 revolution, the main factors that allowed IS to seize control over Sirte and transform it into a centre for its expansion into other territories are to be found elsewhere.

The 2011 civil war and the disruption of Sirte's tribal structures

With its 'sister' town Bani Walid, Sirte was the last stronghold of the Qaddafi regime to collapse in 2011. In contrast to Bani Walid, whose 70,000 inhabitants were almost exclusively from the Warfalla tribe, one of Libya's most numerous and influential tribes, Sirte was home to almost forty tribes of different size, influence across the country and political weight.[1] With around 100,000 inhabitants in 2010, it was not one of Libya's main cities. Yet, from being a small village in the 1940s, the city had gained prominence since the 1970s because of the discovery of oil, and for being Qaddafi's birthplace.

This latter characteristic led the Qaddadfa tribe, while less numerous than other tribes in the city (notably the Ma'dan, the Firjan or the Warfalla) and situated much lower in the tribal hierarchies, to dominate the political and social scene for decades.[2] This was made possible, from the 1970s onwards, by Qaddafi's reconfiguring of tribal alliances to protect the Qaddadfa's position. The tribal confederations (*sufuf*) of the nineteenth century were reactivated, notably the interior *suff*, al-Fugi, which included four clans of the Awlad Sleiman, the Qaddadfa, the Warfalla and the population of the oases of Waddan and Hun, which allowed the Qaddadfa to benefit from the protection of historically more powerful tribes, such as the Warfalla and Awlad Sleiman (in addition to that of major tribes from the east of the country).[3]

From the end of the 1970s, Qaddafi's tribal strategy gradually translated into almost complete domination of the Jamahiriya's structures by members of the Qaddadfa tribe and their allies. Until 1993 (the date of the coup attempt led by Warfalla officers), the Qaddadfa–Warfalla alliance controlled the security apparatus.[4] In the early phase of their creation, in 1977–9, the Revolutionary Committees (RC) recruited in almost all tribes, as well as within all social categories. Gradually, however, the composition of the RC shrank and became increasingly restricted to people from the region of Sirte, and from the Qaddadfa, Warfalla, Magarha and Awlad Sleiman tribes. Leadership positions were concentrated in the hands of members of the Qaddadfa tribe.[5] Several figures from Sirte, such as Said Qaddaf al-Dam, Sirte's governor, or Omar Ashkal, the head of the RC, played a prominent role in the overall power system.

In the 1990s, the creation of the Popular Social Leadership (PSL, *al-qiyada al-sha'biya al-ijtima'iya*) reinforced the tribal dimension of the power system and the key role entrusted to elements of the Qaddadfa tribe. With the PSL, tribal elders respected and influential within their tribes were entrusted with a major role as intermediaries between the power centre and the communities at the local level, thus becoming key to the system of power and social control.[6]

The city of Sirte was directly affected by this evolution. It had already become a showcase of the 1969 revolution, notably through the implementation of an ambitious programme of public works. After 1988, most government departments and the General People's Congress were relocated from Tripoli to Sirte, while Tripoli formally remained Libya's capital.

At the city level, the Qaddadfa's hegemony over the social and political scene created tensions with other tribal components of the city, especially with the tribes that were more numerous and had played an important role in tribal wars and alliances of the nineteenth and early twentieth centuries. As in the historical confederations that had set the confederation of the interior (*suff al-fugi*) against the coastal confederation (*suff al-bahar*), the Qaddadfa on the one hand and the Firjan (originally from Tarhuna, Sirte and the east) and the Ma'dan (which populate the region located between Sirte and Misrata and correspond to the lower, popular class in Misrata) on the other hand belonged to rival camps in the competition for power and influence on the local scene.[7] Yet mechanisms of social regulation and control and at times Qaddafi's direct intervention in local conflicts never allowed these tensions to escalate or threaten the Qaddadfa's domination over the city and the surrounding region.[8]

The battle of Sirte, and the violent destruction of a symbol

In 2011, as the uprising expanded across the country, Sirte remained mostly loyal to the regime. Few sons of the city joined the revolutionary forces. Those who did so were mostly Islamists with a jihadist background who had fought abroad in the 1990s and 2000s (Afghanistan for the oldest, Iraq for the youngest) or had been jailed in the infamous Abu Salim prison before being liberated by the regime on the eve of the uprising in early 2011. They established Sirte Revolutionaries' Brigade (*katibat thuwwar sirte*), as well as the Gulf Martyrs' Brigade (*katibat shuhada al-khalij*, headed by Ali Iq'aim) in the neighbouring town of Nawfaliya. These groups, which included fighters from all tribes, fought against the loyalist forces alongside other revolutionary brigades from across Libya.

What remained of Qaddafi's most powerful security brigades, including the remains of the 32nd Reinforced Brigade (also known as the 'Khamis Brigade', after Qaddafi's youngest son who headed it) and of the Muhammad Magarief Brigade, was concentrated on the objective of defending the city. Qaddafi himself had withdrawn to his hometown, along with his son Mu'tasim, who led the loyalist forces.

Like Bani Walid, Sirte offered fierce resistance for weeks to the revolutionary forces directly supported by the North Atlantic Treaty Organization (NATO) military coalition and other foreign sponsors from the region. The final battle started in August 2011, after several previous unsuccessful attempts to capture the city from forces loyal to Qaddafi. It was preceded by a series of NATO airstrikes. Revolutionary brigades then converged towards Sirte from Misrata in the west, Brega in the east and desert positions in the south. They then imposed a one-month siege on the city before they could take control of it, during which they suffered heavy losses. After weeks of intense shelling and street fighting, Sirte was left devastated, with its infrastructure massively destroyed. Many homes were ransacked and looted by fighters, water mains destroyed, streets and buildings flooded, while Mu'amar Qaddafi and his son Mu'tasim were killed by pro-revolutionary fighters; dozens of people captured in the city were accused of being pro-Qaddafi fighters, then detained and sometimes killed by the victors. But many of the city's inhabitants had previously left the city to escape the fighting, either becoming displaced within Libya or, for those better off or with foreign connections, moving abroad.[9]

The fall of the city was celebrated across the country by supporters of the revolution, many of whom considered that the time had come for revenge against Sirte and its inhabitants, who had to pay the price for their support of the regime for more than four decades. Members of the Qaddadfa and Warfalla tribes, who had been pillars of the regime and its security institutions, were targeted: identity-based arrests and detentions became common for residents of Sirte, many of whom could no longer leave the city limits because of the risk of reprisals by pro-revolutionary elements.[10]

Wide-scale destruction in the city as well as the coalition of revolutionary forces from across the country left Sirte's people isolated and excluded from the rest of Libya, while harbouring deep resentment and anger at having lost to foreign-led forces acting for regime change. Stigmatization and marginalization were indeed a reality. Together with the city of Bani Walid, Sirte was still perceived as both the stronghold of former regime supporters and the symbol of the 'defeated' in the war. As transitional institutions were set up by the 'victors' (i.e. the revolutionary forces, the cities and political currents that supported them), one of their main objectives was to avoid by all means the return of the former regime and its support networks. Political exclusion started well before the adoption of the Political Isolation Law by the first elected parliament in May 2013.

The local communities from Sirte, whatever their direct or indirect role in Qaddafi's ruling system, were de facto excluded from the establishment of the post-Qaddafi order. They themselves strongly opposed this new order, which they perceived as imposed by foreign powers and which they thought had led to the destruction of Libya.

The military domination by jihadist revolutionary forces

The death of Qaddafi and the fall of the city to the pro-revolutionary forces led to a dramatic change in the security landscape of the city. The military capacity of the tribes which had been most influential at the social level (especially the Qaddadfa and Warfalla) was destroyed, and while other tribes (like the Firjan) would attempt to fill the vacuum and establish a new distribution of power in their favour, they found it difficult to assert themselves in the post-war environment. They were stigmatized as Sirte's tribal leaders at the country level, considered remnants of the former regime, and also lacked sufficient military might to assert their power on the ground.

After October 2011, force on the ground was largely in the hands of the revolutionary brigades that had fought against Qaddafi. Sirte's Revolutionaries' Brigade (*katibat thuwwar sirte*), headed by Makhlouf bin Naser al-Firjani and dominated by jihadist fighters, remained the dominant power, as most of the other revolutionary brigades from across Libya left the city after winning it over. Only a few of them decided to stay, like the Zawiya Martyrs Brigade, originally from Benghazi and headed by Salah Abu Haliqa, a former army officer who defected to the revolution. Conflict was quick to erupt, however, between Abu Haliqa and the jihadists. Attempts by the former to coordinate the action of the different armed groups at the city level failed, the jihadists refusing to take part in such efforts.[11]

In this context, the transitional authorities in Tripoli were facing serious difficulties in their attempts to organize efficient security structures in the city that would be placed under the control of the government. Composed of local youth from the city and its surroundings, the Sirte Revolutionaries' Brigade was eventually considered the most able to ensure security, and so was provided with recognition and resources by the central authorities. The jihadist background of most of its members did not seem to raise concerns, and their prominent role at the city level was reinforced.

One immediate consequence of the war in Sirte was therefore the military hegemony of the jihadist movement in the local context. This was the result of the limited number of pro-revolutionary elements in the city apart from the jihadists, as well as of decisions made by the National Transitional Council (NTC) at the end of the war. Faced with the local communities' lack of military force and fearful of leaving any kind of power and capacity to organize to pro-Qaddafi supporters in the city, the transitional authorities ended up entrusting jihadist fighters with the responsibility for securing Sirte.

At the end of 2011, a Supreme Security Committee (SSC, *lajna amniya 'ulya*) was officially established in Sirte with the aim of integrating the armed brigades devolved from the war into a single entity placed under the control of the transitional authorities in Tripoli (a model which was supposed to be implemented across Libya). In Sirte, the SSC was controlled by the Sirte Revolutionaries' Brigade. Led by Khalifa al-Barq, it included fighters from all the city's tribes (for instance prominent figures like Abdelhadi Zarqun, from the Warfalla tribe), many of whom were former Islamist detainees, like Salah al-Sid al Firjani.

For Sirte's jihadists, joining the Security Committee did not mean acceptance and recognition of the new Libyan authorities. Rather, they saw this as an opportunity to benefit from the resources allocated by the transitional authorities to groups entrusted with security tasks on the ground. Hence, not only could jihadist elements operate rather freely in the political and security vacuum resulting from the 2011 events in Sirte; but also, since Libya's transitional authorities could not rely on any other significant military force supportive of the 2011 revolution, they further empowered the jihadist elements in Sirte.

Tribal hierarchies contested

Beyond the severe impact on the city's infrastructure, the months of civil war and extreme violence had a major influence on the social and political structures in Sirte and the neighbouring towns. While the Qaddadfa tribe had been hegemonic for decades, the collapse of the regime, the death of Qaddafi and the deep resentment towards all individuals and communities who had supported his regime led to a major political vacuum and dramatic social disruption.

The victory of the pro-revolutionary forces had at least two major consequences for the social fabric and political structures in the city: the political exclusion of the Qaddadfa tribe and their closest allies, the Warfalla; and the severe loss of influence of tribal elders in general within their communities, especially for the youth. The incapacity of tribal leaders from all tribes to protect their people and prevent their violent exclusion from the national social and political arenas had a negative impact on their social status and influence.

However, the war had led to the emergence of a new leadership organized around young militiamen displaying their military force and their will to use it. Within the Magharba tribe in Ajdabiya, for instance, Ibrahim Jadhran soon contested the authority of the tribal leadership, represented by Sheikh Salah al-Atyush. Within the Firjan tribe, the tribe's elders and jihadist pro-revolutionary fighters entered into competition for influence and for the community's leadership. Many of the tribe's elders, now part of Sirte's Council of Notables and Wisemen (*majlis a'yan wa hukama sirt*), had already occupied these same positions of influence within the community under Qaddafi and therefore felt rather fearful, even though they had not played a key role with the former regime.

In this new environment, tribal elders still perceived that they had to organize the protection of their people and their neighbourhoods, and in turn supported the establishment of their own armed brigades. For example, the creation of the al-Jalat brigade instigated by leaders of the Firjan tribe at the end of 2012 aimed to gather pro- and anti-revolutionary fighters from various tribes into one single armed group that would be entrusted with securing and policing the city. Most of its members were from the Firjan and Ma'dan tribes, however, as one of the al-Jalat brigade's objectives was to make sure that the influence and interests of the Firjan tribe would be protected in the evolving local scene, especially with regard to the powerful Sirte Revolutionaries' Brigade.

Against this background, building on the credit earned during the war, revolutionary fighters from the Firjan tribe such as Salah al-Sid and Makhluf bin Naser started making decisions and acting on the ground without referring to the tribal leadership, represented by Sheikh Ajil al-Sadeq. When tribal elders attempted to respond to such affronts to their authority, their focus on the values of respect, reverence and dignity did not fit with the references and modes of action of the younger generation. For the latter, the use of force and ideology was key, and they proved quite successful in convincing young men from all the city's tribes to join them around this more effective platform.

Sirte, a gathering place for jihadists from across Libya and from abroad

The Salafist–jihadist current, initially led by Libyan revolutionary fighters who had taken part in the fight against Qaddafi, was quick to emerge as the dominant military force in Sirte after 2011. Yet its roots ran much deeper than the 2011 revolution and civil war.

While inspired and influenced by developments at the regional and international levels (especially the Afghan jihad against the Soviets), the Salafist–jihadist current which emerged in Libya initially had a rather 'national' dimension and focus. In the 1980s, small groups of Islamists had started advocating taking up arms against the regime instead of working patiently to prepare for the eventual establishment of an Islamic state, as proposed by the Muslim Brotherhood. They were inspired by the experience of scores of young Arabs who travelled to do jihad in Afghanistan, as well as by preachers like Sheikh Muhammad Abd al-Salam al-Bishti, a popular imam in Tripoli, who contributed to spreading the idea that Qaddafi's rule was illegitimate in an Islamic sense.[12]

Around 1990, a number of veterans of the Afghan jihad created the Libyan Islamic Fighting Group (LIFG), known as *al-muqatila*, with the objective of gathering Libyan jihadists under a single umbrella and organizing armed struggle against Qaddafi. While security pressure from the regime initially constrained the group's leaders to work outside the country, they managed to organize the return of some fighters to Libya and attract supporters. Under the leadership of the LIFG, the jihadist movement managed to expand and establish bases in the country, especially in eastern Libya's Green Mountains area. However, the decision to begin direct confrontation with the regime in the mid-1990s led to huge losses for the group. Part of the leadership escaped abroad, while another part of the group was imprisoned in Tripoli's Abu Salim prison.[13] The shared experience of fighting abroad, as well as the experience of repression, and imprisonment and the consequent links between inmates would all constitute a strong bond between Salafist–jihadists from across Libya—whatever their region or community of origin—and from abroad.

Qaddafi's policies towards the Salafist–jihadist current and also towards the Islamist opposition changed at the turn of the 2000s. As he stepped up his efforts to widen the circle of his supporters and invest more religious authority in his rule, he developed an interest in Salafism. In the mid-2000s, the regime invited Salafist clerics close to the Saudi establishment to Libya. The objective was more specifically to promote the Madkhali Salafist school (named after Saudi cleric Rabi'a bin Hadi al-Madkhali), which promotes a doctrine of obedience to the current political authority (*wali al-amr*), avoiding any political activism or armed resistance against the ruler, whatever his behaviour.[14] Qaddafi's son S'adi entered into discussion with Salafist prisoners and agreed on their liberation, encouraging their *da'wa* (missionary work) activities with support from the state's security agencies. For instance, they could gain control over a number of mosques in Tripoli and across Libya. The regime also attempted to develop a Libyan Salafist current inspired by Libyan, instead of Saudi, figures.[15]

In the mid-2000s, beyond supporting the diffusion of quietist Salafism, efforts to defuse the Salafist–jihadist threat on the regime also included encouraging the departure of the most radical elements to fight abroad in order to avoid destabilization in Libya. After 2005, the Jamahiriya's military intelligence in some instances facilitated the departure of those willing to fight against the American-led coalition in Iraq.[16] The coastal city of Nawfaliya, in particular, located around 100 kilometres east of Sirte and mostly populated by the Magharba tribe, was a departure point for Libyan jihadists. Nine young men from the city left for Iraq at the time, some of whom returned under the agreement concluded between the Qaddafi regime and part of the LIFG leadership at the end of the 2000s.

After attempting to deflect the threat, Qaddafi then initiated a process of rapprochement and reconciliation with major figures among the LIFG leadership imprisoned in Libya. The rationale behind this move was that by convincing the 'intellectual' leadership of Libya's Salafist–jihadist current to renounce violent struggle, and thereby influencing doctrinal change within the current, the regime would lessen the threat of LIFG 'ordinary' members.

Under the leadership of Saif al-Islam Qaddafi and his Qaddafi International Charity and Development Foundation (QDF), and with the support of Libya's internal and external security services, a process of dialogue was engaged with imprisoned figures of the LIFG. In 2009, as a result of the initiative, several leading members of the LIFG issued a 'recanting' document, in which they attempted to redefine the ethics of Islamic *sharia* law and jihad, and publicly refuted the LIFG's decades-long jihad against Qaddafi and his regime. More than 200 jihadists were then released from prison, with the last releases taking place at the beginning of 2011, just days before the beginning of the uprising.

Qaddafi's policies towards the Salafist and Salafist–jihadist currents throughout the 2000s ended up having very mixed results. A quietist Salafist current did develop and expand in Libya, strongly influenced by Saudi preachers from the Madkhali school, but with Libyan figures emerging as well. While advocating obedience to the ruler in place in the political realm, the Salafist doctrine which gradually gained ground across the country included theological principles and religious practices also considered as basic to the Salafist–jihadist current. Their wide diffusion through Libyan society might in some circumstances facilitate the latter's maneuvering on the ground, as for instance in situations of political and social vacuum, with social order being called for by communities.

Within the Salafist–jihadist sphere itself, the end of the uprising and the civil war led to the emergence of a new generation of fighters who did not necessarily recognize themselves in the historical leadership of the LIFG or in the main figures behind the recanting document, such as 'Abd al-Hakim Bilhaj or Sami al-Sa'adi.[17] It also led to jihadist fighters who had spent time in Iraq or other wars coming back to Libya to join the struggle against Qaddafi. They returned with significant military experience, and with connections to the global jihadist movement that would help them access resources key to the competition for power and influence in post-2011 Libya.

The Syrian–Libyan jihadist nexus

The contacts established between Libyan revolutionary fighters and their Syrian counterparts, encouraged by Libya's transitional authorities, also confirmed the global dimension of the Libyan jihadist networks and the role this played in their expansion. Like the policies previously conducted by Qaddafi, the policies of the post-2011 authorities favoured and reinforced the connection of local jihadist groups to global networks. The process of 'globalization' of the Libyan jihadist movement, which had started with the participation of young Libyans in the Afghan jihad and developed with the war in Iraq in the 2000s, gained momentum after the collapse of the Qaddafi regime as key figures within the first transitional governments and some members of the General National Congress (GNC) elected in 2012 encouraged and helped young Libyan revolutionary fighters to go to Syria to support the armed opposition to Bashar al-Assad.[18]

Those who chose to head for Syria had various profiles.[19] The first wave to leave in 2011 included those who had joined a jihadist brigade during the revolution and were willing to pursue the fight in Syria after Qaddafi's death. The majority, however, were less motivated by religious conviction and their desire to join the jihad and more by their solidarity with the Syrian people. Most of them went and joined the Free Syrian Army, without the question of their religious or political loyalties playing a role in their affiliation. The Umma brigade (*liwa al-umma*), for instance, founded by Irish–Libyan Mahdi al-Harati, was part of this movement.

The second wave of departures, in 2012, was different. It included a younger generation of Libyan jihadists who had decided to leave Libya to fight in the Iraqi war against the Americans in 2003, as well as numerous former inmates of the Abu Salim prison in Tripoli. Major jihadist figures, essentially veterans from Afghanistan who were considered 'leaders' of the Libyan jihadist movement, were also part of this wave of departures. These chose to join the ranks of Jabhat al-Nusra or to establish their own combat units, mainly comprising Libyans and foreign fighters. This was notably the case of the Umar al-Mukhtar brigade (*katibat 'umar al-mukhtar*), led by jihadist militant Ziyad Balaam.

While the Libyan fighters' choice to join one or other group in the Syrian rebellion was initially mostly based on opportunity—those who would welcome them on their arrival—at a later stage a large majority of them were part of either Jabhat al-Nusra or the Islamic State of Iraq and the Levant (ISIL). When Libya ceased to be mostly a country of transit or departure towards Syria but also a country of destination—around the end of 2013—these fighters were assigned the mission of establishing and developing in Libya the organization that had welcomed them in Syria.

Returning to their homeland from Syria, the Libyan fighters also brought back fellow fighters from other countries. While the more general Libyan context offered some opportunities for development, the specific situation in Sirte had particular advantages: the political and security vacuum in the city, as well as the influence of jihadist elements since 2011 encouraged them to settle in Sirte.

Sirte under Ansar al-Sharia: a gathering point for jihadists

Sirte soon became a gathering place for jihadists from across Libya and from abroad. The lack of military competitors in a local environment dramatically transformed by defeat in the civil war and the exclusion of the communities that had previously enjoyed the most political and social influence played a key role in the transformation of Sirte into a jihadist hotbed soon after the end of the war.

Over the course of 2012, the Ansar al-Sharia Brigade in Benghazi, officially established in February 2012 and led by a former inmate of the Abu Salim prison, Muhammad al-Zahawi, was rebranded Ansar al-Sharia in Libya, ASL.[20] It started conducting *da'wa* and social activities in Sirte. In a city which had been largely abandoned by the transitional authorities after being destroyed during the war, ASL's activities, although initially not highly organized, were rather welcomed by residents. The group focused on keeping order and combating organized crime (especially drug trafficking), which obviously filled a void in a city whose social and political structures had been seriously damaged. Social activities were also aimed at preparing the ground for the deeper, longer-running establishment of the organization in the city, however. While ASL actions focused on local issues and the organization of local life in the context of a vacuum, the group's proselytizing activities were also fully in line with the ideological milieu of global jihadism: ASL doctrine and agenda focused on pure monotheism (*tawhid*), the excommunication of the unbelievers (*takfir*) and military fight (*jihad*) to purge the Islamic community (*umma*) of unbelievers and implement *sharia*.[21] Socially and militarily, ASL influence grew as the majority of Sirte's jihadists came under the umbrella of the organization, and as a number of ASL elements had to flee Benghazi after the attack against the American consulate in September 2012.

At the beginning of 2013, members of Misrata's al-Farooq brigade, which had fought against Qaddafi loyalists in the city in 2011, also decided to establish a base in Sirte. While originally created in 2011 in the neighbourhoods of al-Ramla and al-Zarquq by jihadist al-Tuhami Abuzayan (from the al-Ramla tribe in Misrata, a law professor at Misrata University), the al-Farooq brigade had failed to convince a significant number of young Misratans to rally. The domination of the jihadist elements over the group also led to an internal split: those among the members who belonged to the 'popular' revolutionary movement stayed in their home city, some of them even returning to civil life, while the jihadists left Misrata to establish themselves in Sirte, where they came to support the Supreme Security Committee, with whom they shared a common jihadist background.[22] In Sirte, the al-Farooq brigade also included sons of the city in its ranks. Here again, ideological allegiance to the jihadist community (and often shared personal trajectories of imprisonment) prevailed over tribal identity: members of the brigade for instance included Abdelhadi Zarqun from the Warfalla tribe; Walid al-Firjani from the Firjan tribe; Fawzi al-'Ayat from the Hawsana tribe; Ali al-Safrani from the Sheki tribe, etc.[23]

In June 2013, the Supreme Security Committee and the al-Farooq brigade joined forces under Ansar al-Sharia Libya, which officially announced its establishment in the city under the leadership of Ahmad Ali al-Tayyar, the Misratan commander of the al-Farooq brigade. The banning of the Tunisia branch of Ansar al-Sharia by the Tunisian authorities in August 2013 after the killing of politicians Shukri Belaid and Muhammad Brahmi accelerated the growth of the local branch of the movement. The city had become a point of convergence of jihadist networks at the regional level. In addition to their social and religious activities, Ansar al-Sharia Libya had also established training camps for foreign fighters and were part of weapon transit networks between the region's main conflict areas (Mali, Tunisia, Libya, Syria, etc).

In the security field, the jihadists gathered within Ansar al-Sharia had few competitors at the local level, as local communities remained militarily weak after the civil war, being on the defeated side. In 2013, the Zawiya Martyrs Brigade led by Salah Abu Haliqa was among the few groups to hold out in the face of Ansar al-Sharia. However, several episodes of clashes and armed confrontations between the two groups led eventually in March 2014 to the departure of the Zawiya Martyrs Brigade and its return to Benghazi from where it originally came. From then on, Ansar al-Sharia enjoyed almost complete control over the city. Although the al-Jalat brigade set up by the Firjan tribe attempted to compete and play a role in the security field, its strength remained very limited compared with the jihadists. The Dignity (*Karama*) campaign launched in Benghazi also resulted in a major shift within Ansar al-Sharia, whose focus was now primarily on military action instead of *da'wa*.[24]

Against such a background, the declaration of the Caliphate by Abu Bakr al-Baghdadi and the establishment of the Islamic State in the Levant (Iraq and Syria) had a dramatic impact on local developments in Sirte.

The Islamic State in Sirte: unrivalled dominance

While al-Baghdadi's declaration of the Caliphate triggered a split in the Levant between supporters of al-Qaeda and the new Islamic State organization, this development had particular reverberations in Sirte. Many among the ASL leaders initially had reservations about al-Baghdadi's move. The members of the Libyan Salafist–jihadist sphere had developed ties with their Syrian counterparts since 2011, and most of them had joined brigades affiliated with Jabhat al-Nusra in Syria. Because of these links, Sirte's jihadists tended to side with Jabhat al-Nusra in the conflict that opposed the latter to the new proclaimed Islamic State organization.

In June 2013, however, some among Sirte's jihadists had facilitated and organized the visit of the Bahraini preacher Turki al-Bin'ali to the city. A disciple of Salafist–jihadist preacher Abu Muhammad al-Maqdisi,[25] al-Bin'ali had conducted an ambitious programme of religious teachings, giving speeches in local mosques, on Radio Tawhid,[26] and teaching ASL members from the city, as well as dozens of others coming from Benghazi, Derna and other Libyan cities. The preacher's visit seemed to have considerable impact over ASL members and the leadership.

The links established by Turki al-Bin'ali with ASL members in Sirte, as well as the feeling that IS was the rising force within the global jihadist sphere, resulted in a new balance of forces between supporters and opponents of IS within ASL in Sirte. A new leadership favourable to al-Baghdadi emerged, causing opponents to the new trend to flee the city and return to Benghazi, where they joined ASL in their fight against Haftar's forces there. In return, the emergence of a pro-IS leadership in Sirte resulted in new Salafist–jihadist elements from Benghazi and eastern Libya moving into the city. There they rapidly seized control of the mosques and religious institutions, entering into conflict with the city's mufti and the local *awqaf* (endowments) office responding to Tripoli's Dar al-Ifta. The head of the *awqaf* office, 'Abdallah Hawilat, refused to pledge allegiance to IS. After escaping an assassination attempt, he eventually fled the city to seek refuge in Bani Walid.[27]

While the IS leadership initially seemed to have chosen to focus its strategy of development in Libya on the eastern coastal city of Derna, historically a hotbed of Libya's jihadist movement, the local situation in the city proved less favourable to the group than expected. The Islamic Youth Shura Council (IYSC, *majlis shura shabab al-islam*) formed in Derna by Libyan jihadists returning from Syria pledged allegiance to IS in October 2014. Even though they could rely on wide networks, well-rooted in Derna's local society and connected to the global jihad, they were also faced with local groups enjoying both social influence and military strength. The Abu Salim Martyrs Brigade (*katibat shuhada buslim*), in particular, constituted a direct competitor to IS-affiliated IYSC in its strategy of territorial control and expansion. The brigade entered into direct military confrontation with the IYSC, getting support from military forces from other eastern cities (revolutionary brigades from al-Bayda and Tobruk, the Fursan al-Qataan brigade, the Hassan al-Jabar brigade, etc). The city of Derna was also directly targeted by Haftar's Dignity operation: Libyan air force fighters conducted aerial raids against militants in the city in November 2014, while the Haftar-allied forces laid siege to the city in March 2015.

The difficulties faced by IS in consolidating its presence in Derna made Sirte a more conducive environment and a possible alternative for the development and expansion of IS in North Africa. The city had become a hub and gathering point for Libyan and international jihadists since 2012 and had passed into almost complete military domination by pro-IS Ansar al-Sharia militants after mid-2014. In addition, the tribal leadership which used to dominate the social scene had been seriously weakened by defeat in the civil war, both militarily (with its armaments largely destroyed) and socially (with the authority of local tribal elders contested by young militiamen, most of whom belonged to the Salafist–jihadist trend and whose counter-authority stemmed from their access to global networks to obtain financial and military resources).

Control over Sirte: a strategic asset for IS expansion

Under control by Ansar al-Sharia militants, Sirte had already demonstrated that it had many assets that could prove key to IS expansion in Libya and North Africa. Over the course of 2012–14, ASL militants had used the strategic location of the city (in Libya's central region, a crossroads for routes going west, east and south through wide desert areas) and its modern transport infrastructures (notably its port) to smuggle fighters, migrants and weapons in and out of the city. By so doing, they could significantly increase the number of fighters, including foreigners (from Tunisia, Sudan, Yemen, Chechnya, Morocco, Algeria, etc), who could be mobilized to fight alongside them. In addition, the proximity to Libya's main oil installations (Sidra, Ras Lanuf, al-Brega) contributed to the plan that, at a later stage, control over the region's riches might provide IS with significant revenue.

ASL's military hold over the city and *da'wa* activities, as well as the attempts of key figures from global jihadist networks (notably Turki al-Bin'ali, who was to become IS mufti) to rally Sirte residents to their cause, facilitated IS's progressive and rapid implantation in the city and its surroundings. More than the appeal of the group's ideology and objectives, what enabled IS to take root in the city was the unwillingness and incapacity of local communities to confront the threat. This was demonstrated for the first time as early as December 2014, when IS had not even officially announced its presence in Sirte.

Control over the Gulf of Sidra had been a key challenge for all the political and military forces competing for power in Libya since 2012, and even more since 2014, when Libya became divided into two sets of rival political and military coalitions ('Libya Dawn' and 'Dignity') and institutions (established in Tripoli and in al-Bayda/Tobruq). In mid-December 2014, the two rival blocks entered into direct confrontation over the so-called 'Oil Crescent', then under control by federalist forces loyal to Ibrahim Jadhran. On 14 December, an attack on Sidra's oil terminal carried out by Operation Sunrise (*Shuruq*), led by Misratan forces and allied with Libya Dawn, was repelled by Dignity forces. Mediation efforts by influential figures from both camps led to the retreat of Misrata's forces. Yet the episode constituted the first opportunity for IS elements to signal their presence in the region and demonstrate their strength. While the Misratan forces had come to an agreement with Sirte's local military forces—essentially Ansar al-Sharia and the al-Jalat brigade—to secure its supply lines from Misrata to Sidra and Ben Jawad, the agreement did not last long. On 27 December fourteen members of the Firjan tribe in the al-Jalat brigade, who were entrusted with the protection of Sirte's electric power plant, were slaughtered.[28] While there was initial questioning that they might have been killed by Misratan forces, this later proved to have constituted IS's first show of force in the area.[29]

IS undertook the communication of its presence, now referred to by official IS channels as the Tripoli province (*wilayat trablus*), with Sirte as its capital. In February 2015 IS released a video showing the beheading of twenty-one Egyptian Christians, whom they had abducted in the previous weeks. It took them little time to announce their complete seizure of the city of Sirte. On 8 February 2015, an important convoy of IS members entered the town of Nawfaliya, which had been among Libya's main departure points for Libyan jihadists to Iraq in the 2000s. ASL members in the city provided logistical support on the ground to facilitate this move, despite the split that the issue of allegiance to IS provoked within the organization.[30] In June 2015, the town of Harawa, populated by members of the Awlad Sleiman tribe, was in turn seized.

IS take over Sirte

IS encountered little, if any, resistance when it established its rule over Sirte and the neighbouring towns. Sirte's inhabitants had largely been left to themselves to reorganize civil life and conduct reconstruction in the city since 2011. The behaviour of IS leaders and its members (Libyans, Arabs and nationals of other countries) when they officially seized control over the city in early 2015 contributed to the residents' relative quiet in the face of the new rulers.

Sirte's residents shared a common fear of foreigners, whether armed groups from the city of Misrata or foreign fighters with IS, and there was a feeling that the threat could come from anywhere. Yet for the tribes which did not support the revolution (especially the Qaddadfa, Warfalla, al-'Amamra), IS presence and control over the city initially did not constitute a threat any more serious than that of the armed groups which had been ruling the city since October 2011. For many, there was no major difference between *Daesh* (the Arabic acronym for IS) and the 'militias' (the armed groups that had dominated the city since 2011). Therefore, they initially remained relatively indifferent to the emergence of IS.

IS leaders initially focused on imposing order in the city and on religious 'education'. Particular emphasis was put on *da'wa* activities, which did not encounter serious resistance given the strong Salafist influence among local tribes. Diffusion among young people was facilitated in the region of Sirte by the cultural void and the absence of activities available to the youth, as well as by the social pressure exerted over young people living in small, relatively closed tribal communities. In such a context, the presence of one or two influential figures was sufficient to attract followers among youth groups. *Da'wa* activities, and especially the enforced attendance at lectures and ideological classes organized for the city's residents, had a particular impact on the teenagers.

The IS leaders were also careful not to go against the tribal elders and figures considered as supporters of the former regime (notably from the Qaddadfa and Warfalla tribes). In contrast to common practice in Libya between 2011 and 2016, they avoided framing their discourse in pro- and anti-revolution terms, or using the narrative and symbols of the revolution and the post-2011 regime. By focusing on belonging to the Islamic community, they had far more chance of gaining favourable attention from members of the local tribes, who had been subjected to marginalization and exclusion since 2011. This strategy initially secured IS the relative indifference and neutrality of most members of the defeated tribes. And indeed, some among pro-former regime tribes even displayed interest in joining IS. They did so on an individual basis, however, rather than as members of a specific tribal group. Most often they did so out of pragmatism, rather than ideological identification.

One of the tools that IS used to attract followers among former regime supporters was the value they gave to the theme of repentance: an individual's political past was of little importance, provided that he repented of his past actions. Those who repented and swore allegiance to IS were considered full members of the group; in addition to becoming part of an organization that was becoming increasingly influential, both at the local and global levels, they benefited from immunity regardless of the role they had played in the service of the former regime. This proved attractive to some among the civil leadership of the Qaddafi brigades who were wanted by the judicial authorities or the revolutionary groups. IS policies provided them with a form of protection that they could not get from any other authorities, including their own tribal elders, defeated in the war and subsequently significantly weakened.[31]

Some also joined IS because it could provide them with access to weapons, something that their community leaders who remained in Sirte could not offer them, being largely deprived of access to networks—either within Libya or outside—which could help them regain the military power lost during the war. Also, the desire to take revenge against the city of Misrata, seen as the main agent of the 2011 war and the subsequent destruction of the city, constituted in some cases a further incentive to support the new power, whatever its ideological and religious basis.[32]

Sirte's tribal leaders' helplessness

Overall, resentment and competition between the tribes in Sirte and Libya's central region largely facilitated IS's efforts to gain control over the city and expand its influence. IS leaders were well aware of the tensions and competition between tribes and tribal leaders at the city level and in the region. They knew the depth of the divide between members of the pro-February (i.e. revolutionary) current (even though these members had joined the pro-revolution wave late, when it had become clear that by doing so they would be on the winners' side) and members of the pro-September (i.e. former regime) current (especially from tribes that had been key pillars of the Qaddafi regime) and attempted to use it to their advantage. They had limited success in this endeavour, however, as they could not use tribal bonds as a mobilizing force in their favour. When members of the Qaddadfa or the Warfalla joined the organization or provided support, they could only do so as individuals, and not in the name of the tribe.

The disruption of relations of power and authority within the tribes also played a role in the initial reluctance and difficulty of tribal elders reacting to the jihadist threat. For instance, while the elders of the Firjan tribe were willing to lead an effort to confront IS, fighting the jihadist organization would have meant alienating members of their own tribe (mostly the youth), many of whom took part in the 2011 uprising alongside jihadist armed groups or joined these at a later stage.

Security-wise, the military weakness of the communities that had historically been the most influential and powerful (the Qaddadfa and Warfalla under Qaddafi, as well as the Firjan previously) now allowed the jihadist elements to seize almost complete control over the city. Most of these were not from the city itself, but came from other Libyan cities or from abroad. Over the course of 2013 and 2014, this trend even intensified as Ansar al-Sharia networks smuggled an increasing number of foreigners into the city, often with the knowledge and support of Libyan military and political leaders close to the Salafist–jihadist current.[33] The beginning of Haftar's military offensive against Islamist armed groups in Benghazi—the Dignity campaign—also led many Salafist–jihadist Islamists to seek refuge in Sirte after May 2014.

With Misrata having withdrawn its forces from the whole region after the end of the Sunrise operation, IS fighters found themselves with few opponents capable of confronting them militarily. In Sirte, the massacre committed at the electric plant had led the al-Jalat brigade to start preparing for a confrontation with the extremist forces controlling the city. Yet IS immediately made it clear when they seized Sirte that they would not tolerate any other group carrying weapons in the city. They requested from the al-Jalat brigade leadership that they surrender theirs, which they refused to do. This did not lead to immediate confrontation, however, as the balance of military force between the al-Jalat brigade and the local communities it stemmed from (especially the Firjan tribe) on the one hand, and the jihadists on the other hand, was too uneven.

The feeling of increased threat led tribal elders from the city to gather and discuss the situation and ways to present a common front against IS. Yet agreement could not be reached within Sirte's Council of Notables and Wisemen on how to confront the jihadist threat. In particular, conflict arose within the council on the name under which the battle against IS should be conducted, and under whose leadership. The head of the Firjan tribe, Sheikh al-Sadeq 'Ajil, argued that they were ready to take the lead in this fight, and wished to do so in the name of the 'February revolution', claiming that they would get support from their Misratan neighbours. This was unacceptable to the Qaddadfa tribe leadership, represented by Sheikh Abdelhamid Basbsin from Abu Hadi, who refused to participate and fight if the battle was not led by local communities altogether, without sponsorship from the groups and communities deemed responsible for the 2011 war (especially the Misratan neighbours).[34]

The majority of tribes in Sirte followed the Qaddadfa in this decision and refused to join forces with the Firjan leadership, illustrating the remaining social influence of the Qaddadfa tribe in the city, despite the military weakness resulting from the war and the loss of political influence in the post-war context.[35] The elders of the Firjan tribe remained isolated on the local scene and subsequently with limited capacity to confront IS directly.[36] Despite requests for support presented to General Haftar and his forces, the al-Jalat brigade did not receive any significant assistance.[37]

By contrast, the connection of ASL and IS to global networks that enabled them to obtain weapons and money, as well as social influence (including via global media networks), undoubtedly proved appealing to young people eager to escape from what they perceived as traditional patterns of power and authority and to become more influential within their communities. This was even more the case for young people originating from tribes that could have benefited from the post-2011 disruption of political and social structures, like the Firjan.

IS repression of the Salafists' attempts at resistance

Within a few weeks, however, the relationship between IS forces and Sirte's residents profoundly changed. The number of foreigners smuggled into the city increased dramatically and IS started harassing and exerting violence against the population, without discrimination as to tribal loyalty or neighbourhood residence. While the *da'wa* activities had not been opposed in the first phase of IS control, the degree of coercion now imposed on Sirte's residents, especially the youth, as well as the *sharia*-based punishments now vigorously imposed, were deeply resented by the people. As pressure increased on the residents in their daily lives, they started leaving the city to seek refuge in other cities (the majority to Tarhuna, Bani Walid, Misrata, but also to Tripoli, Zliten, etc.).[38]

While the IS leaders did not encounter any major resistance by the local communities at first, their ambition to exert complete control over local religious institutions and to use them to rally sons of the city to their cause backfired. Contrary to the military and political aspects, in the religious field they found themselves faced by local competitors. The Salafist current, whose influence was strong among local tribes, started to react as they felt directly threatened by IS intervention in their territory.

Control over religious discourse and the city's mosques became a major point of contention between the two groups. Salafist Sheikh Khaled bin Rajab al-Firjani, who spoke at the Cordoba mosque in

Sirte's neighbourhood number 3, was among the most prominent religious figures to criticize IS publicly and refuse to let them use his mosque for sermons. He entered into a war of speeches with IS preacher Hassan al-Karami, from Benghazi, speaking from the Rabat mosque, located in the same neighbourhood. Clashes erupted on several occasions.

Yet, while the Firjan leadership had tried to mobilize the Salafists early on to confront IS directly, their call was not heard until Sheikh bin Rajab was killed in August 2015. The cleric's assassination prompted an immediate armed uprising against IS in neighbourhood number 3, in which Firjani fighters from the al-Jalat brigade fought alongside the Salafist youth against IS. As fighting broke out, two of the jihadist group's commanders—Saudi Abu Huzaifa Ansari and Egyptian Abu Hammam Masri—were killed. The battle lasted for days, but IS shelling of the whole neighbourhood eventually resulted in local resistance being crushed. Many residents were killed,[39] including civilians and local leader Mabruk al-Firjani. Military defeat led most of the Salafist youth to leave the city to join the Yarmuk brigade based east of Misrata, or the 604th Infantry Battalion established in Tripoli by Khaled bin Rajab's brother.[40] Members of the al-Jalat brigade left for Tobruk, where they joined General Haftar's forces.[41] IS was now in complete control of the city, with the very few groups that could have opposed its domination having been militarily defeated and chased out of the city.

It was only in May 2016, after the jihadist organization started directly targeting the city of Misrata and raising concerns among Western governments regarding its capacity to conduct military operations in Europe, that a wide-scale military offensive was launched against IS in Sirte and its surroundings. Branded Solid Foundation (*al-bunyan al-marsus*), the coalition of forces that confronted IS was dominated by armed groups from Misrata. Almost five years after the fall of Qaddafi's regime, the city remained the major military force in western Libya, which made it an indispensable military partner for the internationally-supported government established in Tripoli. Libyan local forces, though powerful and experienced, did not match up to the IS fighters established in Sirte, however. Significant foreign assistance (including American aerial support) and several months of bombardment were needed before the city could be recaptured from IS.

Conclusion

The 2011 uprising and the period of internal conflict and instability it opened up in Libya created a space for the various armed groups born out of the war to consolidate their power and influence over local territories, people and nascent political institutions. The jihadist movement, in particular, gained strength as a result of the war, as the past fighting experience of its members and the global networks of support (human, military, financial) it could mobilize made joining jihadist groups relatively attractive.

While jihadists had historically found a propitious ground to develop in some areas of eastern Libya, the coastal city of Sirte quickly became a gathering point for jihadists from across Libya and from abroad (especially the Middle East and North Africa and the Sahel region) after the death of Qaddafi in October 2011. Sirte's Revolutionaries' Brigade, the local jihadist brigade which took control of the city after its fall, was soon joined by individuals and groups with a similar ideological outlook which first rallied under the banner of Ansar al-Sharia (ASL) in 2013, then under the banner of the Islamic State (IS) in 2015.

Most of Sirte's residents and tribal leaders had no more ideological affinity with the Salafist–jihadist groups in power than did the rest of the Libyan population. Yet they did not put up major resistance to ASL and IS, which therefore managed to establish and consolidate their presence in the city and its surroundings. The reasons behind this apparent passivity, sometimes understood as outright support, have much to do with the previous 2011 war and its consequences for the local communities.

In addition to its impact in terms of destruction and marginalization, the externally-supported civil war had had a dramatic impact on the relationships between Sirte's residents and the rest of the Libyan people. Symbolizing Qaddafi's regime and his crimes in the eyes of many of their fellow countrymen, they were socially ostracized and excluded from the definition of the post-Qaddafi political order. Defeat in the war had already deprived them of their military capability.

In an overall environment now characterized by the multiplication of local conflicts and of acts of revenge, this meant that Sirte's local communities did not have the ability to defend themselves. Military domination at the city level had deserted the powerful Qaddadfa–Warfalla tribal coalition and passed to local jihadist armed groups.

The relations of power and authority within and between the local communities had also been deeply disrupted. The political elimination of the Qaddadfa tribe opened the way for competition between former rivals to assume leadership in the city, as the authority of tribal elders from all tribes was now contested by young fighters who founded their legitimacy on new values: military might and action. In this context, the jihadists obviously had the upper hand and encountered no major obstacle to establishing their military domination over the city.

The consolidation of jihadist power was also helped by the incapacity of Libya's transitional authorities to fulfil their security and public order duties in Sirte after the 'liberation' of the city. They subsequently decided to outsource security to the dominant military forces on the ground after 2011, which meant to armed brigades dominated by jihadists who therefore obtained direct support (financial and military) from the central government in Tripoli.

The networks established between jihadists from across the Middle East and North Africa since the 1980s, as well as the experience of imprisonment shared by many among Libya's Islamist and jihadist spheres, were quickly mobilized and contributed to reinforcing the position of Sirte as a new jihadist platform in Libya and in North Africa. Ansar al-Sharia, which then appeared as the helm of the Salafist–jihadist movement in Libya, seized control of the city in 2013 without encountering resistance.

While ASL facilitated the arrival of scores of foreigners (including fighters) to Sirte through its global networks, it also included many sons of the city within its ranks. Ideology and common fighting experiences were key to belonging, not tribal bonds: like the various jihadist groups which had pledged allegiance to the organization, ASL included members of all the city's tribes, as well as Libyans from other regions and cities, and foreigners.

When events and developments on the global jihadist scene led to the emergence of the Islamic State in 2014, Sirte followed the trend. After some internal dissent, IS supporters galvanized themselves and took control of the city at the beginning of 2015, bringing together the majority of the jihadist elements that had dominated the city since late 2011, as well as foreigners present in the city who had so far kept a low profile.

Once again, the emergence of IS and its seizing control over the city did not initially trigger significant reaction from Sirte's residents and their tribal elders. Left without support from Libya's rival central authorities (in Tripoli and in al-Bayda), local communities did not have the capacity to oppose this ultimate development. The new IS leadership did not meet any major opposition, as it chose to focus on *da'wa* activities and maintaining public order, without claiming to represent the 2011 revolution. In Sirte, which remained largely hostile to the revolution, such positioning was initially rather well received.

IS governance revealed itself to be different from that of its jihadist predecessors, however. The new organization was not content with the mere indifference or passivity of local residents to its rule, and attempted to play on tribal divisions and gain support from the tribes defeated in the 2011 war. While this strategy led to individual members of the Qaddadfa and Warfalla tribes rallying to the organization or offering support, IS did not manage to get massive loyalty from these tribes.

Yet competition and resentment between local tribes and their elders did deter local communities from joining ranks and opposing IS. The Firjan tribe, for instance, which was willing to take the lead in confronting IS, realized that they were too weak to act in an isolated capacity and had to renounce the effort.

The increased violence and coercion used by IS towards Sirte's residents (notably through compulsory ideological training and the implementation of punishments for those violating allegedly Islamic rules) pushed those who could afford it to leave the city.

Eventually, it was the IS leadership's attempts to seize control over the whole religious field (the religious discourse as well as the city's mosques) which triggered reaction from within the local communities. After the assassination of Salafist Sheikh Khaled bin Rajab al-Firjani in August 2015, the Salafist current in Sirte succeeded where the Firjan tribal leadership had failed: military confrontation eventually took place with IS members, on the initiative of the Salafist current in the city.

Even though the military action, which involved Salafist and Firjan fighters, was severely repressed by IS and resulted in the jihadists reinforcing their grip over the city, it underlined a major shift in the balance of force in post-2011 Sirte: with the weight and influence of the tribes having been seriously weakened by the war and its consequences, the Salafist–jihadists and the Salafists now appeared as the two dominant forces on the local scene.

The eventual defeat of IS in Sirte by forces external to the city—led by the city of Misrata and supported by foreign militaries—also highlighted that local communities now find it increasingly difficult to confront and constrain jihadist groups, which can obtain considerable support from global networks.

CONCLUSION

Virginie Collombier

Despite the frequent overlap between areas where tribes remain a dominant form of socio-political organization and areas where global jihadist groups have taken root over the last two decades, the tribes have nothing inherently specific that would make them more vulnerable to the influence of jihadism. It is more the pragmatic and interest-based strategies developed by both that have laid the ground for cooperation between global jihadists and tribesmen in specific contexts. As illustrated by the different case studies gathered in this volume, the weakening or collapse of state power, deep socio-economic transformations and civil warfare, as well as the subsequent crisis of tribal leadership and community cohesion have constituted a fertile ground for the development and rooting of jihadist groups in various tribal areas of the Middle East and Africa.

The strategy of jihadist groups to expand their global influence and control over territories, from al-Qaeda and its affiliates in the 1990s to the Islamic State more recently, has evolved over time and to adapt to contextual specificities. Borderlands, remote areas difficult to access or decoupled from direct state influence, have traditionally been used by jihadist militants in search of protection, like in mountainous Yemen or

Egypt's Sinai. There, their encounter with local tribes did not automatically lead to cooperation, however. On the contrary, their acceptance depended on the tribes' goodwill and perception of their own interests. In Yemen, the tribes' readiness to cooperate was often motivated by their desire to increase their power and bargain capacity with other tribes and the Yemeni and Saudi governments. In Egypt's Sinai, different jihadist generations have established themselves, initially regarding the area as a retreat from the 'infidel' society, but then also gradually creating bonds with the local communities and attracting some Sinai tribesmen into their ranks.

Both tribal and jihadist groups have attempted to reinforce their respective power through an interaction in which military manpower and intelligence of local power networks were traded by tribesmen in return for the ideological/religious legitimacy provided by global jihadists, as shown in the case of Afghanistan. Tribes have used outside actors to change the balance of power in their favour in local conflicts, against local competitors or against a state perceived as predatory or repressive. Alliance with the jihadists, therefore, was first and foremost part of a political and military strategy rather than a religious act. In the context of weakened states, tribesmen also expected jihadists to provide local order and basic services to their communities. For their part, the jihadist groups have realized that they needed to come to terms with the local context to gain legitimacy and support among local communities, as the globalized jihad of al-Qaeda often contradicted the agenda of local actors. This has led to major changes in the strategy of al-Qaeda in Yemen or of the various offshoots of al-Qaeda and of the Islamic State in Iraq, for instance: in both cases, global jihadists managed to win support and take root locally when they started 'localizing' their agenda. What determined tribal communities' cooperation and the capacity of the jihadists to anchor was indeed a combination of factors which rendered the interaction potentially profitable to both sides.

Warfare and the crisis of state power, in particular, have been central to the diffusion and penetration of global jihadism in tribal areas. They have led to the re-emergence of the tribe as a key socio-political structure to offset the state's deficiencies or mere absence. From Afghanistan to north Cameroon through Yemen and Libya, the failure of states to exert political and social control positioned tribal or community structures as the only alternative to fulfil major functions (from security and law enforcement and conflict resolution to basic services provision), both to local and external actors. This has incapable of maintaining the clientelistic networks key to their social and political control. Moreover, the sense of alienation/exclusion or the repression exerted by governments against specific communities (the local tribes in Egypt's Sinai, the Sunni community in Iraq, the Kanuri community in Cameroon, the tribes allied with Qaddafi in Libya) have also triggered renewed community solidarity, often in defiance of a state perceived as illegitimate or even as a threat.

The main players of global jihadism have seized the opportunity provided by the new regional and international context. While this was already the case in the 1990s, in Afghanistan or in Yemen for instance, the phenomenon has gained momentum as a result of the political turmoil in the Middle East and North Africa since 2011. The collapse of states and its impact on border control, in particular, gave a boost to jihadist transnational networks as the circulation of ideas, manpower, weapons and money was facilitated across the Middle East and North Africa and beyond. Civil warfare in Libya, for instance, contributed to the connection of Egyptian Salafist figures from the *Awlad 'Ali* tribe with radical, violent Islamist groups operating in eastern Libya through their transnational networks. Similarly, because of the weakness of the new state structures and the defeat of the local tribal leadership in the civil war, the Libyan city of Sirte became a gathering point for jihadists from across the region. In the borderlands between north Cameroon and Nigeria, the closure of the border and the reinforced security measures did not disrupt the existing smuggling networks, but rather contributed to the further expansion of criminal networks and to widening the social basis of the Boko Haram insurrection, as a result of the new war economy that has developed in the area.

Throughout the cases studied in this volume, the expansion of global jihadist groups in tribal areas reveals the deep crisis of the tribal system and of the tribal leadership, rather than a natural proximity between tribal structures and their vision of society on the one hand and jihadist groups and tribesmen's agenda on the other hand. The interplay between tribes and jihadists can be at least partly explained by the deep political as well as socio-economic changes that have shaken the tribal structures and weakened community leadership. As the case of Boko Haram illustrates very well, community bonds are only one reason to account for the jihadist expansion across borders or among specific tribes and communities. In north Cameroon, as in Libya's Sirte or in the Afghan province of Helmand, jihadist groups have mobilized fighters and supporters beyond ethnic or tribal links: the new communities they have created are indeed largely trans-ethnic and trans-tribal and rely on new networks of power and interests.

Tribes do not act as collective actors: in Iraq, in Egypt, in Libya, tribesmen have joined jihadist groups as individuals, not as members of a corporate group. It is certain factions, families or households who have cooperated with al-Qaeda and IS in Iraq; in Sirte, Ansar al-Sharia and IS attracted individuals from the same tribes that led the fight against them. Most often, those who decided to join the ranks of jihadist groups were young men who belonged to the middle and lower ranks among tribes. They have come to understand that they could benefit from alliance with those jihadists coming from abroad, to challenge the structures of leadership and authority in place. For them, it has been a way to rebel against the hierarchies, privileges and corruption of their own leaders ruling from the capital city or from abroad (in Iraq or in Cameroon, for instance), or to contest the legitimacy and authority of tribal leaders whom they felt had failed to protect the community (as in Sirte). In many ways, the rise and expansion of al-Qaeda, Boko Haram and the Islamic State can therefore be seen as a generational conflict and a social revolution. In the face of delegitimized and contested tribal hierarchies, global jihadism provides new models and instruments of influence and power, as well as new resources for tribesmen to use in their local power games.

Ideology, and religious discourse, are of course part of these resources. However, the case of the Awlad 'Ali tribe in the borderland between Egypt and Libya well demonstrates that neither politicized Islam nor jihadism has much to do with the tribes as particular forms of socio-political organizations. While global jihadism in the Sunni world can mostly be seen as a derivation of the Salafist school of thought, which is considered close to the tribesmen's conservative view of religion and society, this proximity per se cannot account for the shift of some tribesmen towards radical forms of contestation and violence. The different cases gathered in this volume show that global jihadism interacting with local tribal structures has indeed constituted a political–military movement, more than a purely religious one. It is repression by state authorities, economic and political marginalization and civil warfare that often explained the shift towards radicalization of some within local communities, as shown by the expansion of IS in the Libyan city of Sirte, in Egypt's Sinai or among the Kanuri community in the Lake Chad region, for instance.

In areas where both the state and local community leaders were weakened and delegitimized, the provision of public social services by jihadist militants has largely contributed to making their ideological stance accepted by local tribesmen for whom the enforcement of local order was a priority, or who were in search of new moral figures to lead their communities. The religious discourse that jihadists used to justify their actions, as well as the security and order they provided locally, at least to some extent account for much of the legitimacy they acquired and which made their rooting possible in tribal areas. Moreover, ideological indoctrination of the local communities, especially the youth, including through forced attendance of religious courses, proved key to the jihadist rooting in tribal areas, especially when no alternative discourse was available or considered legitimate.

Sectarian dynamics and conflicts also constituted an important trigger for the expansion of jihadist militancy in Sunni tribal areas, as shown by the cases of Iraq and Yemen, where the Shi'a-dominated government and the rise of the Huthi movement were respectively perceived as a major threat to Sunni tribesmen; they also largely contributed to the growing appeal of al-Qaeda and IS.

The sense of threat—perceived or actual—that members of local tribes and communities experience in the face of an environment undergoing deep socio-economic, political and military transformations have constituted a key determinant of their relationships with global jihadist forces over the past two decades. As shown throughout this volume, it has led to forms of cooperation in specific contexts where tribesmen and jihadists had a common interest in building bridges between the local and the global, beyond and sometimes against the state.

Direct threat has also been key to the expansion of global jihadist forces in tribal areas: the use of force—or the threat of it—against local communities severely weakened by socio-economic transformations and civil warfare and with no leadership capable of protecting them (including militarily) largely made up for IS gains in Iraq, in Libya, in Egypt or in the Lake Chad region. Absent or delegitimized, the local political and religious elites could not keep up with the attacks conducted on them by foreign forces more powerful militarily and ideologically, and allied to local contesters. When the jihadists could not win the support of local tribes and their leaders, they worked towards neutralizing them, by using force when necessary.

Whether local tribesmen have so far managed to retain the upper hand on global jihadist forces or not, the different case studies gathered in this volume highlight the ambiguous relationship that links them together; mostly it has its roots in the feeling of being under threat, experienced by local communities in the face of socio-economic transformations, political turmoil and civil warfare. While global jihadists have seen the collapse of community leadership and cohesion and the weakness of states as an opportunity for expansion, the new challenges of governing at both the local and the state levels need to be better understood and addressed. In the relationship between the tribes and global jihadism, it is indeed the crisis of the state and of the mechanisms for governing areas in crisis which is revealed. This is certainly not a crisis that can be solved solely by military means or through the reform of religious discourse.

APPENDIX I

SHEIKHS WHO APPEARED IN PLEDGE OF ALLEGIANCE (AL-BAYA'A) VIDEOS TO ISIS'S LEADER ABU BAKR AL-BAGHDADI—NINEVEH, MARCH 2015

This unpublished chart, established by the researcher Omar Mohammed, shows that most of the leaders who attended the pledge of allegiance to Al-Baghdadi do not actually represent their tribes, and thus do not hold any status within their communities.[1]

	Tribe[2]	*Tribal leader*	*Observations*
1	Albu Badran	Unknown (or refuse to communicate out of fear)	–
2	Albu Hamdan	Rashid Hamdani	The real sheikh (leader) is Salem Mullah Allu.
3	Tay	Sfuk Hamadi Al-Hanash	He is not representative of the tribe, which consists of many other clans and lineages. He is one of the sheikh's relatives.[3]
4	Al-Nuaim	Ahmed Al-Nuaimi, Saad Al-Nuaimi	The Al-Nuaim tribe is composed of five clans whose actual leaders did not attend the ISIS meeting. ISIS mentioned Ahmed Al-Nuaim as the Al-Nuaim tribe's representative.[4]
5	Al-Abadah	Unknown (or refuse to	Their leader (sheikh) did not attend the meeting; ISIS replaced him with

		communicate out of fear)	Adil Al-Asad Abadi, a member of the tribe and ISIS as well.[5]
6	Al-Akeedat	Unknown (or refuse to communicate out of fear)	–
8	Al-Luhaib	Unknown (or refuse to communicate out of fear)	Only a few members are shown at the allegiance ceremony to ISIS, although they are in conflict with the organization today.[6]
9	Bani Rabia	Unknown (or refuse to communicate out of fear)	–
10	Al-Hamdon	Unknown (or refuse to communicate out of fear)	The tribe was involved militarily with ISIS and the Wali (governor) of Mosul, Radwan Talib Al-Hamdoni, who was one of those who planned the occupation of the city. Al-Hamdon's clans are not in favour of ISIS; this is the case for Bayt Al-Shamlah and their leader Sheikh Ahmed Abdullah Al-Shamlah.[7]
11	Al-Baqara	Omar Joma'a Albjari	The real leader is Sheikh Joma'a Al-Dawar, currently based in Amman, Jordan, who announced his official position against ISIS.
12	Al-Juhaysh	Unknown (or refuse to communicate out of fear)	See Al-Zubaid tribe, 18 below.
13	Al-Sabawi	Unknown (or refuse to communicate out of fear)	Fighting now against ISIS.[8]
14	Al-Shrifat	Unknown (or refuse to communicate out of fear)	One of Shammar's clans, missing at the meeting of allegiance. It is one of ISIS's enemies in the Rabia region.[9]
15	Bani Ezz	Unknown (or refuse to communicate out of fear)	Their number is insignificant in Nineveh. Yet those from Al-Anbar are ISIS's allies.
16	Albu Mutaywit	Unknown (or refuse to	Extremely involved with ISIS. It has taken control of Sinjar under ISIS

		communicate out of fear)	orders and formed a military power in Sinjar.
17	Al-Rashid	Faisal Al-Rashidi	Completely unknown.
18	Al-Zubaid	Unknown (or refuse to communicate out of fear)	One of the biggest tribal confederacies in Iraq, whose branch in Nineveh is the Al-Juhaysh tribe which consists of seventeen clans.[10] None of their official leaders appeared in the allegiance ceremony, and those who were present were loyal to ISIS. Their loyalty goes so far as to execute their legitimate leader, Ali Hussein Yousef Aljehesh, as well as seventy members of their tribe.[11]
19	Al-Hyanien	Unknown (or refuse to communicate out of fear)	Their legitimate sheikh leader was absent, and those who appeared were ISIS members from that same tribe.
20	Al-Sumaidie	Qahtan Sumaidie	No one knows or recognizes him.
21	Albu Hayat	Unknown (or refuse to communicate out of fear)	They are a small clan from Al Hyanien, but ISIS keep calling them a tribe.
22	Al-Khafaja	Unknown (or refuse to communicate out of fear)	There are very few in Nineveh.
23	Al-Jawalla	Unknown (or refuse to communicate out of fear)	Small clans from Tay tribe. Their official representative was missing.
24	Al-Janabat	Unknown (or refuse to communicate out of fear)	There are very few in Nineveh, and those who attended were from Al-Anbar.
25	Albu Ajeel	Unknown (or refuse to communicate out of fear)	Their numbers are small in Nineveh. The attendees were from Tikrit, and members of the tribe in Nineveh who follow their sheikh in Tikrit, Sheikh Abdul Karim al-Neda.

APPENDIX II

JIHADIST GROUPS ASSASSINATING TRIBAL LEADERS IN SUNNI AREA SINCE 2006[1]

	Sheikh name	*Tribal name*
1	Idriss Shahatha Nasser	Albu Hama
2	Salih Elias Yassin	Al-Ekiedat
3	Falah Al-Farhat	Al-Farhat
4	Ali Al-Jaban	Al-Jaban
5	Shahatha Al-Jazaa	Albu Mutaywit
6	Rashid Al-Zaidan	Al-Lahib
7	Abdul Bari Al-Lahibi	Al-Lahib/head tribal associate
8	Abdul Karim Al-Lahibi	Al-Lahib/head of Nineveh tribal associate
9	Ibrahim Al-Mirir	Al-Lahib
10	Fawzi Mohsen Abo	Al-Hayaleen
11	Mahmoud Al-Sabawi	Sbaaoyen
12	Abdul Aziz Al-Tabour	Al-Jubour
13	Ahmed Al-Ramah	Al-Ramah
14	Mohammed Obaid Al-Hamdani	Albu Hamdan
15	Barzan Hazem Al-Badrani	Albu Badran
16	Said Abbas Al-Jubouri	Al-Jubour
17	Mohammed Taher Al abid-Rabbo	Sheikh Jubour tribe
18	Khaled Al-Zubaidi	Al-Zubaid
19	Sabhan Qassab	Al-Anaza
20	Salim Yusuf Alkikah	Alkikah
21	Ahmed Naif	Al-Mirir
22	Amer Ali Aldaaod	Sheikh of tribe of Albu Hamdan

23	Mohammed Khaled Al-Sharabi	Al-Sharabien
24	Ryan Abed Rabbo	Al-Jubour
25	Raad Al-Alyani	Al-Juhaysh

NOTES

INTRODUCTION

1. Eickelman 1998: ch. 6. There is an important academic literature on tribes in the Middle East, which endeavours to highlight the dynamic and versatile dimension of the tribal phenomenon: see for instance the seminal Khoury and Kostiner 1991; and Abdul-Jabar and Dawod 2004.
2. The journal of ISIS in English, *Dabiq* (issue 3), explicitly states that a good jihadist has to break with his tribal background and has to become a 'stranger', that is, somebody with no affiliation with any kind of previous community: 'Those who break off from their tribes. Ibn Mas'ūd (*radiyallāhu 'anhu*) said that the Prophet (*sallallāhu 'alayhi wa sallam*) said, "Verily Islam began as something strange, and it will return to being something strange as it first began, so glad tidings to the strangers." Someone asked, "Who are the strangers?" He said, "Those who break off from their tribes", reported by Imām Ahmad, ad-Dārimī, and Ibn Mājah, with a sahīh isnād. So those who left their tribes—the best of Allah's slaves—rallied together with an imam and a jamā'ah upon the path of Ibrāhīm.'
3. The same ambivalence towards tribes is to be found among 'ideological' states, like the Baathist regimes in Iraq and Syria, or the communist regime in Afghanistan (1978–92). They officially rejected tribalism as opposed to the concept of 'nation' or 'people', but they never hesitated to play on the tribal 'grammar' to ensure state control. On Syria, see Khaddour and Mazur 2013; on Afghanistan, Roy 1990a.
4. On a very different ideological level, the way that in 1994 and 1996 pro-Taliban tribes were able to re-integrate their children who had been prominent communist cadres before the fall of the communist regime in 1992 is remarkable, and shows the resilience of tribal affiliations to ideological commitments. This is also valid for jihadists.

5. Independently of their ties to jihadist groups, there is an interesting approach to the transnational connections of Syrian tribes in Dukhan 2014.
6. McCants 2015: 898–903.

1. IRAQI TRIBES IN THE LAND OF JIHAD

1. Hosham Dawod is an anthropologist at the Institut Interdisciplinaire d'Anthropologie du Contemporain (IIAC/CNRS, Paris) and was director of the Institut Français du Proche-Orient (IFPO) until September 2014. His field is the Middle East, and more specifically Iraq and the Kurdish population. He has published numerous books and studies on ethnicity, tribalism, kinship and power in Iraq.
2. See Searle 2008: 62–6. Apart from providing data, the article mainly praises the merits and the knowhow of the US Special Forces in the tribal areas of Al-Anbar province.
3. Dawod 2012.
4. In some areas, it is possible to hear the term *qabila*, which Iraqis use to mean tribal confederation. The Iraqis also use the term *'asha'ir*, which means tribes in plural, to refer to a tribal confederation. The Shammar tribal confederation, for example, is called *'asha'ir shammar* and/or *qabilat shammar*. In other regions of the Middle East and North Africa, the term that is most used to refer to one *'ashira* is *qabila*. People in these regions similarly use the terms *fakhdh* and *hamula*.
5. As everywhere else, the same term can have different meanings in different areas. In southern Iraq, the term *hamula* means 'clan', whereas in central and north-west Iraq, the term used is *fakhdh*. We must take into account that we are not just dealing with the logic of terminological classification, because very often each *fakhdh* and each *hamula* has its own sheikh (leader). These are therefore tribal sub-units that have a significant social and political role to play. See Salim 1970, particularly ch. 5, 'The Lineage, Clan and Tribe'; Batatu 1978, especially ch. 6, 'The Shaykhs, Aghas and Peasants'; al-Wardi 1965, especially ch. 3 and 6.
6. Claude Lévi-Strauss makes a connection between Boa's analysis of the Kwakiutl house and European noble houses. By underlining the similarity between these institutions, he defined the house as 'a moral person holding a state made up of material and immaterial wealth which perpetuates itself through the transmission of its name down a real or imaginary line, considered legitimate as long as this continuing can express itself in the language of kinship or of affinity, and most often, of both', in Lévi-Strauss 1983, p. 174. See also Lévi-Strauss 1984, pp. 189–241; idem 1986: 1217–22; idem 1987: 34–7, a discussion

between Claude Lévi-Strauss and Pierre Lamaison. The later writings by Lévi-Strauss on the house [*maison*] have provoked a large number of colloquia, seminars, articles and other types of anthropological literature around the world: see, for example, Macdonald 1987; Carsten and Hugh-Jones 1995.

7. Eickelman 2017: 57–68.
8. To have a better understanding of what has become the Arab tribes, see Hammoudi 2017: 11–56.
9. On the segmentarist discourses and analysis, see particularly Middleton and Tait 1952; Gellner 1969; Hart 1981; Akbar and Hart 1984.
10. On nomadic culture in Iraq and the Mashriq countries in general, see al-Wardi 1972; Thahir 1986, especially ch. 2, pp. 203–39.
11. Dawod 2001, pp. 21–41.
12. See various seminars given by the great Ayatollah Mohammad Sadiq al-Sadr (several years before his assassination in 1999 by the Iraqi powers that be). These seminars were collected and printed in a pamphlet which was rapidly banned in Iraq and then secretly distributed: 'Al-Fiqh al-'ashari' (Tribal Jurisprudence).
13. Sakai 2003, pp. 136–61.
14. Baram Amatzia, a professor at the University of Haifa, advised the US troops to take the tribes into consideration: 'Such support could be extremely useful as coalition forces face growing agitation from a few influential radical Shiite clergy and daily armed attacks coming from Sunni Arab supporters of the Baath regime embittered by the loss of their privileges and hoping to bring Saddam back to power.' He emphasized the internal divisions of the various tribal groups that were exacerbated by summary executions of prominent members under Saddam: 'Members of these disgruntled sub-tribal groupings may prove invaluable to the United States in providing information about weapons of mass destruction, financial transactions, hide sites, or other regime activities.' See Baram 2003; and Baram 2001, pp. 301–29.
15. McCallister, Kyle, Alexander 2003, s.l., p. 1.
16. Ibid., p. 8.
17. Bazzi 2003: A05; Ciezadlo 2003: 1; Graham 2004: 37–49; Gilmore 2004; Harris 2004.
18. Pollack 2004.
19. Hashim 2006.
20. Media and specialists in the field saw the role that General Petraeus played in Iraq between 2006 and 2009 only as major, but far from unique. In the same period of time and during the implementation of the Surge Strategy, the number of American soldiers and officers in Iraq far exceeded 150,000, with a number of army units reporting to

specific chains of command. While the press focused on the actions of General Petraeus, since he was the commander of the Multi-National Force in Iraq, other generals who were no less prominent were doing silent work on the ground. Such was the case of Marine General John Allen, who was the Deputy Commanding General of Multi-National Forces West in Al-Anbar province between 2006 and 2008, before he was called to serve in Afghanistan and then returned to his country. Even when he was recalled by his government, he did not sever his ties with some tribal leaders in western Iraq. His nomination as Special Presidential Envoy for the Global Coalition against ISIL between September 2014 and October 2015 certainly came as a result of his military experience on the ground and also of his relations with local tribal actors.

21. Kilcullen 2009; Kilcullen 2006: 103–8.
22. McFate 2005a; McFate 2005b: 42–8.
23. Gonzales and Price 2007; Gonzales 2005; Gusterson 2007: 155–75; Ricks 2006; Assayag 2008: 135–68; Dawod 2011; Sahlins 2011.
24. Iraq's 'tribal awakening' movement, or *sahwa*, was established by tribal leaders in Al-Anbar province from 2005 to fight al-Qaeda in Iraq in direct collaboration with the American military and Iraqi security forces. In fact, the tribes viewed al-Qaeda as an element of destabilization. After the implementation of the Surge strategy and the disarmament of Shiite militias between 2006 and 2008, the *sahwa* was maintained in northern and western Iraq and undertook civilian and surveillance militia tasks. Amounting to some 100,000 members in 2008, the majority were integrated into the Iraqi armed forces and the rest employed as security personnel deployed especially in Sunni areas. However, the former PM Nouri Al Maliki's government years (2006–14) witnessed a twofold development: on the one hand, the *sahwa* was weakened until it eventually ended; on the other hand, what remained of it was politicized and put to the service of the government. The increasingly confession-sensitive army, in addition to sectarian tensions, the alienation of Sunnis, and the aggressive rise of *Daesh* have deeply shaken the *sahwa* as an anti-jihad power.
25. Department of Defense 2007.
26. Klein 2007.
27. Numerous testimonies of abuse against tribes that cooperated with US troops have been reported by the media. See for instance Graff 2007.
28. These are the same experts who call for the promotion of tribalization of political relations in the whole Middle East region, such as Amatzia Baram: "Provided it maintains a solid cadre of specialists in tribal affairs, the central government in Baghdad has a good chance of

being able to use the tribal system to increase social stability in rural areas and keep the country in one piece. By contrast, an attempt to ignore the tribes or dismantle the tribal system would be destabilizing and could even increase the chances of armed conflict.' Baram 2003.

29. See Eisenstadt 2007, a US Army Reserve Lt. Col.; and the account of Operation Alljah by Lt. Col. William F. Mullen, commander of the Marines 2nd Battalion, 6th Regiment: 'As for the awakening, that is more of a tribal thing. Tribes have little influence inside Fallujah because of how mixed up the population is', in 'Operation Alljah and the Marines of 2nd Battalion, 6th Regiment', *Captain's Journal* 2007a. See also 'The Special Forces Plan for Pakistan Mistaking the Anbar Narrative', *Captain's Journal* 2007b.
30. In Eisenstadt 2007.
31. Dawod 2013.
32. Khaddour and Mazur 2017.
33. *Oil Report*, classified documents in the researcher's possession, dated 26 May 2015.
34. Coker 2016.
35. Freeman 2016; Ellyatt 2016.
36. Mohammed 2016.
37. Dawod 2004.

2. *KTO KOVO?* TRIBES AND JIHAD IN PUSHTUN LANDS

1. Mike Martin is a former British Army officer who has worked, travelled and lived all over the world in order to try and understand conflict. His previous books include *A Brief History of Helmand*; *An Intimate War: An Oral History of the Helmand Conflict*; and *Crossing the Congo: Over Land and Water in a Hard Place*. He is a War Studies Visiting Research Fellow at King's College London.
2. Apart from a brief period of calm post-2001, Helmand has at all times since 1980 faced competition for the tribes' allegiance between different outside ideological players.
3. Oxford 2010.
4. Ibid.
5. Chimhundu 1992: 87–109.
6. Personal experience as a Pushtu-speaker who spent nearly two years in Helmand.
7. Ahmed 2013: 125.
8. Hopkins and Marsden 2012: 44.
9. Martin 2014: 128.

10. Gebrewold 2013: 131.
11. Abou El Fadl 2007: 221.
12. Peters 1979: 118.
13. http://www.bbc.co.uk/news/world-middle-east-27930414, accessed 7 November 2015.
14. Oxford 2010.
15. Qutb 1978: 31.
16. Lewis 1993: 4, 10.
17. Esposito 1998: 41, 179.
18. http://www.longwarjournal.org/archives/2015/08/ayman-al-zawahiri-importance-jihadist-media.php, accessed 7 November 2015.
19. http://www.presstv.com/Detail/2015/02/14/397545/Importance-of-unity-in-defeating-Israel, accessed 7 November 2015); Kepel 2006: 265.
20. Whilst the importance of Muslim unity is ubiquitous among jihadi groups, the definition of a 'Muslim' is not; for example, see ISIS targeting Shia Muslims in Iraq and Syria currently.
21. Heacock 2013.
22. http://www.atlanticcouncil.org/blogs/egyptsource/a-new-sinai-battle-bedouin-tribes-and-egypt-s-isis-affiliate, accessed 7 November 2015.
23. Lackner 2014: 19–25.
24. Shay 2010: 37.
25. Weiss and Hassan 2015: 200.
26. Ibid.: 68.
27. http://www.wsj.com/articles/saudi-officials-linked-to-jihadist-group-in-wikileaks-cables-1435529198, accessed 7 November 2015; Kepel 2006: 61–2.
28. http://robertreich.org/post/80522686347, accessed 7 November 2015.
29. Dawisha 2002: 282.
30. https://www.foreignaffairs.com/articles/2001–01–01/will-nation-state-survive-globalization, accessed 7 November 2015.
31. Immerman and Goedde 2013: 97.
32. Baram 1997: 1–31.
33. Weiss and Hassan 2015: 134.
34. Martin 2014: 73.
35. Grosby 1995: 1.
36. See, for example, Crawford 1979 for modern accounts of this old phenomenon.
37. Gat 2006: 50.
38. Human Rights Watch 1999.
39. For example, Collier and Hoeffler 2002.

40. Collier 2000: 91.
41. Collier 2000: 1.
42. Kaufman 2006: 45–6.
43. Kaufman 1996: 108.
44. Kalyvas 2006.
45. Kalyvas 2006: 10.
46. Kalyvas 2006: 365.
47. Kalyvas 2006: 376.
48. Kalyvas 2006: 364.
49. Ahmed-Ghosh 2003.
50. http://www.independent.co.uk/voices/isis-in-afghanistan-is-a-disaster-waiting-to-happen-10099198.html, accessed 7 November 2015.
51. Khan 1981: 33.
52. Martin, *An Intimate War*, pp. 25–6.
53. Ibid., p. 31.
54. David Edwards, *Before Taliban: Genealogies of the Afghan Jihad* (Oakland, CA: University of California Press, 2002), pp. 237–8.
55. Olivier Roy, *Islam and Resistance in Afghanistan* (Cambridge: Cambridge University Press, 1990), p. 114.
56. Victoria Schofield, *Afghan Frontier: Feuding and Fighting in Central Asia* (London: I. B. Tauris, 2003), pp. 336–9.
57. Farrell and Giustozzi 2013: 845–71.
58. 'Isis sparks turf war as it enters Helmand', *The Times*, 14 January 2015.
59. 'Musa Qala is small military victory for Taliban but big propaganda boost', *Guardian*, 27 August 2015.
60. See, for example, AfghaNews, *Provincial News*, vol. 8 (London, April 1990). (AfghaNews was Jamiat's official newsletter.)
61. Interviews with Hafizullah Khan and Malem Mir Wali, Kabul, 2012.
62. Interviews with ex-mujahidin and police commanders, Helmand, 2011.
63. Interviews with government officials, Helmand, 2011.
64. Interview with Noorzai tribal elder, Helmand, 2012.
65. Giustozzi and Ullah 2006: 5.
66. Edwards 2002: 235–76.
67. Interview with Malem Mir Wali, Kabul, 2012.
68. Interview with Sher Mohammad Akhundzada, Kabul, 2012.
69. Interview with ex-militia commander, Helmand, 2011.
70. Roy 1990b: 121.
71. Interview with former engineer on canal projects, Helmand, 2012.
72. Interview with ex-Khalqi police commander, Helmand, 2011.
73. Interview with ex-militia commander, Helmand, 2012.
74. Interview with Sher Mohammad Akhundzada, Kabul, 2012.
75. Interviews with tribal leaders, Helmand, 2012.

76. Giustozzi and Ullah 2006.
77. Martin 2014: 85.
78. Scott 2008: 6.
79. Interview with tribal leader, Helmand, 2012.
80. Interviews with ex-mujahidin commanders, Helmand, 2011–12.
81. Interview with professional, Helmand, 2012.
82. Interview with Noorzai tribal leader, Helmand, 2012.
83. Interview with ex-Hizb commander, Helmand, 2011.
84. Interview with ex-Harakat commander, Helmand, 2012.
85. Interview with tribal leader, Helmand, 2011.
86. Interview with Kharoti commander, Helmand, 2011.
87. Giustozzi 2000: 266.
88. Interview with Jabbar Qahraman, Kabul, 2012.
89. Multiple interviews with ex-mujahidin commanders, militia commanders and Helmandi notables, 2011–12.
90. Interview with mujahidin commander, Helmand, 2010.
91. The so-called 'negative symmetry', where both sides agreed to reduce their financial support of elements fighting in the conflict.
92. Giustozzi and Ullah 2006.
93. Interview with senior Barakzai tribal leader, Helmand, 2011.
94. Davis 1998: 51.
95. Interview with Alizai elder, Helmand, 2012.
96. Nojumi 2002: 135.
97. Interviews with tribal elders, Helmand, 2011–12.
98. Martin 2014: 78.
99. Interview with Baluch elder, Helmand, 2012.
10. Interview with militia commander, Helmand, 2011.
101. Interview with ex-mujahidin commander, Helmand, 2011.
102. Interview with ex-mujahidin commander, Helmand, 2012.
103. Martin 2014: 108.
104. Martin 2014: 125.
105. Farrell and Giustozzi 2013: 845–71.
106. Interviews with Taliban commanders, Helmand, 2012.
107. Personal experience as a British military officer in Afghanistan, 2008.
108. http://www.bbc.co.uk/history/events/nato_increases_the_number_of_troops_in_afghanistan, accessed 7 November 2015.
109. Martin 2014: 195–231.
110. Coghlan 2009: 143.
111. Interviews with Taliban commanders, Helmand, 2012.
112. Interviews with Taliban commanders, Helmand, 2012.
113. Personal communication, Claudio Franco, 2012.
114. Clark 2011: 15–16.

115. 'Funds for Taliban Largely Come from Abroad: Holbrooke', *Dawn*, 28 July 2010.
116. Interviews with Taliban commanders, Helmand, 2012.
117. Martin 2011: 13.
118. Interviews with Taliban commanders, Helmand, 2012.
119. Interviews with Taliban commanders, Helmand, 2012.
120. Martin 2014: 249.
121. http://www.bbc.co.uk/news/world-asia-31290147, accessed 7 November 2015.
122. Telephone interviews with Helmandi notables, 2015.
123. http://www.theguardian.com/world/2015/oct/20/taliban-threaten-southern-afghan-city-of-lashkar-gah, accessed 7 November 2015.
124. Graeme Wood, 'What ISIS really wants', http://www.theatlantic.com/magazine/archive/2015/03/what-isis-really-wants/384980/, accessed 7 November 2015.

3. TRIBES AND POLITICAL ISLAM IN THE BORDERLAND BETWEEN EGYPT AND LIBYA: A (TRANS-) LOCAL PERSPECTIVE

1. Thomas Hüsken is a senior research fellow at the department for ethnology of the University of Bayreuth. His main fields of research are political anthropology, with a particular focus on non-state forms of power and the anthropology of development. In particular, he has studied the economy of the *Awlad 'Ali* Bedouin in the Egyptian–Libyan borderland. From the beginning of the Libyan revolution in 2011, Thomas conducted several months of fieldwork in Libya (2011, 2012, 2013, 2014). His most recent work deals with the interlacing of state and non-state forms of political organization and conceptions of order in the Egyptian–Libyan borderland.
2. In 2011, the former German Agency for Technical Cooperation (GTZ) merged with the German Development Service (DED) and the society for International Education and Development (InWent) into the German Agency for International Cooperation.
3. Hüsken and Roenpage 1998.
4. Hüsken and Roenpage 1998: 56ff.
5. Abd Al-Malik, Al-Qasr, June 1994.
6. Miftah Riziq, Ramadan 1994.
7. Dawod 2015; Hüsken and Klute 2015.
8. Evans-Pritchard 1949; Gellner 1969; Assad 1970.
9. Cole 2003: 235.
19. See Abu-Lughod 1989: 280ff.

11. Abu Lughod 1989; Dresch 1989; Eickelman 1989; Dawod 2004; Hüsken 2009; Marx 2014; Prager 2014.
12. Barth 1969; Elwert 1997.
13. I refer to Hobsbawm and Ranger's (1983) notion of invented traditions to make a clear statement against essentialist or primordial understandings of the tribe.
14. Dawod 2015: 1.
15. See Dawod (2015) on Sunni tribes in Iraq.
16. Schielke 2010: 1.
17. Asad 1986.
18. Roy 1999. A broader discussion of the historical genesis of Islamism is not part of this chapter.
19. Hüsken and Roenpage 1998: 36.
20. The Arabic term *watan* can be translated as nation, territory or homeland. In the usage of the *Awlad 'Ali*, it stands for tribal territory. In practice, the *watan* of the *Awlad 'Ali* is subdivided into territories that belong to sub-tribes and clans according to the segmentary lineage system of *Awlad 'Ali* society. Thus, the *Awlad 'Ali* would not speak of the *watan* of the *Awlad 'Ali* but only of the *watan* of a given sub-tribe/clan. In the days of pastoral nomadism up to the 1940s, the *watan* was never an entirely demarcated unit. The *watan* could shift in size and place due to social, political and economic relations and also because of conflict between different tribes. Just 200 years ago, the *watan* of the *Awlad 'Ali* was almost entirely located in the west of the Libyan Cyrenaica, when intertribal conflicts—mainly with the *Obaidat* tribe—forced them to move east into Egypt.
21. Although the *Awlad 'Ali* are only a small minority among the autochthonous oasis population and other groups, their role as traders and tenants of land and pasture has a long history. See Rusch and Stein 1988.
22. These numbers are rough estimations given by my key informants and the governorate administration in Marsa Matrouh in 2011. The official numbers of the Egyptian census speak of 400,000 inhabitants in the entire governorate of Matrouh (http://www.capmas.gov.eg). Some *Awlad 'Ali* politicians claim that there are more than 5 million *Awlad 'Ali* residing in Egypt. Abdelsatar Hetita (belonging to the *Awlad 'Ali*), a journalist from the newspaper *Al-Sharq Al-Awsat*, stated at a conference in Florence in 2014 that there were around 10 million *Awlad 'Ali* in Egypt. In any case, with below 3 per cent of the total population, tribal groups are a small minority in Egypt.
23. For a more detailed account of the process of sedentarization, see Hüsken and Roenpage 1998: 29ff.

24. Administratively, Matrouh governorate is divided into eight districts or centres. Each of them is known as a Markaz. These are, from east to west: El-Hammam, Al Alamein, El-Dabaa, Matrouh, Siwa, El Negeela, Sidi Barani and El-Salloum. The governorate comprises eight cities, forty-three villages and 182 sub-villages.
25. As in the case of Egypt, these numbers are only rough estimations based on the information given by key informants and local politicians.
26. The *Obaidat* are the leading tribe in the eastern part of Cyrenaica. Several men from the *Obaidat* have been part of the Libyan political establishment, before, during and after Qaddafi. Well-known figures are Fatah Junis Obaidi, minister under Qaddafi and leading general of the revolutionary forces, and Suleiman Mahmud Obeidi, one of the young officers in the days of Qaddafi's revolution, later general of the Libyan border troops in Tobruk and the first general to defect from Qaddafi in favour of the revolution in 2011.
27. See Marx 2014.
28. Hüsken and Klute 2015.
29. Hüsken 2009, 2013.
30. Cole and Altorki 1998.
31. Hüsken 2016.
32. Hüsken 2009: 119f.
33. I have no exact information about the number of preachers who are active in the borderland. According to my personal observation and the information from my informants, Salafist preachers practise in almost every larger settlement or city such as Marsa Matrouh, Sidi Barani, Al-Alamein, Saloum and Tobruk. Beside my studies of the two preachers and their followers, I have conducted fifteen semi-structured interviews with key informants in Marsa Matrouh, Al-Hamam, Sidi Barani, Tobruk and Benghazi. These key informants are tribal politicians, Islamic and Christian religious leaders (like the head of the Coptic community in Marsa Matrouh and leading members of a Sufi *Tariqa*) but also businessmen, military personnel, political activists and one Libyan colleague. In addition, I have a corpus of information that derives from numerous conversations and discussions about the issue with friends and hosts, like that with my mentor Abd Al-Malik mentioned above. All the names of people are changed in order to ensure their anonymity.
34. I met Sheikh Mohammad on a regular basis (usually every ten days) during my field studies on tribal politics in the borderland of Egypt and Libya (2007–13). After the riots against the Copts in Marsa Matrouh in 2010 (in which Sheikh Mohammad played a prominent role as agitator and inflamer) he refused to see me again. Members

of the mosque also started to turn down my requests for meetings, criticized my presence in the region and publicly accused me of being an Israeli spy.

35. Roy 1999.
36. The portrait is based on three biographical interviews I conducted with Osman in 2009. In addition, I conducted participant observation among Osman's followers (including group discussions and interviews) in 2009, 2010 and 2011. During the revolutions in Egypt and particularly in Libya, Osman became prominent as an organizer of food and medical supplies from Egypt to Libya, which I personally accompanied. From late 2011, when Osman intensified his cooperation with the radical Libyan Islamist camp, Sheikh Osman refused to see me again.
37. Pargeter 2008.
38. Hüsken 2009.
39. Hüsken 2009: 120f.
40. Cole and Altorki 1998: 199ff.
41. Roughly 10–20 per cent of the population of Marsa Matrouh originate from the Nile valley.
42. Hourani 1992.
43. Hüsken 2013.
44. Bayat 2010: 192.
45. Hüsken 2013.
46. Since I also fall under the restrictions of gender segregation, my research here is quite limited. I have only two female conversational partners among the *Awlad 'Ali* with whom I can address these issues openly. A female researcher would have much better access and I can only hope that a female anthropologist will soon come to work in this very interesting field.
47. Apt 2011: 2f.
48. Hüsken 2009, 2013, 2015.
49. The *Senussia* order (1837–1969) in which the *Awlad 'Ali* were integrated has almost entirely disappeared from the collective memory or is considered 'un-Islamic'. Although many places and settlements in the borderland carry the prefix *Zawiya* (endowment of the *Senussia* order), people have little knowledge about their own historical legacy or express reservations about the *Senussia* order.
50. *Sharia* (Islamic law) defines and protects the status of Christians and Jews as *Ahl al-Kitab* (people of the book) or *Ahl al-Dhima* (protected people).
51. At the same time, these radical Islamic groups feel little reservation when it comes to illegal activities (such as the smuggling of arms) for the benefit of their fellows in Libya.

52. Benda-Beckmann 1994.
53. '*Urf* literally means 'tradition', or more specifically 'the way things have been done'.
54. Ibid.
55. Pre-Islamic customary laws in the Middle East were gradually integrated into the emerging corpus of Islamic law or continued to coexist with *sharia*. It is therefore not surprising that both systems share basic elements of legal procedure and judgement (see Kraus 2004: 256ff.).
56. Hüsken 2013: 222f.
57. According to Father Bejemy (the local bishop), between 1,500 and 2,000 Copts live in Marsa Matrouh.
58. http://www.asianews.it/news-en/Crowd-of-3-thousand-Muslims-attack-a-Coptic-Christian-community,-25-injured-17876.html;http://www.churchinchains.ie/node/320; http://www.deseretnews.com/article/700016283/Muslims-attack-Coptic-Christians-in-northern-Egypt.html?pg=all
59. Land is becoming a scarce resource because of intensive construction in the tourism sector, and most Bedouin do not hold official land right titles.
60. Hüsken 2013.
61. Sheikh 'Aissa, Saloum, 23 March 2011.
62. I personally observed these transports during my fieldwork in 2011.
63. In 2011, I crossed the border between *Saloum* (Egypt) and *Amsa'ad* (Libya) several times without being checked by official border personnel or customs.
64. From that time on, research participant observations among these actors became impossible for me (see footnote 194) and my information is based on interviews with informants from Tobruk, Derna and Benghazi via social media.
65. Lacher 2015a: 33f; Fitzgerald 2015.
66. Hüsken 2013: 225f., Lacher 2015b.
67. Intermediary elites are positioned between the state and local populations (Klute, von Trotha 2004).
68. Both offices were introduced by the Egyptian state but subsequently appropriated by the *Awlad 'Ali* (see Hüsken and Roenpage 1998: 85f.).
69. Abu-Lughod 1989: 287.

4. SUFI JIHAD AND SALAFI JIHADISM IN EGYPT'S SINAI: TRIBAL GENERATIONAL CONFLICT

1. Abu Haniyeh and Abu Rumman 2015.

2. Interview with Belal Fadl, 2015.
3. Shoqeir 1916.
4. Al-Banna 1999.
5. El-Sherif.
6. Noaman and El-Sherif.
7. Interview with a mujahid, 2011.
8. Salman 2014.
9. Ibid.
10. El-Bolok and Khaled 2012.
11. Salman 2014.
12. Ibid.
13. King 2007.
14. Salman 2014.
15. Khalaf 2013.
16. Interviews with the leading domestic representative of the Palestinian community in Al-Arish, 2013–14.
17. El-Bolok and Khaled 2012.
18. Interview with a former MB leader in Al-Arish, 2013.
19. Meharram 2013.
20. Interview with a local expert on Islamist groups, 2013.
21. Group interview with local activists in Sheikh Zuwaiyyed, as part of the uncompleted project on documenting the Egyptian Revolution, Arab Centre for Research Policy Studies, 2011.
22. Alexandrani 2013, 2014.
23. Alexandrani 2015.
24. Nasser's digital archive.
25. Heggi 2014.
26. Interview with a veteran conscript, 2015.
27. Alexandrani 2013.

5. THE GLOBAL AND THE LOCAL: AL-QAEDA AND YEMEN'S TRIBES

1. Marieke Brandt is a researcher at the Institute for Social Anthropology (ISA) of the Austrian Academy of Sciences in Vienna. Her research focuses on tribalism, tribal genealogy and history, and tribe–state relations in south-west Arabia. She is the author of *Tribes and Politics in Yemen* (2017), and wishes to thank Marie-Christine Heinze and Mareike Transfeld for comments on the manuscript draft.
2. This approach has been elaborated by Eickelman (2002), Eickelman and Piscatori (2004) and Al-Rasheed (2007).
3. For a summary of this discussion, see Gingrich 2015.

4. For a comparative overview of different models of tribal leadership among two main Yemeni tribal confederations, see Brandt 2014.
5. See, for example, Mundy 1995.
6. For further details on the history of Zaydism and the growth of Zaydi thought, law and doctrine, see the studies by van Arendonk 1960, Madelung 1965 and vom Bruck 2005.
7. Serjeant 1969: 285.
8. For an elaboration of al-Shawkānī's intellectual biography, see Haykel 2003.
9. Vom Bruck 2010: 187; Haykel 2003: 226.
10. Various authors provide information on Muqbil al-Wādiʿī. See, for example, Burgat and Sbitli 2002; Haykel 2002; Bonnefoy 2011 *passim*. On the Salafi movement in Yemen, see Dresch and Haykel 1995: 413; Haykel 2002; Burgat and Sbitli 2002; Bonnefoy 2011.
11. Weir 1997 and 2007: 296–303; vom Bruck 2005: 131–5, 145–62.
12. On the Ḥūthī conflict and the Ṣaʿdah wars, see, for example, International Crisis Group 2009; Hamidi 2009; Salmoni et al. 2010, and Brandt 2016.
13. See, for example, Wedeen 2008: 198; Johnsen 2013 *passim*.
14. Bonnefoy 2011: 256–7.
15. Phillips 2011: 42–3.
16. Phillips 2011. For a similar approach, see Wedeen 2008: 148–85.
17. ʿAṭwān 1996.
18. Author's interviews with members of the Hamdān al-Jawf and Wāʾilah tribes.
19. See also Weir 2007: 112–20.
20. See Dresch 1989: 312.
21. Selznick 1949: 13–15.
22. For details of the Saudi influence among Yemen's borderland tribes, see Brandt 2016.
23. Cited in Loidolt 2011: 111.
24. On marriage relations between tribes and AQAP members, see Johnsen 2009; Levinson and Coker 2010.
25. Loidolt 2011. *Qabyalah* ('tribalness') is a system of ethical values, a set of value-laden ideal characteristics of the tribesman connoting honour, courage, pride and protection of the weak. See Adra 1982: 139–58.
26. Bonnefoy 2011: 273–8.
27. In 2009, locals estimated the number of jihadis in the Kitāf camp at several hundred (author's interview).
28. Unlike Muḥammad b. Shājiaʿ, these families and persons have not been mentioned previously in the literature or the press. Since the disclo-

sure of personal names may endanger these persons and their families, this study refrains from publication of their full names.

29. Miller and Gerth 2001.
30. In June 2009 nine foreigners (seven Germans, a Briton and a South Korean) disappeared in Ṣaʿdah province. See *Wikileaks*, 24 June 2009. In January 2010, the kidnappers demanded the release of several prisoners affiliated to al-Qaeda. See *Der Spiegel*, 16 January 2010.
31. See, for example, Bergen 2001: 173.
32. Interview with a sheikh from north-east Yemen who worked for the National Security Apparatus (*amn qawmī*).
33. Gochenour 1984: 326.
34. International Crisis Group 2013: 12.
35. For an overview of Yemen's stalled transition process, see Lackner 2016; Heinze 2016.
36. On the complex relationship between AQAP, tribal militias and the army, see Cigar 2014.
37. Zimmerman 2015a; 2015b: 24–5.
38. CTC 2011: 16.
39. Kendall 2016a.
40. Cigar 2014: 34.
41. Kendall 2015.
42. Cigar 2014: 38–9.
43. Kendall 2016a.
44. Basil and Shoichet 2013.
45. Salisbury and Mohsen 2015; Zimmerman 2015a; Kendall 2016a.
46. Kendall 2016b.
47. Zimmerman 2015c.
48. Kendall 2016b.
49. Augustin 2015: 13–14.
50. Zimmerman and Diamond 2016.
51. Kendall 2016b.
52. See, for example, Weir 2007: 49–51.
53. Zimmerman 2015c; Kendall 2016b.

6. BETWEEN THE 'KANURI' AND OTHERS: GIVING A FACE TO A JIHAD WITH NEITHER BORDERS NOR TRIBES IN THE LAKE CHAD BASIN

1. Claude Mbowou is a research fellow at Paris 1 Panthéon Sorbonne in a research program focusing on civil wars. His PhD research in political science focused on the transnational diffusion of the Islamist insurgency in the Lake Chad basin through numerous field surveys between

the far-north of Cameroon, north-east of Nigeria and south of Chad. This chapter was translated from French by Eleonora Narbone.

2. Renart and Garçon 2014; Higazi 2015; Higazi 2013: 137–64.
3. On the role of populations and information exchange in civil war mobilizations, see Kalyvas 2006.
4. Durkheim 1893, 1986.
5. Goffman 1986.
6. As it happens, the idea that this rapid spread is due to cultural and linguistic continuities between Borno, Nigeria, northern Cameroon, Chad and Niger also tends to support the idea of community solidarity. Thus, the International Crisis Group's report points to a cultural-linguistic continuity between the Kanuri of Borno state, Nigeria and the Kanuri of Mayo-Sava and Mayo-Tsanaga departments in Cameroon. The current leader of Boko Haram, Abubakar Shekau, is himself Kanuri. These sociological factors facilitate the covert penetration of Boko Haram elements into this part of Cameroon. International Crisis Group 2014: 8.
7. The Kanuri people of today are descended from an ethnic entity whose historic territory was close to Lake Chad: in Borno and Yobe states in Nigeria, as well as in Niger, Chad and northern Cameroon, where they are largely resident in the Mandara mountains region, in Mayo-Sava department. On the evidence, they number around 2 million across these countries. The Kanuri are known for being deeply rooted in a mix of Islam and traditional culture that strongly shapes their identity. They were the architects of the Kanem-Bornu Empire's power; dominant from the seventh to the nineteenth century (1893), this empire covered present-day Nigeria's north-east, Cameroon's Extreme North Region and north-west Chad. See Hiribarren 2017.
8. See Ousmane 2015.
9. This has been amply illustrated by, for instance, the August 2014 attack in Kolofata, in which hundreds of armed men attacked Deputy Prime Minister Amadou Ali's villa, kidnapping his wife and sixteen others as well as the Lamido (local sultan) and members of his family; and by many other murders and assaults in the neighbourhood, which have continued to multiply.
10. Through participation in hostage rescues, information exchange with the military and civil authorities, and appeals for the community to be included in the village vigilance committees.
11. Interviews with former Cameroonian hostages, Karena and Bargaram villages, July 2014.
12. A few figures on Cameroon: total population (2012): 20,386,799; rural population as a percentage of the total: 51 per cent; population

density: 37.5 inhabitants per sq km; Human Development Index (HDI) ranking (2012): 0.495, 19th in Africa; poverty rate: 39 per cent; primary education rate (2011): 77 per cent, 12th in Africa. Compare these with the figures for Extreme North Region: total population (2005): 3,111,792, or 19 per cent of the national population, making it the most populous region, and the youngest (51 per cent under 15); rural population: 77%; population density: 90.8 inhabitants per sq km; poverty rate: 65%; primary education rate (2011): 47 per cent.

13. During a mini-summit in Paris on Nigerian security, attended by the French, Cameroonian, Nigerian and Chadian heads of state.
14. It is true that there were many more symbolically charged and publicized assassinations, attacks and particularly kidnappings of Westerners in Cameroon before 2014 (notably of the Moulin-Fournier family in February 2013 and of Father Georges Vandenbeusch at Nguetchewe on 13 November 2013; he was freed on 1 January 2014). However, it was the attack on Fotokol on 2 March 2014 that really sounded the first alarm bells and tipped the strategic scales, creating the conditions that led Cameroon to declare war in May 2014.
15. Dobry (2009) refers to brutal transformations that engender situation-specific logics, which in turn constrain actors' perceptions, calculations and tactics.
16. Interviews with families of the displaced, Mora, June 2015.
17. In Rousseau's sense of this notion, based on a contractual conception of the State. See Bourdieu 2012: 541.
18. About Cameroonian nationalism, read Joseph 1977; Mbembe 1996.
19. From *al-Hajj* (pilgrimage) in Arabic, meaning 'one who has completed the pilgrimage'. This title ultimately supports the conflation of the two registers: the religious and the socially prosperous.
20. Over the last ten years, many schools with reduced numbers of classes have been built in this region with European funds. But, for the most part, they have never been or are no longer used, to the extent that some of these buildings are already in ruins.
21. That is, the state's capacity to transform society profoundly, irrespective of classic variables like development of a centralized administration. See King and Le Galès 2011: 453–80; or, for more detail, Mann 1986: 113, who defines infrastructural power as 'the capacity of the State actually to penetrate civil society, and to implement logistically political decisions throughout the realms'.
22. On the border dispute surrounding Darak Island in Lake Chad, see Halirou 2008.
23. In the whole of the Extreme North Region, scarcely 2 per cent of the road network had been tarmacked (667 of 30,616 kilometres in

total). Most of the little that was resurfaced has now completely deteriorated, as a result of negligence and war.

24. Official figures suggest 0.5 civil registration centres per 1,000 inhabitants in Cameroon's Extreme North Region. There is no available data on the current number of centres that are actually operational.
25. Whereby third-party witnesses guarantee the applicant's declaration of identity.
26. Normally, while the applicant waits for a national ID card to be produced and provided by the central police administration, a receipt is sent directly to them by the local identification office, to last for a maximum of one year.
27. This loan is ideally repaid upon payment for the cotton, with an interest rate of up to 10 per cent, or with interest calculated on the basis of the cotton's sale price.
28. About this notion, read Thompson 1971: 76–136; Lonsdale 1992: 265–504; Siméant 2010: 142–60.
29. Interviews, Mora and Hilé, Makari, July–August 2014.
30. Interviews and personal observations, Magala Kébir, August 2014.
31. Depending on global market fluctuations, prices in Nigeria could vary from 300 to 2,000 CFA francs, whereas the state offered a fixed price. On the cotton agro-industry, its crisis and the mobilization of peasant work in Cameroon, see Vadot 2014: 45–67; and Liba'a 2014: 426.
32. Equivalent to hamlet and district chiefs in the traditional sense.
33. Liba'a (2014: 335) reports that, for example in the village of Mesteuk, the inspection commission comprising the brigade commander and representatives of the Company was able neither to seize the cotton nor to influence the Nigerians, because the latter had the people's support.
34. Interview, August 2012.
35. 2,000 CFA francs (€3) a day at the locality checkpoints, and 24,0000 CFA francs (€38) of gas money a month for those teams given motorbikes.
36. Around 30 euro cents.
37. Interview, August 2014.
37. Interview, August 2014. In one example of such pressures, the chief of Roua village (Mayo-Tsanaga) reportedly declared, 'He who dares to sell his cotton in Nigeria absolutely must leave the village, because we are nothing without the Cameroonian Cotton Company.' Interview, 10 May 2012, by B. Djoda and M. Doudou, in 'Mutation de la filière cotonnière et commercialisation clandestine du coton graine vers le Nigeria dans le secteur SODECOTON de Mokolo: cas de la zone SODECOTON de Roua'. Dissertation for DIPES II (Diplôme de professeur de l'enseignement secondaire général deuxième grade),

Geography Department, Ecole normale supérieure of Maroua University. Cited in Liba'a 2014: 336.

39. Fieldwork observations, February–May 2013, border areas; interviews and observations, July 2014. The banning of motorbike travel and the limitations of travel on the Amchide–Mora road were concrete measures that would go beyond any previously announced security precautions. See Comolli 2015: 87–91.
40. Arms from Libya, Sudan or raids on the Chadian stocks pass through Logone and Chari departments and very often enter Nigeria through Fotokol village, or further south through Amchide. Between January and April 2014, eight Boko Haram weapons caches were discovered in Fotokol, Kousséri, Goulfey, Makari and Mokolo. See 'Cameroun—Extrême-nord: l'armée saisit 300 kalachnikov à Goulfey', *Repères*, 2 April 2014; *Daily Independent*, 2 April 2014; and 'Cameroun—Extrême-nord: une cache d'arme de Boko Haram découverte dans le Logone et Chari', Cameroon-info.net, 28 March 2014.
41. This abduction was described by the insurgents as retaliation against the French military action in Mali a few weeks earlier. See Gambrell 2013.
42. Cameroon's deputy prime minister, Amadou Ali, who is of Kanuri ethnicity, personally led these negotiations.
43. On that dispute, see Olinga 2009.
44. Interviews with the civil and judiciary authorities of Kousséri and N'Djamena, November 2011.
45. Rumours were spreading that the Cameroonian government had paid 3 billion CFA francs on behalf of the French state in exchange for the hostages' liberation, though France has always opposed financial negotiation with Boko Haram.
46. Interviews, Tckakamari and Doublé, July 2014.
47. Speech by the Senior Divisional Officer at a meeting with Makari village chiefs, August 2014.
48. Interviews, Doublé, August 2014.
49. On the military intervention in these villages, see Amnesty International 2015: 41.
50. 'The politics of the belly' is a translation of the French term *la politique du ventre*, popularized by Bayart 1993.

7. SIRTE'S TRIBES UNDER THE ISLAMIC STATE: FROM CIVIL WAR TO GLOBAL JIHADISM

1. It has up to one million members established across the country, notably in Sirte, Sebha and Benghazi.
2. Baghni 1996: 66.

3. Hamida 1994: 51–3.
4. The Qaddadfa notably played a key role in the regime's security brigades, which constituted the real core of the security apparatus. They gave birth to several generations of military leaders, including Qaddafi himself, Hassan Ashkal, Omar Askhal, Khalifa Hanish, Messaoud Abdelhafid, Said Aouidet, Ahmed and Sayid Qaddaf al-Dam, Mu'amar Qaddafi's sons.
5. Ouannes 2009: 186–7.
6. Ouannes 2009: 198–202.
7. In the nineteenth century, to confront the *suff al-fugi*, the Ottoman state rallied the *suff* of the coast, al-Bahar. *Suff al-Bahar* included most of the population of the coastal *makhzani* towns of Khums, Zlitan, Misrata, Tajura; the tribes of Awlad Salim, Hussun, Abadlla, Ma'dan, Firjan, Magarha of Fezzan tribesmen; and the populations of Sukna and Zella.
8. Administrative divisions were also largely drawn along tribal lines, and influence was mainly linked to the ownership of land. In the smaller towns surrounding Sirte, for instance, Nawfaliya was mostly inhabited by members of the Magharba tribe (whose centre is in Ajdabiya), Harawa by members of the Awlad Sleiman tribe, Al-Wadi al-Ahmar by al-Zayayna, while Ben Jawad and Ras Lanuf were rather a mix of several tribes, like central Sirte.
9. According to the UN Office for the Coordination of Humanitarian Affairs, by the end of October 2011 an estimated 80,000 people had fled from Bani Walid and Sirte, many of them to areas around Tripoli, Misrata and Benghazi. The International Medical Corps (IMC) reported that some 10,000 people from Sirte city centre had taken refuge on the outskirts of the city.
10. Residents of the town of Bani Walid and members of the Warfalla tribe shared the same fate in western Libya.
11. Author's interview, local activist who took part in Abu Haliqa's efforts to organize this 'coordination meeting', January 2017.
12. Pargeter 2008: 93–4.
13. Abu Salim prison was infamous as a high security prison, filled with scores of political prisoners and Islamists, where inmates suffered mistreatment and abuse.
14. Lacroix 2011. After the outbreak of the 2011 uprising, Sheikh Madkhali issued a directive urging his followers to support the insurgency. Many of them remained loyal to the regime or stayed on the sidelines.
15. Two figures from the Libyan Amazigh community, in particular, played a key role in this strategy of 'nationalization' of the Salafist *madkhali* school: Majdi Hafallah, from the city of Yefren, and Muhammad Abu

Sawa, from Nalut. Author's interview with Amazigh activist familiar with Islamist militancy in western Libya, January 2017.
16. Author's interviews with observers from Misrata and Ben Jawad who conducted interviews with relatives of some of the jihadists who went to Iraq at the time, January 2017.
17. Lacher 2015a.
18. Author's interview with local observer from Misrata, December 2016.
19. Collombier and Trabelsi 2016.
20. Zelin 2012.
21. Zelin 2015.
22. Author's interview, local observer from Misrata, December 2016.
23. Author's interview, local observer from Ben Jawad, January 2017.
24. Fitzgerald 2016; Zelin 2015.
25. Al-Maqdisi is considered the spiritual mentor of the al-Qaeda leader in Iraq, Abu Musab al-Zarqawi.
26. Radio Tawhid was established by young people from Sirte, before it was seized by the military council and placed under the control of the city's Supreme Security Council.
27. Author's interview, local observer from Ben Jawad, January 2017.
28. Author's interview, local activist from Ben Jawad, December 2016.
29. 'Misrata tatawwaq fitna ma'a sirt ba'd majzarat junud fi-l madina' (Misrata attempts to limit divisions with Sirte after the massacre of soldiers in the city), *Al-Hayat*, 27 December 2014, http://bit.ly/2qVXlJX
30. IS demanded that the residents of the town pledge allegiance to al-Baghdadi. Ghedan Saleh al-Nawfali, the initial leader of ASL in the city, refused and announced that he would leave the group. But other elements of ASL in Nawfaliya did pledge allegiance.
31. Author's interview, member of the Qaddadfa tribe from Sirte, January 2017.
32. Ibid.
33. Author's interview, local observer from Misrata, December 2015.
34. Author's interview, local activist from Ben Jawad, January 2017.
35. Author's interviews, local activist from Ben Jawad, January 2017; member of the Qaddadfa tribe from Sirte, January 2017.
36. In the neighbouring town of Harawa, essentially populated by members of the Awlad Sleiman tribe, local community leaders also remained isolated and lacked support from other communities or from the government. First, the Awlad Sleiman of Harawa were marginalized geographically. They shared borders in the east with the Zway and Magharba tribes, and in the west with the Warfalla tribe, all of these unwilling to enter into confrontation with any party. The Awlad

Sleiman also adopted an overall pro-revolutionary, pro-Misrata stance during the 2011 revolution, which had a negative impact on their relations with their immediate neighbours.

37. Author's interviews, local activist from Ben Jawad, January 2017.
38. According to Sirte city council, some 19,000 families fled after June 2015. Source: United Nations High Commission for Refugees, December 2016; author's interviews with local residents from Bani Walid, February 2016.
39. Accounts of the number of fatalities diverge, but some estimates mention up to thirty-eight people. See http://www.ohchr.org/EN/NewsEvents/Pages/DisplayNews.aspx?NewsID=16329&LangID=E
40. Wehrey 2016.
41. Markaz dirasat al-janub al-libi li-l-buhuth wa-l-tanmiya (Southern Libya Centre for Research and Development), 'Tanzim al-dawla fi-l-mintaqa al-gharbiya wa-l-janubiya: al-wujud... al-makhatar wa-l-dawr al-mustaqbali' (Islamic State in the western and southern regions: presence, dangers and future role), February 2016.

APPENDIX I

1. Mohammed 2016.
2. This chart was extracted from a video titled 'Nineveh tribes renew their allegiance to Al-Baghdadi' which ISIS broadcast in 2015.
3. Aljazeera.net: http://goo.gl/P4zkuE
4. Butun 'Ashirat Alnu'aim: http://www.alnoor.se/article.asp?id=229534
5. Ubada Trieb website: http://3badah.com/?page_id=25
6. 'New crime for ISIS against an entire village; mass executions of the village's men and children at Alhud village'. *Mosul Eye*, 1 January 2016, https://www.facebook.com/552514844870022/photos/a.552572524864254.1073741828.552514844870022/839974049457432/?type=3&theater
7. An-Nassabun: http://www.alnssabon.com/t25313.html
8. 'Mobilization of a number of Nainawa tribes south of Mosul, leading to fluster of ISIL'. *Mosul Eye*, 3 February 2016, https://www.facebook.com/permalink.php?story_fbid=856257084495795&id=552514844870022
9. An-Nassabun: http://www.alnssabon.com/t25313.html
10. Zubaid tribe website: http://goo.gl/vte3tl
11. *Buratha News*: http://burathanews.com/news/285233.htm. Alkhalij: http://www.alkhaleej.ae/alkhaleej/page/b4d5b00a-827b-4cf0-82f5-d100bd95383e

APPENDIX II: JIHADIST GROUPS ASSASSINATING TRIBAL LEADERS IN SUNNI AREA SINCE 2006

1. *alhayat*: http://goo.gl/S7tKb

BIBLIOGRAPHY

Abdul-Jabar, Faleh and Dawod, Hosham (eds), 2004. *Tribes and Power, Nationalism and Ethnicity in the Middle East*. London: Saqi Books.

Abou El Fadl, Khaled, 2007. *The Great Theft: Wrestling Islam from the extremists*. London: HarperCollins.

Abu-Lughod, Lila, 1989. 'Zones of Theory in the Anthropology of the Arab World', *Annual Review of Anthropology*, vol. 18: 267–306.

Abu Hanieh, Hassan and Abu Rumman, Mohammad, 2015. *The "Islamic State" Organization: The Sunni Crisis and the Struggle of Global Jihadism*. Amman: Friedrich-Ebert-Stiftung Jordan & Iraq.

Adra, Najwa, 1982. 'Qabyala: The Tribal Concept in the Central Highlands of the Yemen Arab Republic', PhD thesis, Temple University, Philadelphia.

Ahmed, Safdar, 2013. *Reform and Modernity in Islam: The Philosophical, Cultural and Political Discourses Among Muslim Reformers*. London: I. B. Tauris.

Ahmed-Ghosh, Huma, 2003. 'History of Women in Afghanistan: Lessons Learnt for the Future or Yesterdays and Tomorrow: Women in Afghanistan', *Journal of International Women's Studies*, vol. 4.

Akbar, S. and Hart, D. (eds), 1984. *Islam in Tribal Societies. From the Atlas to the Indus*. London: Routledge & Kegan Paul.

Alexandrani, Ismail, 2011. 'Citizenship in Neo-Islamism and Post-Islamism'. Conference on Islam, Citizenship and New Media. Cairo: Netherlands-Flemish Institute.

———, 2014a. 'Sinai's undeclared war', http://mondediplo.com/2014/09/05sinai

———, 2014b. 'The War in Sinai: A Battle against Terrorism or Cultivating Terrorism for Future?' Arab Reform Initiative, http://www.arab-reform.net/continuation-securitocracy-egypt#sthash.0sRTotb6.dpuf

al-Rasheed, Madawi, 2007. *Contesting the Saudi State: Islamic voices from a new generation*. Cambridge: Cambridge University Press.

al-Wardi, Ali, 1965. *Dirasa fî Tabi'at al-mujtama' al-'iraqi* (A Study of the Nature of Iraqi Society). Baghdad.

———, 1972. *Lamahat ijtimaiyya min tarikh al-Iraq al-hadith*. Baghdad.

Amnesty International, 2015. 'Human Rights under fire: Attacks and violations in Cameroon's struggle with Boko Haram', 16 September.

Arendonk, Cornelis van, 1960. *Les Débuts de l'Imamat Zaidite auYémen*. Leiden: Brill.

Asad, Talal, 1986. 'The Idea of an Anthropology of Islam', Occasional Papers Series. Washington, DC: Center for Contemporary Arab Studies, Georgetown University.

Assayag, Jackie, 2008. 'L'anthropologue en guerre. Les anthropologues sont-ils tous des espions?' *L'Homme*, nos. 187–188.

ʿAṭwān, Abdulbārī, 2001. 'My weekend with Osama bin Laden', *Guardian*, 12 November (original interview published in *al-Quds al-ʿArabī* on 27 November 1996).

Augustin, Amira, 2015. 'Aden wird siegen: Der Südwiderstand', *INAMO*, vol. 21: 11–16.

Baghni, Amr, 1996. *Abhath fi tarikh libia*, Markaz dirasat jihad al-libiyin.

Baram, Amatzia, 1997. 'Neo-Tribalism in Iraq: Saddam Hussein's Tribal Policies 1991–96', *International Journal of Middle East Studies*, vol. 29, no. 1.

———, 2001. '"La maison" de Saddâm Husayn', in Pierre Bonte, Edouard Conte and Paul Dresch, *Emir et Présidents, Figures de la parenté et du politique dans le monde arabe*. Paris: CNRS Editions.

———, 2003. 'The Iraqi Tribes and the Post-Saddam System', Brookings Institution: Iraq Memo, no. 18, 8 July, http://www.brookings.edu/views/op-ed/fellows/baram20030708.htm

Basil, Yousuf and Shoichet, Catherine, 2013. 'Al Qaeda: We're sorry about Yemen hospital attack', CNN, 22 December, http://edition.cnn.com/2013/12/22/world/meast/yemen-al-qaeda-apology/

Batatu, Hanna, 1978. *Old Social Classes and Revolutionay Movements of Iraq*. Princeton, NJ: Princeton University Press.

Bayart, Jean François, 1993. *The State in Africa: The politics of the belly*, 2nd edn. London: Longman.

Bazzi, Mohammed, 2003. 'On Their Terms; US soldier reaches out to understand Iraqi tribal system', *Newsday*, 21 December.

Benda-Beckmann, Franz von, 1994, 'Rechtspluralismus: analytische Begriffsbildung oder politisch-ideologisches Programm?', *Zeitschrift für Ethnologie*, vol. 118, no. 2: 1–16.

Bergen, Peter, 2001. *Holy War, Inc.: Inside the Secret World of Osama bin Laden*. New York: Free Press.

Bonnefoy, Laurent, 2011. *Salafism in Yemen: Transnationalism and Religious Identity*. London: Hurst & Co.

Bourdieu, Pierre, 2012. 'Sur l'État'. Collège de France lecture series, 1989–1992.

Brandt, Marieke, 2010. 'Regimes of Piety Revisited: Zaydī Political Moralities in Republican Yemen', *Die Welt des Islams*, vol. 50, no. 2: 185–223.

———, 2014. 'Inhabiting Tribal Structures: Leadership Hierarchies in Tribal Upper Yemen (Hamdān & Khawlān b. ʿĀmir)', in André Gingrich and Siegfried Haas (eds), *Southwest Arabia across History: Essays to the Memory of Walter Dostal*. Vienna: Verlag der Österreichischen Akademie der Wissenschaften, pp. 91–116.

———, 2017. *Tribes and Politics in Yemen: A History of the Houthi Conflict*. London: Hurst & Co.

Burgat, François and Sbitli, Muhammad, 2002. 'Les Salafis au Yémen ou La modernisation malgré tout', *Chroniques Yéménites*, vol. 10: 123–52, http://cy.revues.org/137#tocto1n1

Captain's Journal, 2007a, 22 August, http://www.captainsjournal.com/2007/08/22/operation-alljah-and-the-marines-of-2nd-battalion-6th-regiment/

———, 2007b, 26 November, http://www.captainsjournal.com/2007/11/26/the-special-forces-plan-for-pakistan-mistaking-the-anbar-narrative/

Carsten, Janet and Hugh-Jones, Stephen, 1995. *About the House: Lévi-Strauss and beyond*. Cambridge: Cambridge University Press.

Chimhundu, Herbert, 1992. 'Early missionaries and the ethnolinguistic factor during the "invention of tribalism" in Zimbabwe', *Journal of African History*, vol. 33, no. 1.

Ciezadlo, Annia, 2003. 'A scholarly soldier steps inside the world of Iraq's potent tribes,' *Christian Science Monitor*, 30 December.

Cigar, Norman, 2014. 'Tribal Militias: An Effective Tool to Counter al-Qaida and its Affiliates?' Carlisle Barracks: Unites States Army War College Press.

Clark, Kate, 2011. 'The Layha: Calling the Taliban to Account', *Afghan Analysts Network*.

Coghlan, Tom, 2009. 'The Taliban in Helmand: An Oral History', in Antonio Giustozzi (ed.), *Decoding the New Taliban: Insights from the Afghan Field*. London: Hurst & Co.

Coker, Margaret, 2016. 'How ISIL's Secret Banking Network Prospers', *Wall Street Journal*, 24 February.

Cole, Donald P. and Altorki, Soraya, 1998. *Bedouin, Settlers, and Holiday-Makers. Egypt's Changing Northwest Coast*. Cairo: American University in Cairo Press.

Cole, Donald P., 2003. 'Where Have the Bedouin Gone?' *Anthropological Quarterly*, vol. 76, no. 2: 235–67.

Collier, Paul, 2000. 'Doing Well out of War', in M. R. Berdal and D. M. Malone (eds), *Greed and Grievance: Economic Agendas in Civil Wars*. Boulder, CO: Lynne Rienner Publishers.

Collier, Paul and Hoeffler, Anke, 2002. 'Greed and Grievance in Civil War'. Oxford: Centre for the Study of African Economies, Working Paper Series.

Collombier, Virginie, 2015. 'Bani Walid: quelle place pour les "vaincus" de la révolution?' *Moyen-Orient*, no. 25, Jan./March: pp. 42–7.

Collombier, Virginie and Trabelsi, Seif Eddin, 2016. 'The Organization of the Islamic State in Libya: from Strategy to the Reality on the Ground', in L. Narbone, A. Favier and V. Collombier (eds), *Inside Wars. Local Dynamics of Conflicts in Syria and Libya*. Fiesole: European University Institute.

Comolli, Virginia, 2015. *Boko Haram. Nigeria's Islamist Insurgency*. London: Hurst & Co.

Crawford, Young, 1979. *The Politics of Cultural Pluralism*. Madison, WI: University of Wisconsin Press.

CTC (Combating Terrorism Center at West Point), 2011. 'A False Foundation? AQAP, tribes, and ungoverned spaces in Yemen', ed. Gabriel Koehler-Derrick. West Point: CTC, https://www.ctc.usma.edu/posts/a-false-foundation-aqap-tribes-and-ungoverned-spaces-in-yemen

Davis, Anthony, 1998. 'How the Taliban became a military force', in William Maley (ed.), *Fundamentalism Reborn? Afghanistan and the Taliban*. Lahore: Vanguard Books.

Davis, John, 1987. *Libyan Politics: Tribe and Revolution*. Oakland, CA: University of California Press.

Dawisha, Adeed, 2002. *Arab Nationalism in the Twentieth Century: From Triumph to Despair*. Princeton, NJ: Princeton University Press.

Dawod, Hosham, 2001. 'Etatisation de la tribu et tribalisation de l'Etat', *Esprit*. Paris.

———. *Tribus et pouvoirs en terre d'Islam*. Paris: Armand Colin.

———. 'Tribus et armée américaine en Irak', *Le Journal de l'Ecole de Paris du Management*, no. 88.

———. 'Construction et déconstruction du pouvoir en Irak: le cas de Nouri al-Maliki', *Carnet de l'Ifpo*, October.

———. 'Les réactions irakiennes à la crise syrienne', in François Burgat and Bruno Paoli (eds), *Pas de Printemps pour la Syrie? Les clefs pour comprendre les acteurs et les défis de la crise (2011–2013)*. Paris: La Découverte.

———. 'The Sunni tribes in Iraq: between local power, the international coalition and the Islamic State'. Norwegian Peacebuilding Resource Center (NOREF).

Department of Defense, 2007. *U.S. Army Counterinsurgency Handbook*, with foreword by Lt. Gen. David H. Petraeus and Lt. Gen. James F. Amos. New York: Skyhorse Publishing.

Dobry, Michel, 2009. *Sociologie des crises politiques*. Paris: Presses de Sciences Po.

Dresch, Paul, 1989. *Tribes, Government and History in Yemen*. Oxford: Clarendon Press.

Dresch, Paul and Haykel, Bernard, 1995. 'Stereotypes and Political Styles: Islamists and Tribesfolk in Yemen', *International Journal of Middle East Studies*, vol. 27: 405–31.

Dukhan, Haian, 2014. 'Tribes and Tribalism in the Syrian Uprising', *Syria Studies*, vol. 6, no. 2.

Durkheim, Emile, 1893, 1986. *De la division du travail social*. Paris: PUF.

Edwards, David, 2002. *Before Taliban: Genealogies of the Afghan Jihad*. Oakland, CA: University of California Press.

Eickelman, Dale F., 1998. *The Middle East and Central Asia, an Anthropological Approach*, 3rd edn. Upper Saddle River, NJ: Prentice Hall.

———, 2002. *The Middle East and Central Asia: An Anthropological Approach*, 4th edn. Upper Saddle River, NJ: Prentice Hall.

Eickelman, Dale F. and Piscatori, James, 2004. *Muslim Politics*. Princeton, NJ: Princeton University Press.

Eickelman, Dale F., 2017. 'Tribal "Belonging" Today, Implications and Transformations', *Omran*, vol. 5, no. 19.

Eisenstadt, Michael, 2007. 'Tribal Engagement Lessons Learned', *Military Review*, September–October.

Ellyatt, Holly, 2016. 'ISIL "making millions" by gaming forex markets', CNBC, 3 March.

Esposito, John L., 1998. *Islam: The straight path*, vol. 4. Oxford: Oxford University Press.

Evans-Pritchard, E. E., 1949, 1973. *The Sanussi of Cyrenaica*. Oxford: Oxford University Press.

Farrell, Theo and Giustozzi, Antonio, 2013. 'The Taliban at war: inside the Helmand insurgency, 2004–2012', *International Affairs*, vol. 89, no. 4.

Fitzgerald, Mary, 2015. 'Finding Their Place: Libya's Islamists During and After the Revolution', in Peter Cole and Brian McQuinn (eds), *The Libyan Revolution and its Aftermath*. London: Hurst & Co., pp. 177–204.

———, 2016. 'Jihadism and its relationship with youth culture and ideology: the case of Ansar al-Sharia in Libya', in L. Narbone, A. Favier and V. Collombier (eds), *Inside Wars. Local Dynamics of Conflicts in Syria and Libya*. Fiesole: European University Institute.

Freeman, Colin, 2016. 'ISIL earning millions by playing the stock market', *Daily Telegraph*, 2 March.

Gambrell, John, 2013. 'Video claims Nigeria sect holds 7 French', Associated Press, 25 February, http://news.yahoo.com/nigeria-french-hostage-family-video-171414745 html

Gat, Azar, 2006. *War in Human Civilization*. Oxford: Oxford University Press.

Gebrewold, Belachew, 2013. *Anatomy of Violence: Understanding the systems of conflict and violence in Africa*. Farnham, UK: Ashgate.

Gellner, Ernest, 1969. *Saints of the Atlas*. Chicago: University of Chicago Press.

Gilmore, Gerry J., 2004. 'Outreach Programs Point Iraqis Toward Road to Democracy', *American Forces Press Service*, 17 February, http://www.dod.gov/news/Feb2004/n02172004_200402172.html

Gingrich, André, 2015. 'Tribe', in James D. Wright (ed.), *International Encyclopedia of the Social and Behavioral Sciences*, 2nd edn, vol. 24. Oxford: Elsevier, pp. 645–7.

Giustozzi, Antonio, 2000. *War, Politics and Society in Afghanistan*. Washington, DC: Georgetown University Press.

Giustozzi, Antonio and Ullah, Noor, 2006. '"Tribes" and Warlords in Southern Afghanistan, 1980–2005'. London: LSE, Crisis States Research Centre Working Paper 2.7.

Gochenour, David Thomas, 1984. *The Penetration of Zaydī Islam into Early Medieval Yemen*, PhD thesis, Harvard University, MA.

Goffman, Erving, 1986. *Frame Analysis. An essay on the organisation of experience*. Boston, MA: Northeastern University Press.

Gonzales, Roberto J. (ed.), 2005. *Anthropology in the Public Sphere: speaking out on war, peace and American power*. Austin, TX: University of Texas Press.

Gonzales, Roberto J. and Price, David H., 2007. 'When anthropologists become counter-insurgents', *Counterpunch*, 28 September.

Graff, Peter, 2007. 'Harsh justice where U.S. relies on Iraq tribes', *Washington Post*, 4 September, http://www.washingtonpost.com/wp-dyn/content/article/2007/09/04/AR2007090400353.html

Graham, Patrick, 2004. 'Beyond Fallujah', *Harper's Magazine*, June.

Grosby, Steven, 1995. 'Territoriality: The Transcendental, Primordial Feature of Modern Societies', *Nations and Nationalism*, vol. 1, no. 2.

Gusterson, Hugh, 2007. 'Anthropology and militarism', *Annual Review of Anthropology*, vol. 36.

Halirou, Abdouraman, 2008. 'Le conflit frontalier Cameroun-Nigeria dans le lac Tchad: les enjeux de l'île de Darak, disputée et partagée', *Cultures and Conflicts*, vol. 72.

Hamida, Ali Abdullatif, 1994. *The Making of Modern Libya. State Formation, Colonization and Resistance, 1830–1932*. New York: State University of New York Press.

Hamidi, Ayman, 2009. 'Inscriptions of Violence in Northern Yemen: Haunting Histories, Unstable Moral Spaces', *Middle Eastern Studies*, vol. 45, no. 2: 165–87.

Hammoudi, Abdallah, 2017. 'Emic and Etic in Re-theorizing "Tribe". A Step Toward an Arab Anthropological Discourse', *Omran*, vol. 5, no. 19.

Harris, Emily, 2004. 'Bridging Gap Between Iraq, Coalition Authority', National Public Radio, 27 June (4 mins 40 sec.) http://www.npr.org/rundowns/segment.php?wfId=1979668

Hart, D., 1981. *Dadda Atta and his Forty Grandsons: the Socio-Political Organisation of the Ait Atta of Southern Morocco*. Cambridge: MENAS.

Hashim, Ahmed S., 2006. *Insurgency and Counter-insurgency in Iraq*. Ithaca, NY: Cornell University Press.

Haykel, Bernard, 2002. 'The Salafis in Yemen at a Crossroads: An Obituary of Shaykh Muqbil al-Wādi'ī of Dammāj (d. 1422/2001)', *Jemen Report*, no. 1: 28–31.

———, 2003. *Revival and Reform in Islam: The Legacy of Muḥammad al-Shawkānī*. Cambridge: Cambridge University Press.

Heacock, Ashley, 2013. *Understanding Mali: Connections and Confrontations between the Tuareg, Islamist Rebels, and the Government*. Amazon Kindle.

Heinze, Marie-Christine, 2016. 'Der Krieg im Jemen vor dem Hintergrund regionaler Dynamiken', *Jemen Report*, vol. 47, nos. 1/2: 104–8.

Higazi, Adam, 2013. 'The origins and transformation of the Boko Haram Insurgency in northern Nigeria', published in French translation as « Les origines et la transformation de l'insurrection de Boko Haram dans le nord du Nigeria », *Politique Africaine*, vol. 130, no. 2.

———, 2015. 'Mobilisation into and against Boko Haram in North-East Nigeria', in K. Tall, M.-E. Pommerolle and M. Cahen (eds), *Collective Mobilisations in Africa. Enough is Enough!* Leiden: Brill, Africa–Europe Group for Interdisciplinary Studies.

Hiribarren, Vincent, 2017. *A History of Borno, From Trans-Saharan African Empire to Failing Nigerian State*. London: Hurst & Co.

Hobsbawm, Eric and Ranger, Terence, 1983. *The Invention of Tradition*. Cambridge: Cambridge University Press.

Hopkins, Benjamin and Marsden, Magnus, 2012. *Fragments of the Afghan Frontier*. London: Hurst & Co.

Hourani, Albert, 1992. *A History of the Arab People*. New York: Warner Books.

Human Rights Watch, 1999. 'Leave None to Tell the Story: Genocide in Rwanda: Obfuscation and Misunderstanding'.

Hüsken, Thomas, 2009a. 'Die neotribale Wettbewerbsordnung in Grenzland von Ägypten und Libyen', *Sociologus*, vol. 2: 117–43.

———, 2009b. 'The Neotribal Competitive Order in the Borderland of Egypt and Libya', in Engel, Ulf and Nugent, Paul (eds), *Respacing Africa*. Amsterdam: Brill, pp. 169–209.

Hüsken, Thomas, 2011. 'Politische Kultur und die Revolution in der Cyrenaika', in Edlinger, Fritz (ed.), *Libyen: Hintergründe, Analysen, Berichte*. Wien: Promedia Verlag, pp. 47–71.

———, 2012. 'Tribal Political Culture and the Revolution in the Cyrenaica of Libya', *Orient, German Journal for Politics, Economics and Culture of the Middle East*, vol. I, pp. 26–31.

———, 2013. 'Tribes, Revolution, and Political Culture in the Cyrenaica Region of Libya', in Malika Bouziane, Cilja Harders and Anja Hoffmann (eds), *Local Politics and Contemporary Transformations in the Arab World*. London: Palgrave Macmillan, pp. 214–31.

Hüsken, Thomas and Roenpage, Olin, 1998. *Jenseits von Traditionalismus und Stagnation. Analyse einer beduinischen Ökonomie in der Westlichen Wüste Ägyptens*. Münster: LIT-Verlag.

Hüsken, Thomas and Klute, Georg, 2015. 'Political Orders in the Making: Emerging Forms of Political Organization from Libya to Northern Mali', *African Security*, vol. 8, no. 4: 320–37.

Immerman, Richard and Goedde, Petra (eds), 2013. *The Oxford Handbook of the Cold War*. Oxford: Oxford University Press.

International Crisis Group, 2009. 'Defusing the Saada Time Bomb', *Middle East Report* 86, 27 May.

———, 2013. 'Yemen's Military-Security Reform: Seeds of New Conflict?' *Middle East Report* 139, 4 April.

———, 2014. 'Cameroun: Mieux vaut prévenir que guérir', *Africa*, no. 101, https://www.crisisgroup.org/fr/africa/central-africa/cameroon/cameroon-prevention-better-cure

Johnsen, Gregory D., 2009. 'The Expansion Strategy of al-Qa'ida in the Arabian Peninsula', *CTC Sentinel*, September, https://www.ctc.usma.edu/wp-content/uploads/2010/08/Pages-from-CTCSentinel-YemenSI-2009-art2.pdf

———, 2013. *The Last Refuge: Yemen, Al-Qaeda, and the Battle for Arabia*. London: Oneworld.

Joseph, Richard A., 1977. *Radical Nationalism in Cameroun. Social origins of the UPC rebellion*. Oxford: Clarendon Press.

Kalyvas, Stathis N., 2006. *The Logic of Violence in Civil War*. Cambridge: Cambridge University Press.

Kaufman, Stuart, 1996. 'Spiralling to Ethnic War: Elites, Masses and Moscow in Moldova's Civil War', *International Security*, vol. 21, no. 2.

Kaufman, Stuart, 2006. 'Symbolic Politics or Rational Choice? Testing Theories of Extreme Ethnic Violence', *International Security*, vol. 30, no. 4.

Kendall, Elisabeth, 2015. 'Yemen's Al-Qa'ida and Poetry as a Weapon of Jihad', in Elisabeth Kendall and Ewan Stein (eds), *Twenty-first Century Jihad*. London: I. B. Tauris.

———, 2016a. 'How can al-Qaeda in the Arabian Peninsula be defeated?' *Washington Post*, 3 May 2016, https://www.washingtonpost.com/news/monkey-cage/wp/2016/05/03/how-can-al-qaeda-in-the-arabian-peninsula-be-defeated/

———, 2016b. 'Al-Qaida and Islamic State in Yemen: A Battle for Local Audiences', in Simon Staffell and Akil Awan (eds), *Jihadism Transformed: Al-Qaeda and Islamic State's Global Battle of Ideas*. London: Hurst & Co.

Kepel, Gilles, 2006. *Jihad: The trail of political Islam*. London: I. B. Tauris.

Khaddour, Kheder and Mazur, Kevin, 2013. 'The Struggle for Syria's Regions', *Middle East Research and Information Project*, vol. 269.

———, 2017. *Eastern Expectations: The Changing Dynamics in Syria's Tribal Regions* (Beirut: Carnegie Middle East Centre.

Khan, Mohammad, 1981. *Afghanistan and its Inhabitants*, trans. H. Priestley. Lahore: Sang-e Meel Publications.

Khoury, Philip S. and Kostiner, Joseph (eds), 1991. *Tribes and State Formation in the Middle East*. Oakland, CA: University of California Press.

Kilcullen, David, 2006. 'Twenty-Eight Articles', *Military Review*, vol. 86, no. 3.

———, 2009. *The Accidental Guerrilla: fighting small wars in the midst of a big one*. Oxford: University Press.

King, Desmond and Le Galès, Patrick, 2011. 'Sociologie de l'État en recomposition', *Revue française de sociologie*, vol. 52, no. 3.

King, Mary Elizabeth, 2007. *A Quiet Revolution: The First Palestinian Intifada and Nonviolent Resistance*. New York: Nation Books.

Klein, Joe, 2007. 'Operation Last Chance', *Time*, 9 July.

Klute, Georg and von Trotha, Trutz, 2004. 'Roads to Peace. From Small War to Parastatal Peace in the North of Mali', in Marie-Claire Foblets and Trutz von Trotha (eds), *Healing the Wounds. Essays on the Reconstruction of Societies after War*. Oxford: Oñati International Series in Law and Society, pp. 109–43.

Kraus, Wolfgang, 2004. *Islamische Stammesgesellschaften. Tribale Identitäten im Vorderen Orient in sozialanthropologischer Perspektive*. Wien: Böhlau Verlag.

Lacher, Wolfram, 2015a. 'Libyen: Wachstumsmarkt für Jihadisten', in Steinberg, Guido and Weber, Annette (eds), *Jihadismus in Afrika. Lokale Ursachen, regionale Ausbreitung, internationale Verbindungen*. Berlin: SWP Studie S7. http://www. swp-berlin.org/fileadmin/contents/products/research_papers/2015_RP05_sbg_web.pdf#page=31

———, 2015b. 'Libya's Local Elites and the Politics of Alliance Building', *Mediterranean Politics* (Special Issue, 'Dynamics of Transformation, Elite Change and New Social Mobilization in the Arab World'), vol. 21, no. 1.

Lackner, Helen (ed.), 2014. *Why Yemen Matters: A society in transition*, vol. 10. London: Saqi Books.

Lackner, Helen, 2016. 'Yemen's "Peaceful" Transition from Autocracy: Could it have succeeded?' *International IDEA*, http://www.idea.int/es/publications/yemens-peaceful-transition-from-autocracy/loader.cfm?csModule=security/getfile&pageID=77329

Lacroix, Stéphane, 2011. *Awakening Islam. The Politics of Religious Dissent in Contemporary Saudi Arabia*. Harvard, MA: Harvard University Press.

Lévi-Strauss, Claude, 1983. *The Way of the Masks*, trans. S. Modelski. London: Jonathan Cape,

———, 1984. *Paroles données*. Paris: Plon.

———, 1986. 'Histoire et ethnologie', *Les annales ESC*.

———, 1987. 'La notion de maison', *Terrain*, no. 9.

Levinson, Charles and Coker, Margaret, 2010. 'Al Qaeda's Deep Tribal Ties Make Yemen a Terror Hub', *Wall Street Journal*, 22 January, http://online.wsj.com/article/SB10001424052748704320104575015493304519542.html

Lewis, Bernard, 1993. *Islam and the West*. Oxford: Oxford University Press.

Liba'a, Natali K., 2014. *Crises de la filière Coton au Cameroun. Fondements et stratégies d'adaptation des acteurs*. Yaoundé: Editions Clé.

Loidolt, Bryce, 2011. 'Managing the Global and Local: The Dual Agendas of Al Qaeda in the Arabian Peninsula', *Studies in Conflict and Terrorism*, vol. 34, no. 2: 102–23.

Lonsdale, John M., 1992. 'The Moral Economy of Mau-Mau: The Problem' and 'The Moral Economy of Mau Mau. Wealth, Poverty and Civic Virtue in Kikuyu Political Thought', in B. J. Berman and J. M. Lonsdale, *Unhappy Valley: Conflict and Kenya and Africa*. Athens, OH: Ohio University Press.

Macdonald, Charles et al. (eds), 1987. *De la hutte au palais: sociétés 'à maison' en Asie du Sud-Est Insulaire*. Paris: Editions du CNRS.

Madelung, Wilferd, 1965. *Der Imam al-Qāsim ibn Ibrāhīm und die Glaubenslehre der Zaiditen*. Berlin: de Gruyter.

Mann, Michael, 1986. *The Sources of Social Power, Vol. I: A history of power from the beginning to AD 1760*. Cambridge: Cambridge University Press.

Markaz dirasat al-janub al-libi li-l-buhuth wa-l-tanmiya, 'Tanzim al-dawla fi-l-mintaqa al-gharbiya wa-l-janubiya: al-wujud… al-makhatar wa-l-dawr al-mustaqbali', February 2016.

Martin, Mike, 2011. *A Brief History of Helmand*. Kabul: Afghan COIN Centre.

———, 2014. *An Intimate War: An Oral History of the Helmand Conflict, 1978–2012*. London: Hurst & Co.

Marx, Emanuel, 2014. *Bedouin of Mount Sinai. An Anthropological Study of their Political Economy*. New York: Berghahn.

Mbembe, Achille, 1996. *La naissance du maquis dans le Sud-Cameroun, 1920–1960. Histoire des usages de la raison en colonie*. Karthala.

McCallister, William S. (Major), Kyle, Charles M. (Captain), Alexander, Christopher (Sergeant), 2003. 'The Iraqi Insurgent Movement', 14 November, http://library.nps.navy.mil/home/ Iraqi Insurgent Movement.pdf

McCants, William, 2015. *The ISIS Apocalypse: The History, Strategy, and Doomsday Vision of the Islamic State*. New York: St Martin's Press, Kindle edn.

McFate, Montgomery, 2005a. 'Anthropology and counterinsurgency: the strange story of their curious relationship, *Military Review*, March–April.

———, 2005b. 'Does culture matter? The military utility of cultural knowledge', *Joint Force Quarterly*, no. 38.

Middleton, J. and Tait, D., 1952. *Tribes without Ruler*. London: Routledge & Kegan Paul.

Miller, Judith and Gerth, Jeff, 2011. 'Honey Trade Said to Provide Funds and Cover to bin Laden', *New York Times*, 11 October, http://www.nytimes.com/2001/10/11/world/nation-challenged-al-qaeda-honey-trade-said-provide-funds-cover-bin-laden.html

Mohammed, Omar, 2016. 'Mapping the Tribes of Nineveh, the Future Role of Tribes in Post—ISIS Nineveh', Outlook Study, unpublished paper, March.

Mundy, Martha, 1995. *Domestic Government: Kinship, community and polity in North Yemen*. London: I. B. Tauris.

Nojumi, Neamatollah, 2002. *The Rise of the Taliban in Afghanistan*. New York: St Martin's Press.

Olinga, Alain Didier, 2009. *L'accord de Greentree du 12 juin 2006 relatif à la Presqu'île de Bakassi*. Paris: L'Harmattan.

Ouannes, Moncef, 2009. *Militaires, Elites et Modernisation dans la Libye contemporaine*. Paris: L'Harmattan.

Ousmane, Douwoure, 2015. 'Les Kanuri victimes du délit de faciès', *l'Oeil du Sahel*, 5 August, http://www.camer.be/44279/11:1/cameroun-boko-haram-les-kanuri-victimes-du-delit-de-facies-cameroon.html; http://www.camerpost.com/cameroun-lutte-contre-boko-haram-45-suspects-aux-arrets-a-maroua-

Oxford Dictionary of English, 3rd edn, 2010. Oxford: Oxford University Press.

Pargeter, Alison, 2008. 'Qadhafi and Political Islam in Libya', in Dirk Vandewalle (ed.), *Libya since 1969. Qadhafi's Revolution Revisited*. London: Palgrave Macmillan, pp. 83–104.

Peters, Emrys, 1990. *The Bedouin of Cyrenaica. Studies in personal and corporate power*. Cambridge: Cambridge University Press, 1990.

Peters, Rudolph, 1979. *Islam and Colonialism. The doctrine of Jihad in Modern History*. The Hague: Mouton Publishers.

Phillips, Sarah, 2011. *Yemen and the Politics of Permanent Crisis*. London: Routledge.

Pollack, Kenneth, 2004. 'Spies, Lies, and Weapons: What Went Wrong', *The Atlantic*, Jan./Feb.

Prager, Leila, 2014. 'Introduction. Reshaping Tribal Identities in the Contemporary Arab World: Politics, (Self-)Representation, and the Construction of Bedouin History', *Nomadic Peoples*, vol. 18, no. 2: 10–15.

Qutb, Sayyid, 1978. *Milestones*. Beirut: Holy Koran Publishing House.

Renart, Manuel and Garçon, Lou, 2014. 'Boko Haram. A chronology', in Marc-Antoine Perouse de Montclos (ed.), *Boko Haram, Islamism, politics, security and the state in Nigeria*. African Studies Centre: West African Politics and Society Series, Vol. 2, https://openaccess.leidenuniv.nl/bitstream/handle/1887/23853/ASC-075287668–3441–01.pdf?sequence=2

Ricks, Thomas E., 2006. *Fiasco, the American military adventure in Iraq*. New York: Penguin Press.

Roy, Olivier, 1990a. *Afghanistan: modèles anthropologiques et pacification*. Cahiers du Monde Russe et Soviétique.

———, 1990b. *Islam and Resistance in Afghanistan*. Cambridge: Cambridge University Press.

———, 1999. *The Failure of Political Islam*. London: I. B. Tauris.

Rusch, W. and Stein, L., 1988. *Siwa und die Aulad Ali*. Berlin: Akademie-Verlag.

Sahlins, Marshal, 2011. 'Iraq, the state-of-nature effect', *Anthropology Today*, vol. 27, no. 3.

Sakai, Keiko, 2003. 'Tribalisation as a Tool of State Control in Iraq: Observations on the Army, the Cabinets and the National Assembly', in Faleh A. Jabar and Hosham Dawod, *Tribes and Power, Nationalism and Ethnicity in the Middle East*. London: Saqi Books.

Salim, Shakir M., 1970. *Ech-Chibayish, Anthropological Study of A Marsh Village In Iraq*, 2nd edn. Baghdad: Al Ani Press.

Salisbury, Peter and Mohsen, Ahlam, 2015. 'The Rise of the Islamic State in Yemen', Vice News, https://news.vice.com/article/the-rise-of-the-islamic-state-in-yemen

Salmoni, Barak, Loidolt, Bryce and Wells, Madeleine, 2010. *Regime and Periphery in Northern Yemen: The Huthi phenomenon*. Santa Monica, CA: RAND.

Schielke, Samuli, 2010. 'Second thoughts about the anthropology of Islam, or how to make sense of grand schemes in everyday life', ZMO Working Papers, no. 2.

Schofield, Victoria, 2003. *Afghan Frontier: Feuding and Fighting in Central Asia*. London: I. B. Tauris.

Scott, Richard, 2008. 'Reconstruction and Opium Poppy Cultivation in Central Helmand', Conference on Afghanistan Reconstruction, University of Nebraska.

Searle, Thomas R., 2008. 'Tribal Engagement in Anbar Province: The Critical Role of Special Operations Forces', *Joint Force Quarterly*, vol. 50, no. 3: 62–6.

Selznick, Philip, 1949. *TVA and the Grass Roots: A Study in the Sociology of Formal Organization*. Berkeley and Los Angeles, CA: University of California Press.

Shay, Shaul, 2010. *Somalia between Jihad and Restoration*. Piscataway, NJ: Transaction Publishers.

Shoqeir, Noam, 1916. *Tarīkh Sinaa al-Qadīm wa al-Hadīth* (The Ancient and Modern History of Sinai).

Siméant, Johanna, 2010. '"Économie morale" et protestation—détours africains', *Genèses*, no. 81.

Der Spiegel, 2010. 'Jemen: Geiselnehmer verlangen Freilassung von Terroristen', 16 January, http://www.spiegel.de/politik/ausland/jemen-geiselnehmer-verlangen-freilassung-von-terroristen-a-672301.html

Thahir, Mas'oud, 1986. *Al-Mashrek al-'arabi al-mu'asir, min al-badawa ila ad-dawla al-haditha* (The Contemporary Arab Maghreb: From nomadism to modern state). Beirut: Ma'had al-inma' al-'arabi.

Thompson, Edward P., 1971. 'The Moral Economy of the English Crowd in the Eighteenth Century', *Past and Present*, no. 50.

Vadot, Guillaume, 2014. 'Un travail de pros. Réforme de la Sodecoton et redéploiement des formes de mobilisation du travail paysan en zone cotonnière dans l'Extrême-Nord au Cameroun', *Politique africaine*, vol. 133, no. 1.

vom Bruck, Gabriele, 2005. *Islam, Memory, and Morality in Yemen: Ruling Families in Transition*. New York: Palgrave Macmillan.

Wedeen, Lisa, 2008. *Peripheral Visions: Publics, Power and Performance in Yemen*. Chicago, IL: University of Chicago Press.

Wehrey, Frederic, 2015a. 'Splitting the Islamists: The Islamic State's Creeping Advance in Libya', 19 June. Beirut: Carnegie Middle East Center.

———, 2015b. 'Taking on Operation Dawn: The Creeping Advance of the Islamic State in Western Libya', 24 June. Beirut: Carnegie Middle East Center.

———, 2016. 'Quiet No More?' 13 October. Beirut: Carnegie Middle East Center.

Weir, Shelagh, 1997. 'A clash of fundamentalisms: Wahhabism in Yemen', *Middle East Research and Information Project* 204, vol. 27, no. 3.

———, 2007. *A Tribal Order: Politics and Law in the Mountains of Yemen*. Austin, TX: University of Texas Press.

Weiss, Michael and Hassan, Hassan, 2015. *ISIS: Inside the Army of Terror*. New York: Simon & Schuster.

Wikileaks, 2009. 'Theories proliferate regarding Saada kidnapping/murder', 24 June 2009, https://wikileaks.org/plusd/cables/09SANAA1153_a.html

Zelin, Aron, 2012. 'Libya's Jihadists beyond Benghazi', Foreign Policy—the Middle East Channel, 12 August 2012.

———, 2015. 'The Rise and Decline of Ansar al-Sharia in Libya'. Washington, DC: Hudson Institute, 6 April.

Zimmerman, Katherine, 2015a. 'AQAP: A Resurgent Threat', *Critical Threats*, 11 September, http://www.criticalthreats.org/yemen/zimmerman-aqap-resurgent-threat-september-11–2015

———, 2015b. 'A New Model for Defeating al Qaeda in Yemen', American Enterprise Institute, http://www.aei.org/wp-content/uploads/2015/09/A-New-Model-for-Defeating-al-Qaeda-in-Yemen.pdf

———, 2015c. 'Exploring ISIS in Yemen', *Critical Threats*, 24 July, http://www.criticalthreats.org/yemen/exploring-isis-yemen-zimmerman-july-24–2015

Zimmerman, Katherine and Diamond, Jon, 2016. 'Challenging the Yemeni State: ISIS in Aden and al Mukalla', *Critical Threats*, 9 June, http://www.criticalthreats.org/yemen/zimmerman-diamond-challenging-yemeni-state-isis-in-aden-al-mukalla-june-9–2016

INDEX

INDEX